Leading with Character

Stories of Valor and Virtue
and the Principles They Teach

Leading with Character

Stories of Valor and Virtue
and the Principles They Teach

John J. Sosik
The Pennsylvania State University

INFORMATION AGE
PUBLISHING

Greenwich, Connecticut • www.infoagepub.com

Library of Congress Cataloging-in-Publication Data

Sosik, John J.
  Leading with character : stories of valor and virtue and the
principles they teach / by John J. Sosik.
       p. cm.
  Includes bibliographical references.
  ISBN-13: 978-1-59311-541-8 (pbk.)
  ISBN-13: 978-1-59311-542-5 (hardcover)
  1. Leadership. 2. Leadership–Case studies. I. Title.
  BF637.L4S67 2006
  158'.4–dc22

                                      2006019761

CONTENTS

FOREWORD

There are literally thousands of books available that promise to provide the keys to successful leadership. They range from autobiographical accounts written by world and corporate leaders, to leadership lessons from great historical figures, to leadership gurus giving informed opinions based on their research, observations, and/or experiences. However, John J. Sosik has created something unique and special. Solidly grounded in research, Sosik draws forth the lessons about leading with character derived from the work of the best leadership scholars. This is not a dry, scholarly dissertation, however, but an accessible and practical guide to understanding how to lead with positive virtues and character.

When examining leadership, social scientists have typically concentrated on whether leaders are able to move groups toward their goals. Successful leadership, therefore, is focused on performance and achieving certain outcomes. To many, this approach has seemed incomplete and unsatisfying. It tells us nothing about whether the leader and the outcomes are good or bad. This is what leadership scholars often refer to as "the Hitler problem"—he was effective in leading, but as far from being a *good* leader as is humanly possible. This book helps us to better understand what good leadership is in a way that most people think about it—an effective leader, but one with character: A leader that we can admire and try to emulate.

John J. Sosik takes a novel approach to illustrate 23 principles of leading with character strengths and virtues, using well-known individuals who personify each. Some are obvious—the courage of Martin Luther King Jr., and Rosa Parks, the humanity of Mother Theresa, and the patience and commitment of Nelson Mandela. Others are subtle and not the expected leadership types—TV's Mr. Rogers, poet Maya Angelou, and the Beach Boys'

Leading with Character, pages vii–viii
Copyright © 2006 by Information Age Publishing
All rights of reproduction in any form reserved.

Brian Wilson. Through these latter examples, Sosik makes us realize that good leaders do not have to be saints and they do not have to be people elected to high office. Leaders come in many forms, but all can be leaders of character and represent positive virtues.

For many years, there has been talk of a leadership vacuum—a shortage of good and great leaders. In more recent years, with horrendous leadership failures and ethical scandals, there has been greater attention paid to bad leadership. To many people, this represents a grim future. This book, however, focuses on positive leadership and helps us to both understand good leadership and to learn how to become better leaders ourselves. Most importantly, John's is an authentic voice urging us to become better leaders and better human beings and providing guidance on how to do it.

—Ronald E. Riggio
Henry R. Kravis Professor of Leadership and Organizational Psychology
Director, Kravis Leadership Institute
Claremont McKenna College

Ronald E. Riggio, Ph.D. is one of the foremost scholars on charismatic and transformational leadership. He has served on the faculties of several colleges and universities, has served as the editor of several social science journals, and has published over 70 books, book chapters, and research articles in the areas of leadership, organizational psychology and social psychology. His professional background includes the publication of his most recent book *Transformational Leadership* (2nd ed., with Bernard M. Bass; Mahwah, NJ: Erlbaum). Dr. Riggio has also served as an organizational consultant to several businesses and organizations across the United States since 1980.

PREFACE

A 2005 Harvard University study of confidence in leadership found that almost two-thirds of Americans think that we are suffering from a leadership crisis in America. The study's respondents showed little confidence in the honesty, integrity and ethics of leaders in sectors ranging from business and religion to local, state and federal government. They also showed little faith in our leaders' knowledge, skills and abilities and their capability to inspire loyalty and enthusiasm from followers. How can this be the case given the increased prominence of leadership topics in our culture today and the proliferation of leadership training in organizations and educational institutions as well?

One possible answer is that we are ignoring what really constitutes leadership. We may have focused too much attention on issues of style, including charisma, impression management, and influence tactics, while ignoring issues of the true substance of leadership–character and virtue. Constant threats to personal and organizational integrity make leadership more challenging than ever. Today's leaders must navigate through cutthroat, morally challenging, and sometimes downright negative and nasty environments. To survive in this demanding context, some leaders skillfully play the role of a dynamic leader because they know the game well and possess the right "style." However, these leaders often do not possess the appropriate character strengths or "substance" required to be true to themselves and others. At first, these leaders are perceived by followers as potential saviors. But over time, they are found out as charlatans lacking character and virtue. Other leaders work hard each and every day to present their true selves. These authentic leaders rely on their character strengths to communicate important values and role model appropriate virtues and behaviors for their followers. Being authentic is critical to achieving leadership effectiveness in today's challenging ethical climate. Authenticity and other character strengths are found in world-class leaders such as Warren Buffet, Andy Grove, Condoleezza Rice, Oprah Winfrey, and the 21 other leaders of character profiled in this book. These leaders support collaborative, positive, and virtuous operations that can provide a competitive advantage and form positive cultures. Such cultures can avoid tragic ethical downfalls as we have recently witnessed at Enron, WorldCom, and Adelphia, among other numerous businesses, faith communities, and governments. How can we achieve these levels of performance excellence while avoiding ethical fiascos?

In this book, I argue that authentic transformational leaders of character build constructive cultures by innovating, inspiring, role modeling, and developing followers in ways that bring about positive change. To fully develop the potential of followers requires understanding the virtues and characters strengths associated with authentic transformational leadership. What you will find this book to be is a how-to guide to authentic transformational leadership based on the life stories of a diverse array of famous leaders.

First, a few thoughts on how this book came about. In January 2005, Penn State University launched its innovative Master of Leadership Development (MLD) graduate degree program that develops authentic transformational leaders. This graduate degree program is separate and distinct from our MBA program and is accredited by the Association to Advance Collegiate Schools of Business (AACSB). Students begin the MLD program with a course I developed called "Leadership across the Lifespan." This course covers topics including authentic leadership, adult human development, and positive psychology/organizational scholarship. As I was preparing the syllabus and searching for appropriate texts for the course, I recognized that few, if any, books make thorough connections between leadership behavior and the character strengths now being discussed by positive psychologists and organizational scholars, and called for by organizational stakeholders and society. How, then, could I illustrate to my graduate students that character strengths and virtues represent the "raw material" or substance of authentic transformational leadership?

Would I have to write the book that makes these connections? My instincts told me "yes." But before I set out on a mission to write such a book, I sought the advice of colleagues, students, and clients. Colleagues from the University of Nebraska at Lincoln, University of Pennsylvania, University of Michigan, and the Gallup Organization were pursuing complementary research programs. MBA and leadership students at Penn State were thirsting for a more spiritual and virtuous approach to leadership studies. I knew that I was onto something special when my clients found the topic to be meaningful, but its practice to be woefully lacking in their organizations. After many discussions with corporate, non-profit, and faith community leaders on the role of virtue in leadership, I became convinced that I *had* to write this book. That's because they told me a few things that I didn't like to hear.

They told me that they didn't see many examples of virtuous character and positive leadership in their organizations–but recognized their value to sustained performance impact. They told me that their people spend a lot of time fixing what's wrong in their organizations, and not enough time celebrating and building upon what is right. And they had a hard time telling me about their personal values and what they actually stand for as leaders. But from my work with a few progressive organizations, I knew that such positive leadership and organizational cultures actually could, and *do*, exist. From my research, I knew that many famous leaders have demonstrated that character does count, and forms the foundation of positive leadership and sustained performance excellence. Indeed, I wanted to write a book that would give hope to those individuals whose attitude toward leadership had become jaded because of their work experiences. I was determined that this book would approach leadership from a different perspective–from a view that celebrates what is right with leaders and their organizations; *not* from one that fixates on what is wrong with them. As it turned out, this book was able to do so and thus is unique in several ways. First, it provides many interesting and colorful examples of "world class" authentic transformational leaders from business, history, sports and popular culture that have demonstrated virtue and character strengths and created sustainable growth and extraordinary performance. You are sure to find one or many leaders of character in this book with whom you can identify and draw good ideas for your own leadership development. Second, the book presents 23 clear principles and related action steps that show you how to demonstrate authentic transformational leadership through character strengths and virtues. These practical tools will help you to reap the mental, physical, spiritual and social benefits associated with character and virtue. Unlike some leadership books, the principles and action steps in this book are grounded in research. Third, the book explains how leaders can shape the moral character of future leaders through educational programs, community service, and organizational development initiatives that accentuate the strengths that people possess.

Finally, this book will appeal to a broad audience. Any student of leadership in a wide range of organizations including profit and not-for-profit and faith communities should find the lessons this book teaches helpful. Students in graduate and undergraduate leadership programs and MBA courses should also find it useful. This audience is particularly interested in examining leadership as practiced by highly visible leaders from different walks of life. They know about these people and can connect with the material in this book. Managers who like inspirational writing and motivational speakers will also relate to the story of authentic transformational leadership that I tell in this book. It also can be used in management and leadership training and development courses. The cases, principles and actionable training points in this book will help you to develop your leadership potential. The book shows you how demonstrating and building character strengths in yourself and others can help your career and organization to flourish.

The book is structured into 11 chapters. The first three chapters provide background and foundation material on Bernard Bass and Bruce Avolio's concept of transformational leadership, and the High Six Virtues and Character Strengths identified by Christopher Peterson and Martin Seligman. Chapters 4–9 link particular character strengths to specific actionable transformational leadership behaviors through real life cases and the principles they teach. Chapter 10 reviews the leadership principles and discusses what we, as members of society, need to do to develop leaders of character. Chapter 11 presents testimonials from adult working professionals in industry that describe some of the "grassroots" leaders of character among us.

Several individuals supported my efforts to complete this book and I want to take a moment to acknowledge their efforts. I am very grateful to Dongil (Don) Jung for helping me embellish and clarify some of the material in the early chapters. Thanks to my colleagues at Penn State Great Valley for intellectual stimulation and encouragement on this project. I especially appreciate the advice and support I received from Diane Disney, Denise Potosky, John McCool, Phil LaPlante, Effy Oz, JoAnn Kelly, and Pastor Robert Scott who offered excellent suggestions and motivation to complete the project. I thank my graduate assistants, Thomas Jones and Pamela Reiher, for their research support, and Jennifer Abboud-Smith for drawing the sketches of the leaders featured in this book. I'd also like to acknowledge the support of George Johnson and the folks at Information Age Publishing. Many thanks to those students who submitted e-mails considered for inclusion in Chapter 11. Their contributions show that leading with character is not limited to "world-class" leaders, but also extends to ordinary people who do extraordinary things in everyday leadership roles.

Finally, and foremost, thanks to Sandi L. Dinger who has given me constant encouragement, advice, and support at every stage of this work. I also wish to thank my parents Josephine and John G. Sosik whose faith, guidance and strong work ethic have been a blessing to me over the years.

—John J. Sosik
Malvern, Pennsylvania
May 2006

CHAPTER 1

MAKING THE CASE
FOR AUTHENTIC
TRANSFORMATIONAL
LEADERSHIP

If you think about what you ought to do for other people, your character
will take care of itself.

—Woodrow Wilson

This is a story that defines the essence of outstanding leadership. It is a story that will be told through the lives of 25 extraordinary leaders of character. Their life stories and the principles they teach will help you answer two questions central to your development as a leader and a person: do you possess "the right stuff" for being a leader of character, and how can you develop the full leadership potential of yourself and others in a virtuous way?

If you are interested in this story and in finding answers to these questions, you are not alone. Leadership scholars have pondered these questions for many years. At first, they focused on identifying certain traits, such as confidence, intelligence, and optimism, associated with outstanding leadership and described them in the "Great Man" theories of leadership. It was in these classic theories that the notion of character was first proposed to be the "raw material" of outstanding leadership. However, scholars soon realized that leaders like Hitler, Stalin, Gandhi, and Churchill shared some of the same traits, but produced very different outcomes. So they shifted their focus from traits to behaviors to see what these leaders actually did to produce their results. They then realized that a leader's traits and behaviors don't tell the whole story; we must enter followers and the situation into the leadership equation to tell the whole story.[1]

Sometimes leadership stories are tragic. Consider the ethical scandals involving top corporate leaders at Enron, Arthur Andersen, WorldCom, Tyco and many other corporations in recent years. One highlight of these corporate scandals came on September 20, 2005 when the former CEO of Tyco, Dennis Kozlowski, was sentenced to 25 years in prison and ordered to pay $167 million in restitution and fines. He and his followers had created an organizational culture that ultimately led to their demise. Consider the utter lack of leadership by all levels of government during the Hurricane Katrina disaster across New Orleans and the Gulf Coast area and its devastating effects on people and property. Also consider the unfortunate cases of abuse against faith community members by some priests and ministers who were supposed to be our most trusted spiritual leaders.[2] How much misfortune and destruction of professional and personal lives could have been avoided if the leadership in these cases were guided by character and virtue?

All of these *negative* events have placed notions of character front and center in discussions of what constitutes outstanding leadership. After hearing about these corporate scandals and watching various images of unethical leadership on the news, people today are sick and tired of being negative. They long to learn how to be more positive as human beings and as leaders. They truly want to be leaders who can transform followers into leaders themselves. For example, Bill George, former CEO of Medtronic, longed for such positive influence over others. In his book *Authentic Leadership*, George argues that being positive, ethical and true to yourself is the way to restore confidence in business firms after Enron and WorldCom.[3]

At the same time, leadership scholars around the world have become interested in this topic. They have been working to expand a stream of research on the kind of leadership that involves being ethical, positive, and true to yourself. This form of leadership, as highlighted by George's book, is called *authentic leadership*. It proposes that a leader's character is central to the development of positive relationships with followers.[4] In many ways, it promotes a classic view of leadership which focuses on the individual leader as the "hero," or the "great man or woman." This understanding of leadership is widely shared and easily understood in Western cultures today.

The need to identify authentic leaders who avoid unethical and self-aggrandizing behaviors is more important than ever before. Unfortunately, only a paucity of research has examined the "right stuff" or "raw material" that makes up the kind of leadership that builds up people, teams and organizations. Given these recent trends of developing authentic leadership in organizations for "sustainable growth," it is important for any leader at any level of the organizational hierarchy to understand what particular character strengths are necessary to display authentic transformational leadership. In addition, it is also important to recognize that being authentic or true to oneself may, in fact, not jive with displaying positive and other-oriented behaviors described by writers on authentic leadership. If a leader truly does not possess appropriate character strengths, being true to oneself may actually mean being a "real pain in the behind."

Most everyone wants to try to practice virtuous leadership, but most are not sure how to go about it. I wrote this book as a "how-to guide" so that leaders, like you, could better understand which type of leader they are today, and what character strengths and behaviors they need to exhibit to develop into the type of leader they want to become. It is important for today's leaders, like you, to gain this understanding given the recent emergence of the fields of positive psychology[5] and positive organizational behavior.[6] These fields focus on bringing out what is best in people by focusing on their strengths, rather than fixing what is wrong with them. Growing interest in these fields has helped to accelerate the success of consulting firms, such as the Gallup Organization. Gallup uses assessment tools to identify strengths of individuals, develop their strengths into talents, and then use their talents to establish an appropriate "person-job fit." Gallup claims that these processes improve leadership dynamics and organizational performance.[7]

My approach to writing this book was to build upon psychologists Christopher Peterson and Martin Seligman's seminal work on character strengths and virtues from the positive psychology literature,[8] and leadership scholars Bernard Bass and Bruce Avolio and their colleagues' work on transformational leadership.[9] I integrate these topics to provide you with a better understanding of how virtuous personal attributes can help you to display authentic transformational leadership behaviors. After reading the 25 stories of leaders of character in this book, you should be able to generate some good ideas for your own leadership development as well as the development of your associates. Let's begin by examining why the world needs authentic transformational leadership today more than ever before.

A SOCIETY LOOKING FOR ANSWERS

In the late 1970s, political scientist James MacGregor Burns defined transformational leadership as influence that "occurs when one or more persons *engage* with others in such a way that leaders and followers raise one another to higher levels of motivation and morality."[10] Interestingly, the need for today's leaders to provide higher levels of motivation and morality in our society appears quite pressing. Consider the results of recent studies by the Gallup Organization indicating that 55% of the U.S. workforce is not engaged or motivated by their work, and another 17% is actively disengaged or de-motivated by their work. These adverse results of employee disengagement have been estimated to cost the U.S. economy between $250 and $300 billion every year in lost productivity.

De-motivated workforces are not limited to the U.S. The situation is even worse in other countries around the world, such as Singapore and France. According to Gallup's studies, eighty-four percent of Singapore's workforce is not engaged in their work and 4% is actively disengaged. Sixty-eight percent of France's workforce is not engaged and 6% is actively disengaged.[11] So de-motivation appears to be a world-wide phenomenon that crosses different cultures and societies around the world. As shown in Figure 1.1, identifying

Figure 1.1.   *Is She Engaged?* An important challenge for today's leaders is making work interesting and meaningful for their followers to gain commitment to the organization's mission.

and then dealing with a de-motivated employee can be a challenge. When it comes to motivating employees through transformational leadership, we need to do much better.

We also need to do much better when it comes to displaying transformational leadership that advocates *and* role models behavior according to moral and ethical principles. Results of another Gallup Poll indicate that the state of moral values in the U.S. is not good. Eighty percent of Americans characterized moral values in the U.S. as only fair or poor. Criticism of moral values is not new, but appears to be a consistent societal sore spot. The majority of Gallup Poll respondents polled in 1965, 1991 and 2003 also were dissatisfied with the moral and ethical climate of the country. What's worse is that there is little hope for the future of the state of moral affairs in the nation. Only 16% of Gallup's respondents think that moral values in the nation are getting better, while a whopping 77% say they are getting worse.[12] Have we lost hope in our leaders' ability to reverse this trend?

Motivation and morality are not the only issues that society has grappled with when it comes to leadership. A variety of social problems plague the U.S. and other countries around the world. Over time, these unresolved social problems often result in widespread negativity about leadership, and if left unchecked, can result in anger and violence. For example, racism remains a persistent problem. Although some advances have been made since Dr. Martin Luther King Jr. led the civil rights movement in the 1960s, there are many opportunities for leaders of character to eradicate the plague of racism. Inequities in the distribution of jobs, opportunities, and other economic resources across socio-economic classes are plentiful. While history has shown Marxism and Communism to be failed economic experiments, opportunity knocks for today's leaders to identify other remedies to our economic woes.

Ecological challenges confront us almost everyday. Oil spills, air pollution, noise, traffic congestion, radiation, and urban sprawl are common news topics. The sad problem of urban decay in cities across the U.S. destroys not only public infrastructure and local economies, but also local traditions and culture. The dilemma of finding alternate sources of fuel to reduce our dependence on foreign oil while protecting our environment has perplexed our leaders since the early 1970s. Many ideas and words have been exchanged, but our government and corporate leaders have done little to achieve this delicate balance.

Education is another societal issue ripe for leadership action. The task of providing education that gives as many people as possible a chance at a better life is another great leadership challenge. Providing a high quality education to all appears to be a difficult task. U.S. school systems are plagued by overcrowded classrooms, disciplinary problems, lack of funding, and teachers who can't pass competency exams in their fields. Why do many of our school administrators appear to be so "leadership challenged"?

Within our government, some of our leaders feel that democracy should be spread to all nations around the world. While democracy is a morally justified form of government according to the founders of the U.S. Constitution, our experiences in Iraq, Afghanistan, and the Palestinian factions have led some to question whether democracy is appropriate in all places and in all times. Consider how Palestinian "democracy" has resulted in the election of a government that endorses violence and the destruction of Israel. The context for leadership and its form of government appears to play an important role in determining how world events unfold.

All of these social issues represent leadership challenges that can be taken on by transformational leaders who actively engage with and develop their followers. It also is a well-proven fact that transformational leaders motivate people by inspiration and by sharing similar values, not through a transactional contract. Consider the great leaders of character such as Franklin D. Roosevelt, Rosa Parks, Martin Luther King, Jr., Susan B. Anthony, and Pope John Paul II. These transformational leaders were able to promote positive change in people, groups and organizations. They rallied people around important missions to get them to achieve more than they expected. This book explains how they put their values and virtuous character into action to lead social change.

ORGANIZATIONS IN NEED OF CHANGE

Leadership doesn't occur in a vacuum. The situation, to a large extent, helps to determine leadership effectiveness. The cases of abuse at the Iraqi prison Abu Ghraib; unchecked greed and arrogance at Enron; or lack of transparency and accountability in sex scandals involving some priests in the Catholic Church illustrate an important lesson. That lesson is this: situational power and absolute authority can make good people do bad things and create unethical and evil organizational cultures.

Research by psychologist Philip Zimbardo helps to explain how such situations can arise. In his famous "Prison Experiment," students at Stanford University played roles of "guard" and "prisoner." At the start of the planned two-week experiment, there were no measurable changes among the participating students. However, as they began acquiring and acting out their expected roles and norms as prisoners and guards, their behaviors became noticeably different. The student prisoners actually began to believe and act as if they were inferior and powerless and became very submissive. Meanwhile, the student guards engaged in abusive, authoritative behavior. Zimbardo's experiment demonstrated that people pick up their expected roles and norms much more easily than they think under certain circumstances.[13] Therefore, it is important that top executives and leaders create a more positive work environment for their followers.

Consider the Enron fiasco. Enron CEO Ken Lay provided people with an ideology that the "Enron way" was superior to generally accepted (i.e., ethical) business practices and accounting principles. Minor infractions and "errors in judgment" by associates were ignored and as a result many associates escalated the severity of their unethical actions over time. Lay also presented himself to his associates as a just authority, who represented a role model for accumulating wealth. Once perceived by associates and the media as a positive charismatic leader, Lay transformed himself into an arrogant, intimidating and dictatorial figure. He led with vague and ever-changing rules and harshly enforced compliance with his policies. Lay's actions transformed the landscape of Corporate America in very negative ways and destroyed not only his company, but the financial future of many employees.[14]

Learning from Enron, many organizations are establishing policies and practices to prevent such unfortunate events from repeating themselves. Enron and other examples of corporate corruption raise important questions about the role of leadership in shaping not only employees' ethical standards, but also specific organizational cultures in general. What is most important for us to focus on achieving? What values should guide our behavior at work? How should we balance our individual desires and goals with those of the organization? What should we do when the organization's goals or activities do not align with our own idea of what is right or just? Many corporate employees look to their leaders for ethical guidance in answering these questions.

In addition to the need to lead followers on ethical issues, organizations call on leaders to help them adapt to a dynamic and turbulent business environment. Organizations need to adapt to the challenges of globalization and increased workforce diversity. Issues of unification and separatism, that we've witnessed in Europe, present new business opportunities for leaders. The events of September 11, 2001 highlight the idea that our increasingly Westernized way of life is not universally accepted or valued by all people. How can leaders leverage the power of diversity to understand differences within and between cultures to fully tap into expanding global markets and growth opportunities?

Organizations also need to adapt to the challenges of surviving mergers and acquisitions. When two cultures merge, there are often clashes that can result in the destruction of the union. Like marriages, mergers between organizations face daunting odds against survival and may end up on the rocks. For example, Northwest Airlines and KLM Royal Dutch Airlines experienced many problems with their merger in 1993 because they were both unwilling to adopt their partner's way of doing business. They took their differences to court and subsequently disbanded their alliance in 1998.[15] An emerging stream of research suggests that transformational leadership may help to facilitate the union of organizations undergoing the sometimes difficult change process associated with mergers and acquisitions. How can leaders point out common virtues and character strengths to help merging organizations join forces rather than part ways?

Another form of change is the ever increasing number of organizations downsizing or de-layering. As a result, an organizational leader's span of control, or number of direct reports, increases. Such increases add more hours to an already full work schedule. They also put additional information loads and stress on leaders. These adverse effects often cascade down to subordinates and lower their morale and motivation level. Add to these ill effects the devastating upshot that downsizing produces more "extreme jobs," where workers now put in more than 60 grueling hours a week. And they don't do it because they love their jobs. They do it because they are afraid of losing their jobs.[16] What kind of leadership is needed to put more balance into the lives of corporate workers so that work and family obligations can be fulfilled in a more humane way?

All of these examples of organizational change represent leadership challenges that leaders and executives must handle effectively everyday. The virtues and character strengths discussed in this book are essential to build a more successful leadership style—transformational leadership. Consider the leaders of character such as Lou Gerstner, Lee Iaccoca, Ronald Reagan, Oprah Winfrey, and Mary Kay Ash. These transformational leaders were able to promote positive change in their organizations, industries, and/or governments. They fundamentally changed the way their followers viewed problems, re-structured their organizations and transformed the way their business was conducted. This book explains how they put their values and virtuous characters into action to lead organizational change.

FOLLOWERS HUNGRY FOR PERSONAL GROWTH

Today, followers expect much more from their leaders than ever before. The days of followers being satisfied with a directive or consultative leader are long gone. That's because followers have become much more sophisticated and educated about business and its various functional areas or specializations. Many of the younger followers in your workforce probably grew up in families that encouraged them to voice their own opinions. They were expected to speak up. In school, they were taught using more group-oriented methods, rather than the command and control, mechanical and

Figure 1.2.   *Sharing Leadership.* Many of the leadership roles formerly performed by superiors are being distributed to members of teams, especially in virtual teams that cross physical locations, cultures and time zones.

individual-oriented educational systems of old. They were taught to value life-long learning and personal development. As a result, today's followers expect to partner with the leader. They expect leadership to be *shared.*

This new attitude held by followers raises the bar for the type of leadership that is required to satisfy followers. Considering leadership as simply moving followers from point A to point B to achieve a goal according to a plan is not sufficient for outstanding leadership. Instead, considering leadership as moving followers from point A to point B to achieve a common goal, *while developing them and sharing leadership with them,* is what followers now expect (see Figure 1.2). That's what transformational leadership is all about.

Followers also expect to enhance their career development and personal growth more than ever before in today's highly turbulent and fragile organizations. They want to work in positive environments that value the contributions they make at work and recognize them for their achievements. However, research by the Gallup Organization indicates that the number one reason people leave their jobs is that they don't feel appreciated. To make matters worse, 65% of Americans said that they received no recognition at work in 2003.[17] In this book, I will explain how transformational leaders who possess the character strength of gratitude can help to fix the recognition problem in such organizations.

Building a more positive work environment for employees appears to be a very popular organizational trend. In my consulting work, clients frequently call upon me to assist them with aligning their corporate values with more positive forms of leadership behavior. One client, in particular, is a large pharmaceutical company that has as its values, quality, integrity (a character strength), respect for people (a character strength called "kindness"), leadership (another character strength), and collaboration/teamwork (yet another character strength called "citizenship").

To help my client bring these character strengths to life, I provided training focused on transformational leadership. To demonstrate quality, leaders were trained to encourage followers to continuously improve people and processes. To demonstrate integrity, leaders were trained to consider the ethical implications of their actions. To show respect for people, I trained their leaders to appreciate and leverage the diversity of their workgroups. To demonstrate leadership, leaders were trained to coach and mentor followers. To promote collaboration and teamwork, I trained their leaders to show followers why what they accomplish together is so much more powerful than working alone.

All of these efforts put that client's values into action. These efforts also reflect what James MacGregor Burns meant when he described transformational leadership as beginning "on people's terms, driven by their wants and needs, and must culminate in expanding opportunities for happiness."[18] I elaborate on this topic later in the book.

BAD LEADERS, BAD DECISIONS, BAD OUTCOMES

Are you amazed by the recent dramatic success of Apple Computer and its line of iPod products? Steve Jobs' brilliant strategy of entering the music market has paid off royally in new markets and profits. However, it wasn't always this way. Immediately prior to Jobs' rejoining Apple as CEO in 1997, Apple was led by a series of bumbling leaders who produced lousy results.

The first of these inept CEOs was Michael Spindler, a former Apple COO. Spindler has been described as "the wrong man for the job."[19] Spindler, who failed to display any transformational leadership, lacked several character strengths associated with great leaders. Instead of being socially intelligent, Spindler was impersonal. Instead of being open-minded, Spindler was rigid. While Spindler did lead production of the PowerMac and began licensing of Apple software to Power Computing, his failure to partner with Lou Gerstner and IBM was viewed by some as both arrogant and obtuse.

Problems abounded for Apple as they failed to fill $1 billion in backorders. Besides failing to make a profit in 1995, Apple posted a $68 million loss for the fourth quarter of 1995. In January 1996, Spindler was asked to step down and was replaced by the equally inept Gil Amelio, the former president of National Semiconductor. Amelio was famous for his management-by-exception (i.e., corrective) and cost-cutting approach to leadership. Amelio's halfhearted attempts at leadership focused on executing broad organizational restructuring and downsizing. Unfortunately, Apple continued to hemorrhage dollars to the tune of a staggering $740 million loss for the first quarter of 1996 and $33 million for the second quarter of 1996. By July 1997, Amelio and his leadership of Apple was history because he lacked the character strengths of creativity, social intelligence, love of learning, and hope.

It was Apple's misfortune to have two poor leaders who made bad decisions that resulted in dire organizational outcomes. However, Apple is not alone when it comes to such leadership buffoonery. Consider the case of a school administrator who descended deep into the depths of bad leadership. At first, there were high hopes for this leader. After proving himself as a capable leader of an academic unit, he received great support from both faculty and staff based on the personal friendships he had formed with them. His friendships and apparent concern for people allowed him to be perceived as a "nice person" and "humane leader."

However, he changed as the demands of his top administrative position began to take their toll on him. Once humble and caring, he became much more proud and arrogant. Once fair, just and equitable, he fell victim to cronyism and favoritism. In fact, he seemed to delight in pitting associates against each other, gossiping about others within his clique, and highlighting differences between academic units. Secrecy in the form of closed meetings and quid pro quo deal making (and breaking) were hallmarks of his leadership style. Instead of sharing ideas and a unifying vision, he held faculty and staff accountable for providing ideas, only to fail to support their ideas. Once careful and respectful of others, he now lashed out in loud tirades during administrative meetings.

As time went by, the results of his leadership became apparent. Enrollments dropped, faculty and staff morale plummeted, and the school lost some very talented and committed people. Even as this was happening, he demonstrated a lack of leadership. He abused time, arriving for work late in the mornings, taking extended lunches with friends and family, and rarely working a full five day week. At work, he would often side with "friends" in his clique instead of doing what was best for the school. He missed important deadlines. He failed to provide mentoring to his faculty and make innovative changes to the curriculum. He also refused to convene meetings with staff support areas that the faculty requested. As a result, his legacy was a five-year decline in enrollments, revenue, employee satisfaction, and a culture of mistrust, competitiveness and cynicism among colleagues. Needless to say, he no longer leads the school.

We can do much better! We must do much better. These examples illustrate the need for leaders of character who can face difficult situations and lead the way to positive change. Transformational leaders can bring about this kind of change. They are perceived as trustworthy and strong role models to be admired and respected. They instill pride and respect in their followers. They set aside their self-interests for the good of the organization. As a result, their organizations attain the very highest levels of performance.

PHONY LEADERS AND PHONY PROFITS

Imagine yourself working for a CEO like the infamous Albert J. Dunlap, formerly of Sunbeam. In the mid-to-late 1990s, Dunlap received much media attention as he was lauded for turning around the economic fortunes of several corporations. Efficient and ruthless, he fired thousands of employees and closed plants in passionate pursuit of raising the market value of his firm's stock. His successes at the nine companies he ran from the 1970s through the 1990s, most notably Scott Paper and Sunbeam, became the subject of discussions in top U.S. business schools. He, like Gordon Gecco of *Wallstreet* (the movie) fame, personified the relentless logic of Corporate America: it's all about boosting the bottom line for the stockholders.

Dunlap, who actually preferred to be referred to as "Chainsaw Al" or "Rambo in Pinstripes," has been described as a merciless and cold-blooded person. He was reported to have skipped the funerals of both his parents, failed to support or acknowledge a child from his first marriage, and refused to pay for the cancer treatment of his niece. He apparently took pride in his iron-fisted business toughness, joyfully explaining to the business press how wonderful firings and plant closing are for stockholders.[20] Are you wondering about what this says about Dunlap's character, leadership and definition of business "success"? I hope so.

But was Dunlap really as effective as he appeared to be? Not at all. While Dunlap's methods caused Sunbeam's stock to rise from $12 to $53/share, Dunlap's methods were eventually revealed to be phony. With the help of Arthur Andersen (also the auditor for Enron and WorldCom), he relied on a variety of accounting scams and irregularities to boost the stock price. He bullied retailers into buying more inventory than they could handle. Sunbeam's warehouses became hopelessly over-stocked. Investors panicked and Sunbeam's stock plummeted to $11/share. After the SEC began its investigation into these shenanigans, Dunlap was fired in June 1998. In September 2002, Dunlap agreed to pay $500,000 to settle SEC charges that he defrauded stockholders by inflating sales at Sunbeam.

The story of "Chainsaw" Al Dunlap, along with the scandals at Enron, WorldCom, Tyco, Arthur Andersen, and the much publicized betrayals of trust by some priests, ministers and presidents, illustrates the importance of authenticity for leadership. Dunlap's character helped to create his *lack* of authenticity as a leader. Such leaders are phony. They are not accountable for their actions. They do not "walk the talk." What they say is *not* what they do, and worst of all, their "hearts are deceitful" and they are not true to themselves. As such, how can they be true to others?

The apparent prevalence of inauthentic leaders in corporate and institutional settings has lead to public outrage and calls for authentic leadership development, moral reasoning training, and increased ethical awareness and accountability. Webster's dictionary defines *authentic* as "worthy of acceptance of belief, conforming to fact or reality, trustworthy, not imaginary, false or imitation." To be authentic requires a greater moral awareness of yourself and the effects your actions have on others. It also requires the integrity to face the truth, even though the truth may hurt. Because in the end, as leader or follower, it is the truth that matters most; it is the truth that sets us free.

Let us now turn our attention to describing what it means to be an authentic transformational leader, paying particular attention to how the virtues (and vices) of leaders shape their character.

NOTES

1. Bass, B.M. (1990). *Bass and Stodgill's handbook of leadership: Theory, research and managerial applications.* New York: Free Press.

2. For discussions of ethical scandals in faith communities, see McElvaine, R.S. (2001, November 11). The birth of the myth that men are closer to God. *The Washington Post, p. B.3,* and Paulson, M. (2005, June 26). Catholic bishops retain 'zero tolerance' policy: Will set aside $1M for sex abuse study. *Boston Globe,* p. A.1.

3. George, B. (2003). *Authentic leadership: Rediscovering the secrets to creating lasting value.* San Francisco, CA. Jossey Bass.

4. Gardner, W.L., Avolio, B.J., Luthans, F., May, D.R., & Walumbwa, F. (2005). "Can you see the real me?" A self-based model of authentic leader and follower development. *The Leadership Quarterly, 16,* 343–372.

5. Peterson, C., & Seligman, M.E.P. (2004). *Character strengths and virtues: A handbook and classification.* New York: Oxford/American Psychological Association.

6. Luthans, F. (2002). The need for and meaning of positive organizational behavior. *Journal of Organizational Behavior, 23,* 695–706.

7. Coffman, C., & Gonzalez Molina, G. (2002). *Follow this path: How the world's greatest organizations drive growth by unleashing human potential.* New York: Warner Books.

8.   Peterson & Seligman (2004) as cited in Note 5.

9.   Bass, B.M. (1985). *Leadership and performance beyond expectations.* New York: Free Press; and Bass, B.M., & Avolio, B.J. (1997). *Full range leadership development: Manual for the Multifactor Leadership Questionnaire.* Palo Alto, CA: Mind Garden.

10. Burns, J.M. (1978). *Leadership.* New York: Harper & Row, p.20.

11. Crabtree, S. (2003, December 11). Beyond the dot-com bust. *Gallup Management Journal.* Retrieved December 17, 2003, from http://gmj.gallup.com/content/default.asp?ci=9841; and personal communication with Robert Lockwood, Partner, The Gallup Organization (September 12, 2005).

12. Saad, L. (2004, May 21). Democrats and Republicans agree that U.S. morals are sub par: Outlook for morals worsened over past year. *Gallup Management Journal.* Retrieved August 15, 2004, from http://gmj.gallup.com/content/default.asp?ci=9841

13. Dittmann, M. (2004, October). What makes good people do bad things? *Monitor on Psychology,* 68–69.

14. Swartz, M., & Watkins, S. (2003). *Power failure: The inside story of the collapse of ENRON.* New York: Doubleday.

15. Sleek, S. (1998, July). Some corporate mergers, like marriages, end up on the rocks. *Monitor on Psychology,* 13–14.

16. Tischler, L. (2005). Extreme jobs. *Fast Company, 93,* 55–60.

17. Rath, T., & Clifton, D.O. (2004). *How full is your bucket?: Positive strategies for work and life.* Omaha, NE: Gallup Press.

18. Burns, J.M. (2003). *Transforming leadership.* New York: Atlantic Monthly Press, p. 230.

19. http://asip.helio.no/applehistory/history.html. Retrieved February 11, 2000.

20. Plotz, D. (1997, August 31). Al Dunlap: The chainsaw capitalist. Retrieved September 22, 2005 from http://slate.msn.com/id/1830/.

CHAPTER 2

AUTHENTIC TRANSFORMATIONAL LEADERSHIP

Transformational leadership is a relationship of mutual stimulation and elevation that converts followers into leaders and may convert leaders into moral agents.

—James MacGregor Burns

Take a moment to think about all of the individuals in your life who have shaped your idea of what it means to be a great leader. Perhaps this group includes your parents, or your spouse, or even a favorite teacher. Maybe it includes your mentor, coach, priest, minister, or rabbi. Of those people, who is the one person who has had the most *profound* effect on your development as a leader and as a person? This is the person who inspired and stretched you to achieve more than you thought you could achieve. This is the person who challenged your fundamental ways of thinking and doing things. This is the person who has helped you to put aside your personal interests for the good of a great cause. This is the person who coached and mentored you and made you a much better person. This person is a transformational leader.

Transformational leaders act in ways that turn followers into leaders in their own right. By empowering their followers, they build excitement around an appealing vision that creates performance excellence in very

Leading with Character, pages 15–32
Copyright © 2006 by Information Age Publishing
All rights of reproduction in any form reserved.

challenging economic and political times. They promote positive change in their people, teams and organizations. Adapting to change has become a fact of life for most organizations. Increasingly, organizations are relying on transformational leaders to promote positive changes in employee work engagement and collaboration, creativity and innovation, mentoring of associates, workforce diversity, product and process quality, technology adoption, and strategy execution.

As you may have realized by now, extensive research on transformational leadership has found that there are several very distinctive and unique behaviors that transformational leaders display. And, here is the good news: Research also indicates that you can *learn* to display transformational leadership behaviors to produce these powerful effects on your own people, teams and organizations. In this chapter, I introduce and explain the concepts, behaviors and tactics you need to acquire to be an authentic transformational leader.

WHO ARE TRANSFORMATIONAL LEADERS?

We can identify transformational leaders by *what they do* and *who they are*. This chapter explains what they do (their behaviors). Chapters 4 through 9 explain who they are (their character). A prominent leadership scholar named Bernard Bass, who invented and elaborated the theory of *transformational leadership* in the 1980s, described transformational leadership in terms of a set of four components—leader behaviors and attributions (acknowledgements) made by followers. The display and attribution of these components in an authentic and ethical manner aids in the leader's own moral development. Phony leaders, who only pretend to be transformational, are often motivated by personal quests for fame, wealth, and/or self-aggrandizement. These leaders use followers as a means to an end. Such leaders display *pseudotransformational leadership*.

Werner Erhard is a good example of a pseudotransformational leader. Erhard, a former encyclopedia salesman, became interested in studying several spiritual disciplines such as Zen Buddhism and L. Ron Hubbard's "Dianetics." According to Erhard, his studies in the early 1970s allowed him to gain a type of self-awareness that he packaged into a controversial training program called *EST* (Erhard Seminar Training). His intensive weekend programs included 18- hour days touted to deliver greater self-expression and vitality. Due to his charismatic stage presence, the EST programs became very popular and Erhard gained a cult-like following including many television celebrities such as Valerie Harper of the television series *Rhoda*. His following grew even larger with the success of his *The*

Hunger Project (a study and proposed solution to chronic world hunger) and *The Forum* (a toned-down and streamlined version of EST).

But much controversy arose after Erhard was charged by former followers of physical abuse. He later faced income tax violation charges by the IRS, allegations of domestic violence and allegations of incest with one of his daughters. The daughter later recanted her story after fessing up to taking a $2 million bribe from a reporter. Still, Erhard's "cult of personality," the allegations against him, and his recent name change to "Werner Spits" have painted him as a pseudotransformational leader who appears to be motivated solely by fortune, fame and self-aggrandizement.[1]

Unlike Erhard, many leaders demonstrate transformational leadership in a more ethical way. They exercise their leadership with the intention of helping and developing others, often at the expense of their own personal interests. Vyomesh Joshi, the head of Hewlett Packard's highly profitable printing division, is an excellent example of authentic leader. Joshi became a strong candidate to succeed the former HP CEO Carly Fiorina. He manages the $24-billion printing division with a friendly and nice-guy attitude. His leadership approach is very down-to-earth. His employees give him high marks for his strategic vision, passion for what he is doing, and uncanny ability to get his associates excited about working for him.[2] Although he has an ambitious vision to double his division to a $48 billion entity within the next decade, he wants to accomplish this by developing his employees' full potential.

Vyomesh Joshi doesn't pretend to be someone else other than who he is. He wants to see his followers grow. He believes that this is how he can attain his vision. Unlike Carly Fiorina, Joshi does not relish in delivering charismatic and inspirational speeches in front of media people. No wonder why the article reporting his success story is entitled "A nice guy finishes 1st: Head of HP's profitable printing division known as a likable career guy who motivates."

Leaders such as Joshi display *authentic transformational leadership.*[3] In the training programs that my colleagues and I give, we like to use the following statement to help participants understand what it means for a leader to be authentic:

> When what you say is what you do, and you are true to yourself, then you are an authentic leader.

Let's carefully examine the elements of this statement. "What you say" refers to the words of influence, messages of motivation, or vision statements that you as a leader express to your followers. "What you do" represents your behaviors—your actions and deeds. You need to be very careful about what you say since your followers pay very close attention to your words and deeds. They look for congruity or agreement between what you say and do in order to see if you are "the real deal" or authentic. Being "true to yourself" means that you feel comfortable publicly expressing your private thoughts about your values, ideas, and feelings. It's a tall order to have all three pieces of this statement in place. But it goes a long way in helping you to express the real you and be true to yourself. Once again, the truth will set you free.

Many leaders have brought about positive changes in others through their ethical actions and by being true to their personal values and beliefs. Consider Mary Kay Ash of Mary Kay Cosmetics. Ash gained the commitment of her organizational members by successfully putting her organization's values, career aspirations of women, and Christian values into the practice of making life better for working women.[4] Other authentic transformational leaders include Nelson Mandela, Eleanor Roosevelt, Mahatma Gandhi, and Donald O. Clifton, formerly of the Gallup Organization.

THE FOUR I'S OF TRANSFORMATIONAL LEADERSHIP

Transformational leaders display four important behaviors: idealized influence, inspirational motivation, intellectual stimulation, and individualized consideration. These behaviors, along with follower reactions, a confident and dynamic leader personality, and a challenging situation, converge to create the highest levels of individual, group and organizational performance.[5]

Idealized Influence

Transformational leaders display *idealized influence* (II-B) or pro-social and positive behaviors to role model organizational values such as high levels of ethical and performance standards. When leaders display such behaviors, followers often reflect great admiration and loyalty back at them and make *attributions of idealized influence* (II-A) towards the leader. Followers perceive the leader as trustworthy and worthy of respect and emulation. II-A involves gaining trust, respect and confidence from followers as a result of displaying II-B through setting and role modeling high standards of conduct for yourself and others. As a result, followers are willing to show support for the leader's vision and put extra effort into their work. For example, General Electric's CEO Jeffrey Immelt exemplifies an idealized leader who holds high expectations of ethical behavior for his associates, as illustrated by GE's zero-tolerance policy for financial reporting misconduct.[6]

Inspirational Motivation

Transformational leaders use *inspirational motivation* (IM) to energize their followers to do more than is expected. IM involves speaking optimistically and enthusiastically, articulating an inspiring and evocative vision, expressing confidence, and championing teamwork and high standards of performance. When displaying IM, leaders speak glowingly about a future desired state that they describe in their vision and develop a plan to achieve it. For example, Mary Kay Ash formulated and articulated an inspiring vision for women to pursue opportunities to achieve unlimited personal and financial success in her organization by serving "God first, family second, and career third."[7] Visions inspire leaders and followers to focus on what is most important without being distracted by events of the day.

Intellectual Stimulation

Transformational leaders use *intellectual stimulation* (IS) to get followers and constituents to re-examine assumptions, seek different perspectives, look at problems in new ways, and encourage non-traditional thinking. They encourage followers to re-think old methods of doing things to break through inappropriate or outdated business models. Such leadership behavior encourages followers to be willing to think for themselves, re-engineer work processes and be more creative. IS seeks to get followers to question the status quo and promote continuous innovation and process improvement, even at the peak of success. For example, James Goodnight, CEO of SAS Institute, Inc., has created an organizational culture that promotes creativity and innovation. Goodnight stimulates the minds of his associates to think of superior performance and better products rather than the hassles of distractions, time pressures, and resource shortages that stifle innovation.[8]

Individualized Consideration

Transformational leaders also use *individualized consideration* (IC) with their followers and customers to recognize their unique potential to develop into leaders themselves. They spend time listening, teaching and coaching followers as shown in Figure 2.1. They go out and visit their customers, one by one, to see what they really value. They treat others as individuals with different needs, abilities and aspirations and get them to appreciate the benefits of diversity. They also help others to develop their knowledge, skills and abilities. As a result, followers begin to value personal

Figure 2.1.   Individualized Consideration can be displayed in many ways, including through the role of mentor. You can see how focused and learning-oriented the leader and follower have become.

learning and development and may appreciate the breadth of knowledge, skills and abilities associated with collaborating within a diverse team. IC energizes followers to develop and achieve their full potential through mentoring and appreciation of diversity. For example, Walmart CEO John Fleming, has promoted employee development with formalized mentoring programs, team-based work structures, and management coaching.

To summarize, authentic transformational leaders are genuine regarding their role modeling, formulation and articulation of a compelling vision, challenging others to question basic assumptions about work, and coaching and mentoring others. While not all transformational leaders are able to display each of these behaviors in an authentic manner, those who display them more frequently and consistently are perceived as more authentically transformational than those who do not. However, an important question remains: How can you tell the difference between a pseudotransformational leader and an authentic transformational leader?

WILL THE "REAL" TRANSFORMATIONAL LEADER PLEASE STAND UP?

Do you remember the classic television game show called *To Tell the Truth?* The game involved a famous person and two impostors trying to outwit a panel of four celebrities. The panelists would grill the three contestants with probing questions about history, pop culture, etc. The object of the game was to try to deceive the celebrities into voting for the two impostors. On many occasions, the panel was fooled and sometimes an imposter was deemed too good to be true.[9]

As in the game show, the real world of leadership holds many opportunities to be duped by charlatans. It is natural to wonder how you can tell apart leaders who are "phony" from those who are authentic, and those who are constructive, positive or "good" from those who are destructive, negative or "bad." Consider an illustration.

One day I was discussing with a friend examples of leaders who are clear examples of "good guy" and "bad guy" leader types. While brainstorming the "good guys," Gandhi, Mother Teresa, and Pope John Paul II were among those came to mind. While brainstorming the "bad guys," Adolph Hitler, Joseph Stalin, and Charles Manson were among those who came to mind. My friend pointed out that both of these groups contain leaders who can be considered as charismatic. She was correct.

I went on to explain that *charismatic leadership* is defined as a social influence process that involves the formulation and articulation of an evocative vision—a compelling image of a better future. It provides inspiration to motivate collective action. It demonstrates sensitivity to industry and business trends. And charismatic leadership often involves displaying unconventional and personal risk-taking behavior. These behaviors result in charismatic leaders being role models for followers. The followers become extremely loyal, trusting of, and emotionally committed to the leader and the vision. The followers also learn to find their jobs meaningful and exciting. And they make sacrifices for the collective cause championed by the leader.[10] My friend understood these characteristics, but then noted that "The leaders in these groups may possess similar charming personalities, but what they do with their charisma is very different." She was onto an important distinction.

Socialized versus Personalized Charisma

I explained to her that although the word "charisma" originates from the Greek meaning "gift of grace"—therefore implying that it is a gift from God, charisma is actually ethically neutral. That is, charisma can be used for tremendous good, as in the case of Gandhi. Or charisma can be used for tremendous evil, as in the case of Hitler. What matters is how the power or influence that the charismatic leader holds is used. If it is used to benefit others, the charisma is said to be *socialized*. However, if it is used to benefit oneself at the expense of others, the charisma is said to be *personalized*.

Leadership scholar Jane Howell coined the term *socialized charismatic leadership*, to denote the "good guy" charismatic leaders, who empower others to promote pro-social and ethical collective action. She contrasted this style with *personalized charismatic leadership*, which manipulates others for self-serving and unethical purposes. Socialized charismatic leadership reflects positive influences on followers and can be explained in terms of positive psychology's emphasis on character strengths which correspond to universally recognized values. Socialized charismatic leadership may result in new heights of individual and collective achievements. However, personalized charismatic leadership may result in individual, group and organizational ruin.[11] Therefore, the distinction between socialized and personalized charismatic leaders allows explanation of "good" or "bad" motives underlying how the charisma is used. But as suggested by Figure 2.2, making this distinction is not easy.

Figure 2.2.   *Hi, What's Your Name Again?* Beware of charming leaders. Despite their charming personality and ingratiating behavior, not all charismatic business leaders have their followers' best interests in mind.

Authentic versus Inauthentic Leaders

Our discussion then shifted to the kind of executive leaders at Enron and WorldCom who, knowingly or unknowingly, usurped and/or destroyed their shareholders' and employees' life-long retirement savings. Were these leaders being true to their stockholders' best interests? Certainly not. Were these leaders true to themselves, as they were busy duping their shareholders and associates by "cooking the books" with a myriad of accounting irregularities and frauds? Were they inauthentic leaders? Or were they actually authentic leaders, just being their rotten selves? These are questions that followers need to ask themselves about their leaders (see Figure 2.3).

Pause. Stop. Hit the rewind button. Our conversation seemed to suddenly slam on the breaks. First my friend look shocked. Then she experienced a

Figure 2.3.   *Hmmm, Is He For Real?* Followers look for consistency between their leader's words and actions over time. This helps to determine whether or not the leader is authentic.

Eureka moment as she thought things over again! Our conversation continued as follows:

"You just told me that authentic leaders act ethically and are true to themselves."

"Right."

"You also told me that inauthentic leaders misbehave by putting on a show that does not really reflect their beliefs and values."

"Right again. You're two-for-two."

"But what happens when being inauthentic doesn't necessarily mean being unethical, and being authentic doesn't necessarily mean being ethical or moral? Is it possible that a leader can be true to himself, but being true to himself means being a real jerk, like Saddam Hussein?"

I then stopped in my tracks, smiled and said, "Let's sign you up for the PhD program!" At that moment, I realized that she was onto a very important point. That is, to understand what it truly means to be an authentic transformational leader requires not only examining authentic and inauthentic forms of leadership, but also examining positive and negative forms of leadership, at the same time. What became clear to us is that we must distinguish between four types of leaders in order to understand how character and transformational leadership are related.

FOUR TYPES OF LEADERS

Let's consider leaders along two continuums or dimensions as shown in Figure 2.4. On the first continuum, we will distinguish socialized leaders who use their power for the good of others from personalized leaders who use their power for their own self-aggrandizement. On the second continuum, we will distinguish authentic leaders who act in ways that are true to their personal values and beliefs from inauthentic leaders who act in ways that are not consistent with their values and beliefs. This creates a typology of leaders with four classifications which are labeled "The Saint," "The Politician/Well-Meaning Chameleon," "The Abrasive/Egotistical Hero," and "The Used-Car Salesman."

The Saint

A socialized charismatic leader who is also highly authentic is the leader type which I label as the *Saint.* Consider leaders such as Mahatma Gandhi and Mary Kay Ash. These leaders use their power and influence to help others. Gandhi focused his efforts on gaining independence for India from

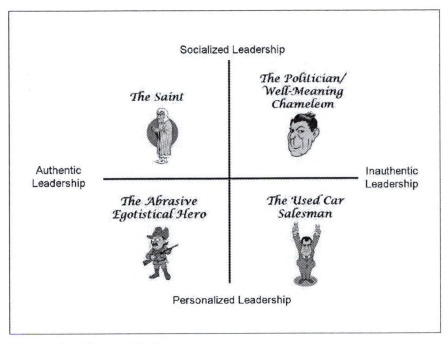

Figure 2.4.   A Leadership Typology.

Great Britain. He also served as a role model for the Indian people on how they should conduct their lives during their struggle for independence and beyond. Mary Kay Ash also used her power in a socialized way. Through her company, Mary Kay Cosmetics, she was able to help women build their self-confidence that they, like men, could enjoy both the joys of family life and the satisfaction of a lucrative career.

Besides focusing on others, Saints also conduct themselves in public in a way that is consistent with their personal or private values and beliefs. Gandhi appealed to his followers to value Indian religious traditions of *sataja-graha* (truthfulness), *ahimsa* (non-violence), and *karma yoga* (spiritual discipline). These were some of the virtues and principles by which Gandhi lived his own life. He practiced them in public and people came to see him as being authentic.

Mary Kay Ash also built virtues into the corporate DNA of her company. She challenged her people to put these virtues into action at work and at home. She could do this because she consistently demonstrated these virtues when she came into contact with others. Mary Kay Ash built her company around the Golden Rule: Treat others as you want to be treated. Leadership based on the Golden Rule is fair and just, and in the end, makes business sense. As discussed in Chapter 3, fairness and justice are virtues that also bring out the best in people. But not every Saint's road to success is paved with cobblestones of fairness.

Such was the case for John H. Johnson, whose rags-to-riches story of leadership and character is quite amazing. Johnson was born into an African-American family in 1918 in Arkansas City, Arkansas. To pursue greater educational opportunities, Johnson's mother moved the family to Chicago in 1936. Johnson struggled through decades of ignorance and prejudice. Remarkably, his resilience, spirituality, focus and social intelligence fueled his success. Over the course of his life, Johnson developed into a man of many talents including media magnet, philanthropist, social activist, publisher, entrepreneur, and business mogul. His first publication, *Negro Digest*, debuted in 1942 as a means for quenching Black America's "thirst for recognition and respect" by dealing with important racial and social issues. Johnson motivated his sales force to base their work on "not your self interest but on their (the customers') interests." Fueled by this success, Johnson launched *Ebony* in 1946 and *JET* in 1951. To this day, both of these publications address important African-American issues of the time.

Despite these successes, Johnson always possessed a friendly down-to-earth personality. He was true to himself and what it meant to be an African American. Over the years, many presidents, politicians, government officials and celebrities appreciated his authenticity. He championed the empowerment and social causes of African-Americans in a tough but ethical way. Johnson exemplifies what I mean when I encourage you to do what you say and say what you really believe in and stand for.

Johnson's socialized charisma yielded many good works and outcomes not just for his people but also for the whole society and perhaps for the whole world. These achievements were recognized at Johnson's funeral in 2005 by many dignitaries and celebrities including former President Bill Clinton, radio celebrity Tom Joyner, publisher Earl G. Graves, Illinois Governor Rod Blagojevich, and the Reverend Jesse Jackson.[12] Perhaps it is this kind of recognition that validates the long-lasting impact that Saints can have by helping others and being ethical and authentic.

The Politician/Well-Meaning Chameleon

A socialized charismatic leader who is inauthentic is the leader type which I label as the *Politician/Well-Meaning Chameleon.* These are the leaders who need to be "all things to all people." They behave in ways that are popular with the majority of people around them at the time. They tend to seek approval from different groups of people. They also depend upon the opinions of others and will act in a manner consistent with what they believe will get others to like them. They lack confidence to act independently of what they perceive to be the popular or accepted position. My research indicates that such leaders possess low levels of confidence in acting independently of popular opinion and set goals cautiously.[13] This type of leader also tends to make impression management a top priority on his agenda.

When Bill Clinton first became president, he was criticized for taking too much time to make decisions. Clinton was a firm believer in including as many points of view in the decision-making process as possible. He also wanted to gain consensus from all of his constituent groups. He had to have their support, even if it meant behaving in ways that may not be consistent with his true ideas and values. At the cost of his authenticity, he wanted to make sure that everyone was "on board" before he made a final decision. All of this stemmed from his need for approval. Being driven by this need is an important aspect of the inauthentic personality of the Politician/Well-Meaning Chameleon.

This type of leader is a social chameleon or actor. Their lack of authenticity stems, in part, from their ability to self-monitor their behavior according to the demands of the situation. Like good actors, they possess a variety of "behavioral scripts" or personas that they enact depending on the situation. In the movie *Zelig*, Woody Allen takes the notion of self-monitoring and turns it into a farce about the ultimate inauthentic leader. Leonard Zelig, the main character of the movie, is inauthentic and wants to "fit in" to the extreme. When he is in a New Orleans jazz club his skin turns black, he takes on stereotypical African-American mannerisms, and convincingly jives with "the brothers." When in Greenwich Village, New York, he grows a long beard, and chants in Hebrew so he can fit in with Hassidic Jews. As a result of his antics, Zelig becomes well-loved and famous, as is the Politician/Well-Meaning Chameleon leader type.

Politicians/Well-Meaning Chameleons adapt easily to a variety of situations. Yet, their ability to change and their display of inconsistent behavior over time detracts from their authenticity. During times of pain and suffering, they may convincingly portray the role of an empathic comforter. For example, during the Spring floods of 1996, President Clinton visited the flood-ravaged people of Northeastern Pennsylvania, "feeling their pain" and promising (and subsequently delivering) relief with compassion. In this instance, Clinton demonstrated the character strengths of kindness and social intelligence.

During times of struggle and challenge, they may convincingly portray the role of an unshakable iron-willed general. For example, during the Monica Lewinsky sex scandal, the same President Clinton looked straight into the eye of the camera, confidently and strongly, and lied to the American people by saying "I did *not* have sex with that woman." While Clinton was found out to be inauthentic over time, he is still admired by many

Americans for the social reforms and economic good times associated with his presidency.

One of our most popular presidents, Ronald Reagan, also shared the ability to self-monitor his behavior based on the demands of the situation. As a trained radio announcer and television/ movie actor, Reagan was able to easily adapt to social relations with many different groups of people. Whether it was joking his way through cabinet meetings, negotiating with Mikhail Gorbachev, or delivering his folksy presidential addresses, Reagan had the knack for putting on a good show. As a result, some of Reagan's staff found him to be sometimes cold and distant, as if every interaction was just another acting performance or role. Regardless of his inauthentic means, Reagan's overarching goal was the safety, welfare, and prosperity of the American people. And they loved him as their President, as if he was their very own grandfather. Like Reagan, the Politician/Well-Meaning Chameleon leader has the best interests of his people in mind. Such leaders may have a plastic appearance, but they certainly possess a heart of gold.

The Abrasive Egotistical Hero

A personalized charismatic leader who is highly authentic is the leader type which I label as the *Abrasive Egotistical Hero*. Their mantra might be "I'm a real bastard and I know it." The Abrasive Egotistical Hero uses his power for personal gain. He demands that his decisions must be followed. He censures criticism, but is the first to bully others using threats and intimidation. He is known to prefer coercive power and punishment to more positive and enduring bases of power such as referent power (based on personal liking) and expertise. My research indicates that such arrogant and abrasive leaders over-estimate their leadership effectiveness and rely on intimidating forms of influence.[14] He is insensitive to others, often ignoring the fact that the leadership process also involves followers. How many managers around you can you identify as Abrasive Egotistical Heroes?

The Abrasive Egotistical Hero doesn't pull any punches. These leaders are known for getting results by being brutally demanding. They are high performers who "deliver the goods." However, their approach and motivation is self-centered. It is more about them than their organization. They are cult-like leaders whose followers *idolize* rather than *idealize* them. Nevertheless, they are genuine and don't try to pretend to be who others want them to be. They are not sugar-coated psycho-babbling phonies. They are truly tough-as-nails taskmasters.

Jack Welch certainly has achieved hero status in the corporate world. Known as "Neutron Jack," Welch came into GE with a warrior mentality that focused on lean and mean operations and being number 1 or 2 in the industry. If GE's business units didn't meet these goals, Welch would ruthlessly sell entire business units or lay people off without blinking an eye. Yes, Welch did add a phenomenal amount of market value capital for GE shareholders. And he did it in a way that was true to his personal values of wealth, fame and self-aggrandizement. GE's success has become a cash cow for his large ego and wallet. While Welch certainly possessed the character strengths of vitality and persistence, he lacked many of the virtues of humanity and temperance associated with socialized charismatic leaders.

Another leader who typifies the Abrasive Egotistical Hero is Steve Jobs of Apple Computer. Some of you may have read about Job's recent victory over cancer and his brilliant graduation speech delivered at Stanford University in May 2005. While Jobs may have grown into a kinder and gentler leader, he was not always that way. Stories abound about his tirades and verbal abuse of Apple employees during the development of the Macintosh computer, his forceful ways of motivating employees to create "insanely great" products, and his ego-maniacal fights with Apple's board of directors. All of this is reported to have driven many people at Apple crazy, making them de-motivated and disillusioned with their work. Indeed, Jobs certainly was true to himself in creating a sense of family (which he never experienced growing up) at Apple and wanting (and then actually making) his people "great" by demanding perfection. This is who Steve Jobs was and still is. This is how he behaved and expected others to behave. With the Abrasive Egotistical Hero, there is no pretense, but the reality is often not very pretty.

Arnold Schwarzenegger has also earned larger than life heroic status. Schwarzenegger's success in bodybuilding during the 1970s is well documented in the movie *"Pumping Iron"*. As an actor, his record-breaking box office victories as "The Terminator" in the 1980s and 1990s also enlarged his already pumped-up ego, and swelled his bank accounts. Sometimes celluloid heroes (remember the Kink's song about old movie stars?) go on to become Abrasive Egotistical Heroes! Schwarzenegger's transition into California politics as its governor, replacing the inept Grey Davis, was met with initial approval and success. However, California residents have recently grown annoyed with Schwarzenegger's ego, rigidness, rubbing people the wrong way, and reference to various individuals as "girly-men," among his other personalized characteristics and actions.

It is interesting that while Schwarzenegger is a former actor, he is remarkably authentic when it comes to his brash governor persona. Schwarzenegger presents a consistently traditional Republican image largely based on the party's traditional values. His brutal honesty, sincerity and concern for his own accomplishments are very evident. Schwarzenegger's pumped-up self-confidence has allowed him to appear to be open to feedback, but whether he acts on the feedback is open to debate. However, his focus appears to be about *himself* and *his* accomplishments as an athlete, actor and politician. He has shown little concern for his constituents' needs. Perhaps when you are used to all the attention that comes with fame and fortune, it is hard to be humble and look beyond yourself.

The Used-Car Salesman

A personalized charismatic leader who is also inauthentic is the leader type which I label as the *Used-Car Salesman*. My sincere apologies go out to those of you with family members who sell used cars. Not all used car salesmen are unethical phonies. But for some reason popular culture has given this group a bad rap. Therefore, the images associated with a used-car salesman may perfectly describe the ideas I am trying to convey to you regarding this type of leader.

What do *you* typically think of when you hear the phrase "used-car salesman?" Be honest. Do the words "sleazy," "huckster," "phony," "weasel," or "cheat" come to mind? Does the phrase "sell your grandmother down the river" come to mind? Yes, I thought so. Based on these images and research on personalized charismatic leaders and inauthentic leaders, I came up with the following profile that describes this type of leader.

The Used-Car Salesman leader type is out for himself. He will use his followers in a slick and cunning way. He comes across as guarded or secretive. He lacks authenticity not because he is naturally cautious and reserved, but because he is downright dishonest. He will try to create an image that he is more capable (or honest) than he is, hoping he can conceal the fact that all that he says and does is based on pretense. In contrast to the Politician/ Well-Meaning Chameleon, the Used-Car Salesman's self-monitoring and acting is done for his own good and at the expense of his followers.

Consider the fortunes amassed by CEOs Ken Lay of Enron, Bernie Ebbers of WorldCom, and Dennis Kozlowski of Tyco. These were fortunes amassed for the CEOs' own self-aggrandizement and self-enhancement— all at the expense of their employees and stockholders. Each of these leaders misrepresented themselves as capable leaders who had all of the answers. They bragged about being smarter than other leaders, smarter than entire industries, and smarter than the IRS and certified public accountants. Their elitist claims created a culture of unethical risk-taking and a sense of being invulnerable. They conned their followers. But in each case, they lost touch with reality and fell down the slippery slope of unethical behavior and cover-ups. How soon did they forget the rhyme that we learned in elementary school: "Oh, what a tangled web we weave, when we first practice to deceive." As Used Car Salesmen, they avoided the responsibility of living authentically and ethically, they ruined entire institutions, and have destroyed the trust granted to corporate leaders by the general public.

The Used-Car Salesman does not only run amuck in corporate settings. They are found in all walks of life. Do you remember the Reverend Jim Bakker, the infamous tele-evangelist of the 1980s? He and his wife, Tammy Faye Bakker came into the homes of countless Americans through their television show, the *PTL Club*. Their popular show allowed the Bakkers to solicit and collect millions of dollars through donations from their faithful viewers, all in the name of the Lord. Bakker lived in extreme opulence, wasting $158 million of these donations on personal excesses and adulterous nights spent with Playboy bunny Jessica Hahn. Over time, Bakker was found out and his public fall from grace was topic of newspapers, and ironically, the evening television news broadcasts. Such is the eventual fate of the Used-Car Salesman leader type, who lack many, if not all, of the character strengths and virtues described in this book.

The typology of leaders described in this chapter provides us with a framework to explain how a leader's character and virtues can help to shape the leadership behavior. An understanding of this framework is needed to reap the benefits of living the good life of the Saint, and to avoid the fate and ignominy of the Used-Car Salesman. These character strengths and virtues are introduced in the next chapter.

NOTES

1. Pressman, S. (1993). *Outrageous betrayal: The real story of Werner Erhard from EST to exile.* New York: St. Martins Press; and Self, J. (1992). *60 Minutes and the assassination of Werner Erhard.* New York: Breakthru Publishing.

2. Breeman, M. (2005, October 2). A nice guy finishes 1st. *The San Diego Union Tribune*, p. D1.

3. Bass, B.M., & Steidlmeier, P. (1999). Ethics, character, and authentic transformational leadership behavior. *The Leadership Quarterly, 10*, 181–217; and Burns, J.M. (1978). *Leadership.* New York: Harper & Row.

4. Fanham, A. (1993). Mary Kay's lessons in leadership. *Fortune, 128*, 68–75.

5. Bass, B.M., & Avolio, B.J. (1994). *Improving organizational effectiveness through transformational leadership.* Thousand Oaks, CA: Sage, and Lowe, K.B., Kroeck, K.G., & Sivasubramaniam, N. (1996). Effectiveness correlates of transformational and transactional leadership: A meta-analytic review. *The Leadership Quarterly, 7*, 385–425.

6. Cook, D.T. (2002, July 2, 2002). Crisis in the corner office: The job of CEO has been reshaped by rising pressures, stock options, and end of boom. *Christian Science Monitor*, p. 1.

7. Mendelsohn, J. (2005, February 6). Tickled pink. *Boston Globe*, p. 19.

8.   Florida, R., & Goodnight, J. (2005). Managing for creativity. *Harvard Business Review, 83*(7), 124–131.

9.   http://www.gsn.com/specific_page_elements.php?link_id=S59.   Retrieved September 29, 2005.

10. Conger, J.A., & Kanungo, R.N. (1998). *Charismatic leadership in organizations.* Thousand Oaks, CA: Sage; and Shamir, B., House, R.J., & Arthur, M. (1993). The motivational effects of charismatic leadership: A self-concept based theory. *Organization Science, 4,* 1–17.

11. Howell, J.M. (1988). Two faces of charisma: Socialized and personalized leadership in organizations. In J.A. Conger & R.N. Kanungo (Eds.), *Charismatic leadership: The elusive factor in organizational effectiveness* (pp. 213–236). San Francisco: Jossey-Bass.

12. Anonymous. (2005, August 29). Remembering John H. Johnson 1918–2005. *JET, 108* (9), 12–42.

13. Sosik, J.J., & Dinger, S.L. (in press). Relationships between leadership style and vision content: The moderating role of need for social approval, self-monitoring and need for social power. *The Leadership Quarterly.*.

14. Sosik, J.J., & Jung, D.I. (2003). Impression management strategies and performance in information technology consulting: The role of self-other rating agreement on charismatic leadership. *Management Communication Quarterly, 17*(2), 233–268.

CHAPTER 3

VIRTUES AND CHARACTER STRENGTHS

Virtue is central to everything we do as leaders.

—John C. Bogle

I am often puzzled by some participants in leadership workshops who have trouble identifying what they stand for (and what they won't stand for) as a leader and as a person. They can easily grasp the transformational and transactional behaviors taught. But when put to the test, they really don't know their personal values, virtues or strengths. They seem to feel uncomfortable disclosing the ideals that their behaviors should reflect. Yet, most successful business leaders do understand the importance of virtue and character to leadership effectiveness. What about you? What do *you* stand for? What won't *you* stand for?

Here is my challenge to you, the reader. During the next three to five minutes, please think about the four or five most important personal values that you have used to guide your behaviors. Don't just make them up for this exercise. Think about the personal values that you have used during the past several weeks or months. Surprisingly, when I do this exercise in graduate leadership seminars, many aspiring leaders have a hard time identifying a set of personal values that are important to them. I bet many readers may face a similar challenge.Some seminar participants protest the exercise by saying that they will be able to develop their core personal values eventually when they become a senior executive down the road. I then challenge them by asking how they will be able to develop their values then if they are clueless now. The banter back and forth persists, but in the end we all learn one important lesson: *Now* is the best time to identify our core personal values and use them for our everyday decisions because they stand for who we are as leaders and human beings.

As part of my graduate leadership seminars, I also have the students interview high-level executives about their life experiences, leadership philosophies and styles. Last year, one of the teams interviewed John C. Bogle, founder and former CEO of The Vanguard Group, one of the world's largest investment management companies. Bogle has become a living legend in the field of index and mutual funds, writing prolifically on the topic, and establishing the Bogle Financial Markets Research Center. During the interview, Bogle talked to the students about the importance of virtue to leadership. According to Bogle, virtue is not elitist, and virtue is not Pollyannaish. Virtue, based on Bogle's experience, is what makes someone a good person, and he highlighted it as the *foundation for outstanding leadership*.[1] Virtue is what leaders use to bring out the best in their followers and in themselves.

Authentic transformational leaders are virtuous. They possess much more than a dramatic and captivating *style*. More importantly, they also possess real *substance*. That substance is the collection of virtues and character strengths that makes them who they are. In this chapter, I explain how virtues and character strengths form the "raw material" or substance of their leadership. Next I describe why virtues and character strengths are important to organizations based on work in the fields of Positive Psychology and Positive Organizational Behavior. The chapter ends by introducing the virtues and character strengths that will be linked to authentic transformational leadership development in subsequent chapters.

THE "RAW MATERIAL" OF LEADERSHIP—VALUES, VIRTUES, AND CHARACTER

A recent CNN/Gallup poll reported that virtue and character strength issues represented the most important factor in determining the voting results in the 2004 presidential election. The perception by voters regarding what values each candidate stood for played a key role in the outcome of the election.[2] I believe that candidates who can project the positive moral values they actually hold, in a way that is believable to and agreeable by voters, demonstrate authentic transformational leadership. Voters need to know what candidates stand for, or what they value. When voters value the same things as the candidates, they become supporters of the candidate.

Values represent notions about what "ought" and what "ought not" to be. Leaders often talk about important values in their speeches to followers. In corporate settings, the values of achievement, helping, concern for others, honesty and fairness are common. Leaders create their visions around these values. That's because history has shown that followers are willing to live and die for the values by which they conduct their lives. For example, the Founding Fathers of the United States created a vision for their independence movement based on the values of "life, liberty and the pursuit of happiness." Even today, we are defending against religious fundamentalists who are at odds with these values.

Leadership scholar, Robert House, proposed that values pervade the entire transformational/charismatic leadership process. According to House, charismatic or transformational leaders possess an unusually strong belief in their own values. They engage in role modeling by displaying "symbolic behaviors" that reflect their cherished values. They motivate followers by exaggerating followers' grievances and promising them specific changes in terms of values. They communicate high performance expectations of, and confidence in, followers by articulating the expectations in terms of values. They formulate and communicate a value-laden vision. And they engage in personal image-building consistent with their espoused values. As a result, followers emulate the leader's behaviors reflecting these values, show trust, loyalty, obedience and unquestioning acceptance of the leader, accept challenging goals, and raise their level of performance expectations.[3]

Consider the role that values played in helping to bring down the Iron Curtain. Historians have noted that Pope John Paul II held strong beliefs in traditional Polish values of human dignity, solidarity and sovereignty. The Pope's articulation of these values in his speeches and exemplification of such values in interactions with communist authorities in Poland and the Soviet Union helped to accelerate the fall of communism.[4] Indeed, cultural values can be a strong force for promoting social change, especially when they represent what is generally accepted as being good and best for humanity.

Generally accepted positive moral values represent *virtues* that describe the traits of "a good person." The great moral philosophers, going back to Aristotle, Plato and Socrates, have pondered the ethics of virtue. Aristotle defined a virtue as a trait of character that is reflected in habitual behavior that is good for a person to have. According to this definition, what a leader thinks, what she wills to do, what motivates her and what she values all shape her behavior and deeds. Behavior and deeds that are repeated over time form the leader's habits. Habits shape the leader's character. For example, if you consistently behave in a way that reflects courage, honesty, loyalty and self-control, then you would be considered to be of virtuous character.

The United States Military Academy at West Point is one of the most effective organizations in shaping the character of individuals. Cadets are transformed into leaders through education that teaches Army values and demonstrates character strengths. This education is reinforced with continuing education, mentoring, self-reflection, and after-action reviews or debriefing sessions. Army values are internalized by the cadets with a strong culture that highlights character strengths through stories, artifacts and traditions. West Point's tradition of developing character, as the bedrock of authentic transformational leadership in its cadets, illustrates the importance of virtue for leadership development.

The Army is not the only organization interested in character development. Character development in children has gained prominence in several school districts in the United States. For example, the North Carolina Public School System has successfully launched a program that highlights many of the character strengths discussed in this book. This school system's mission is as follows:

> All that we do should strive to better ALL of our children, their families, and all of our communities. Shaping, nurturing and developing the total child is a responsibility for us all. Character development, grounded in HIGH EXPECTATIONS and FOSTERING RELATIONSHIPS, embodies all that we as teachers, leaders and role models do EVERY DAY.[5]

The character strengths of authentic transformational leadership reflect many of these themes and set the stage for leaders to create more positive organizations and communities.

POSITIVE PSYCHOLOGY AND ORGANIZATIONAL SCHOLARSHIP

In 1952, Dr. Norman Vincent Peale, a controversial preacher, published an influential book entitled *The Power of Positive Thinking.* The premise of the book is that through better spiritual, mental, physical and emotional health, people can create their own happiness and success in all phases of life. While Peale's book is based on personal anecdotes and Christian religious beliefs rather than rigorous scientific inquiry, it does make an important point. That is, *living a virtuous life and having a positive attitude can reap many benefits.*

Fast forward about 50 years to 2006. Today, many of the ideas that Peale mentioned in his book are being validated by important new research by positive psychologists and organizational scholars. Traditionally, psychologists have focused on pathologies or what is wrong with people. They have helped people to get out of their ruts of depression, anxiety, drug and alcohol addiction, etc. Their job was to take a person who was deemed to be "broken" and to try to fix him. Similarly, traditional organizational scholars have worked to fix what is wrong in organizations. They have focused on team building, cultural transformations, management to leadership style shifts, as ways to deal with a host of other organizational pathologies.

Many types of reinforcement/reward systems used by organizations to improve productivity, effectiveness and performance have mainly focused on something *negative* as a means to control employee behavior. A good example is the use of sick pay. Many organizations provide their employees with paid sick leave as part of the employee's benefits program. Ironically, research has found that organizations with paid sick leave programs experience almost twice the absenteeism of organizations without such programs.[6]

The main reason for this problem is that sick leave programs focus on and reinforce the wrong behavior—absence from work. Instead, positive psychologists argue that organizations should focus on encouraging positive behaviors such as good attendance—not absence. As such, some companies have started to use different forms of "well pay" where they award monetary prizes for those who do not use sick days. For example, General Dynamics has some divisions which hold lotteries with awarding prizes as much as $2,500 in cash and reserved parking spaces. This helps them to reduce the number of work days lost due to sick leave.

In contrast to the approach of traditional psychology and organizational scholarship, the Positive Psychology and Positive Organizational Scholarship movements do *not* focus on what is wrong with people, but on *what is right with people.* Positive psychologists and organizational scholars help people to increase their happiness, productivity, and self-actualization (being the best they can be). They focus on identifying and accentuating a person's strengths, talents, virtues, and positive values to try to bring out the best in people. In this way, positive psychologists and organizational scholars are able to develop character.

Some key findings of the Positive Psychology and Positive Organizational Scholarship movements are worth noting. First, negativity takes its toll on emotional, spiritual and physical health.[7] Have you ever lost sleep at night over worrying about your job, your boss, or your family? How did you feel the next morning? Tired, weak, achy, strung out? If this pattern of thought and worry continued over the short run, what happened next? Did you come down with a cold or other illness? If this habitual way of fretting continued over the long run, did you start to lose your faith in God or yourself? If you answered "yes" to one or more of these questions, you can relate to the research findings of the harmful effects of negativity on human beings.

Second, positive emotions carry the capacity to transform individuals for the better, making them healthier, more socially integrated, knowledgeable, effective and resilient.[8] Positive emotions help individuals to flourish.

When we flourish, we experience goodness from being happy, feeling satisfied, and functioning at our best. We are more open to experiences, less rigid in our behavior, and more open to other people's views and ways of life. We grow by expanding our talents and skills and relationships with others. And we become more resilient after surviving and growing in the aftermath of hardships. Helping people to flourish is what authentic transformational leadership is all about.

People also flourish when they report what is known as "optimal experiences." According to positive psychologist Mihaly Csikszentmihalyi, such optimal life experiences occur when you are "in flow" or "in the zone" while performing tasks you find highly enjoyable. Such optimal flow experiences involve intense concentration and motivation that centers on the process more than on the goal. Flow occurs when your perception of the challenge of the task at hand is equal to your perception of your skills required to complete the task. As a result, you can achieve high levels of performance, creativity and persistence.[9]

Perhaps you have experienced flow at work or at home. While performing a task that really appealed to you, did you experience high concentration, attention and focus on what you were doing? Was your attention limited to your task? Did you feel like you were part of the activity itself, such that you lost sense of your individuality? Did you feel that you were in total control of the action? Did the task itself provide feedback? Did you feel that you were self-directed and intrinsically motivated? If you answered "yes" to one or more of these questions, you can relate to the research findings of the enjoyable and flourishing effects of positive emotions on human beings.

Third, research on individuals, marriages, and high performing business teams demonstrates that there is an optimal ratio of positive to negative comments associated with effectiveness.[10] One study examined the ratio of positive to negative comments made by top management teams. Those teams with a 3:1 ratio of positive to negative comments were most effective. Why 3:1? If all the comments were positive, the teams would have placed more emphasis on maintaining the cohesiveness ("feel good" atmosphere) of the team, at the expense of performance. Research on group cohesiveness has found that an excessively high level of cohesiveness leads to significant amounts of group pressure and group think and eventually stifles creativity in groups.[11] If all the comments were negative, the teams' morale and subsequent performance would decline due to the hostile atmosphere stemming from all of the negativity. It appears that some degree of critical carping or inquiry is necessary to keep teams focused on developing the best ideas, while providing a generally supportive and encouraging atmosphere with positive comments. The results of this study suggest that a healthy balance of positive and negative emotions in teams can lead to positive performance outcomes.

Fourth, positive attitudes (hope, optimism, resilience) have been linked to higher managerial performance and merit-based salary.[12] Hope, optimism, and resilience are part of what organizational scholars call Positive Psychological Capital or PsychCap. This form of capital is a real asset that can fuel productivity and satisfaction at work. A study conducted with Chinese workers revealed that workers who reported higher levels of PsychCap outperformed those with lower levels of PsychCap. In addition, managers who reported higher levels of PsychCap received more merit-based salary increases than those with lower levels of PsychCap. Therefore, it appears that having a positive attitude at work can actually pay off. Taken together, these key findings suggest that a positive approach to life and work that displays virtues and character strengths can produce the benefits that can help you to flourish as a leader and as a person. But first you must reflect upon which virtues and character strengths you possess, and which ones you need to work on.

INTRODUCING THE HIGH SIX VIRTUES AND CHARACTER STRENGTHS

After conducting a comprehensive review of the psychology, philosophy, sociology, religious and historical literatures, positive psychologists Christopher Peterson and Martin Seligman identified 24 character strengths, clustered within six virtues, associated with positive personal qualities and related to beneficial outcomes for individuals.[13] Virtues are core characteristics universally valued by moral philosophers and religious thinkers as exemplars of good character. For example, Judeo-Christian virtues include wisdom, faith, hope, and charity (love). Character strengths are positive traits or psychological processes or mechanisms for displaying the virtues. For example, love of learning is a character strength that reflects the virtue of wisdom.

Figure 3.1 illustrates the High Six Virtues and their associated character strengths. These virtues are wisdom and knowledge, courage, humanity, justice, temperance, transcendence. The thesis of this book is that these virtues and character strengths provide the foundation for authentic transformational leadership, as shown in Figure 3.2.

Wisdom and Knowledge

Good judgment and the appropriate use of intelligence is a core virtue that Peterson and Seligman called *wisdom and knowledge*. This virtue represents cognitive (mental) strengths for acquiring and using knowledge in a beneficial manner. Many leaders throughout history, going back to King

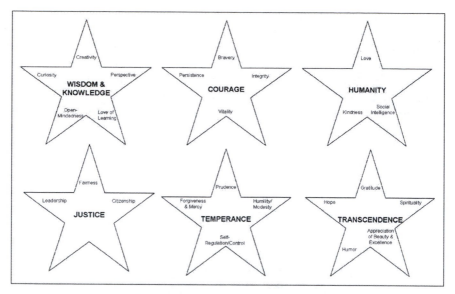

Figure 3.1. The High Six Virtues and Character Strengths (Peterson & Seligman, 2004).

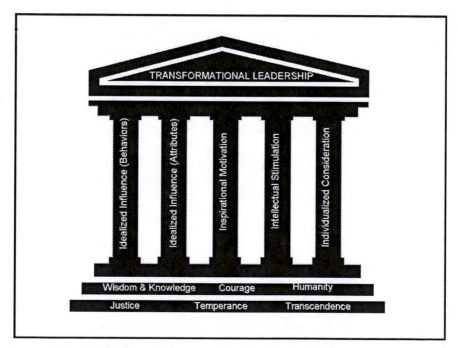

Figure 3.2. A Solid Foundation For Transformational Leadership Behavior.

Figure 3.3.   *Gaining Wisdom and Knowledge in the Information Age.* The Internet and other forms of advanced information technology are helping leaders and followers to solve today's complex organizational problems.

Solomon, have strived to acquire wisdom and knowledge which can be used to influence and help followers to achieve objectives. Today, wisdom and knowledge are more important than ever as illustrated in Figure 3.3. According to Peterson and Seligman, there are five character strengths that reflect the virtue of wisdom and knowledge: creativity, curiosity, open-mindedness, love-of-learning, and perspective.

Creativity

People who are wise and knowledgeable often are creative. They are original and ingenuous in the way they think, talk and perform tasks. Creativity represents "thinking of novel and productive ways to conceptualize and do things."[14] Creativity has been linked to unconventional behavior, nonconformity, flexibility in perceiving and thinking, and risk-taking behavior. Leaders need to be creative to develop innovative strategies for engaging the competition, and to help followers solve the many complex problems that face their organization.

Curiosity

Wise and knowledgeable individuals often have many interests, seek novelty and are open to new experiences. Curiosity represents "taking an interest in an experience for its own sake, finding subjects and topics fascinating, and exploring and discovering."[15] Curiosity has been linked to general positive feelings and emotions, willingness to challenge stereotypes, viewing experiences positively and being close with people, but also to impulsivity, anger and antagonism. Although leaders should be aware of the negative aspects of curiosity, they still need to be curious to learn about people, processes and trends that may provide new strategic directions for their organization.

Open-mindedness

Wise and knowledgeable individuals use good judgment and critical thinking that takes into account alternate viewpoints. They are able to change their minds after weighing fairly all of the evidence. Open-mindedness represents "thinking things through and examining them from all sides, and not jumping to conclusions..."[16] Open-mindedness has been linked to critical thinking, complexity in perceiving and thinking, and ability to predict how others will behave. The downside of open-mindedness is that it may lead to endorsement of authoritarian, dogmatic and ethnocentric ideas. While leaders should fight any impulse to be controlling and dictatorial, they need to be open-minded since they come into contact with a wide variety of individuals, each with their own ideas and culture. Such diversity can provide them with the strategies and resources to accomplish great things. More importantly, it provides powerful ammunition for innovative work processes and outcomes. The Abrasive/Egotistical Heroes described in Chapter 2 lack open-mindedness.

Love of Learning

Wise and knowledgeable individuals enjoy the process of learning new things and are motivated by the intrinsic desire to perform a task that they find enjoyable and enlightening. They enjoy methodically adding to what they currently know. Love of learning represents "mastering new skills, topics, and bodies of knowledge, whether on one's own or formally..."[17] Love of learning is linked to many psychological and physical aspects of wellbeing. These include positive feelings about new things, feeling challenged and autonomous, self-efficacy (believing that you can perform a task successfully), decreased stress, and protection from impairments in perceiving and thinking in later life. Besides reaping these personal benefits, leaders should value learning so they can authentically encourage the continuous improvement of their followers and organizational processes. Finally, love of learning can lead to what many creativity researchers have found to be the most powerful and important source of creativity—intrinsic motivation. When you love to learn something new, it could lead to a new idea regardless of extrinsic rewards that are being promised by your organization.

Perspective

Wise and knowledgeable individuals look at situations from many different viewpoints. They are able to integrate these views into one that is easily understandable by all. Perspective represents "being able to provide wise counsel to others; having ways of looking at the world that make sense to oneself and other people."[18] Perspective has been linked to successful aging, satisfaction in multiple areas of life, and the absence of neuroticism (excessive worrying about the self). Perspective is helpful to leaders for these very beneficial personal reasons. The need for business leaders to reconcile different perspectives is due, in part, to increasingly conflicting data including technological trends and oftentimes confusing consumer preferences. As a leader, you have to be able to come up with effective planning processes and strategies by carefully considering multiple perspectives. Perspective also can help you show followers the what, how and why of becoming more engaged in your work and more committed to your organization's mission. Both the Saints and Politician/Well-Meaning Chameleons discussed in Chapter 2 show great perspective-taking ability in their interactions with others.

Courage

The ability to persist in the face of significant obstacles or danger is a core virtue that Peterson and Seligman called *courage*. This virtue represents emotional strengths for exercising your will despite opposing forces from others and within yourself. Courage is a fundamental core virtue espoused by military training organizations such as the United States Military Academy at West Point. It is also a virtue required for most all aspects of life as shown in Figure 3.4. According to Peterson and Seligman, there are four character strengths that reflect the virtue of courage: bravery, persistence, integrity, and vitality.

Bravery

Courageous individuals demonstrate valor, boldness and heroism. They do not back away from threat, challenge, difficulty or pain. They speak up for what is right even though there is opposition. They act on convictions even at the risk of being viewed as unpopular. Bravery has been linked to favoring and looking out for others, feeling connected with others, entering and sustaining high quality relationships with others, self-confidence, self-efficacy, reflection, tolerance for ambiguity and uncertainty, ability to assess risk, and whistle-blowing. The responsibility of being a top leader can be tremendous. Many challenging and troublesome conditions arise.

Figure 3.4.   *The Face of Courage.* The courage, strength and bravery of the legendary coal miners of the anthracite region of Pennsylvania are recognized in a memorial monument in Nanticoke, PA. Imagine the amount of self-leadership these miners possessed each day in their work.

Many difficult strategic, tactical and ethical decisions must be made. To remain composed in these situations, leaders need to be brave.

Persistence

Courageous individuals remain industrious and persevere despite obstacles, challenges and setbacks. They take great pleasure in finishing tasks that they start. They "get things done" and follow through on their intentions.[19] The ability to execute strategies and initiatives depends upon effective strategic leadership in high-tech organizations. Persistence has been linked to entrepreneurial success, goal attainment, enjoyment of subsequent successes, improvement of skills and resourcefulness, and self-efficacy.

Yet some undertakings are truly impossible and therefore persistence may lead to escalated commitments and resources expended fruitlessly. Leaders need to know the difference. When the mission is highly improbable but not impossible and the outcome is a significant improvement in the lives of others, perseverance is the fuel that makes it happen. As Nelson

Mandela and Mother Theresa can attest to, the road to leadership development of the self and others can be long and hard. Leaders must persevere.

Integrity

Courageous individuals act with honesty and authenticity. They are not pretentious. They are true to themselves. Demonstrating integrity involves "speaking the truth but more broadly presenting oneself in a genuine way and acting in a sincere way."[20] Integrity is a core feature of the construct of authentic leadership. Integrity has been linked to positive moods, life satisfaction, self-actualization, openness to experiences, empathy, conscientiousness, trust, and effective workplace relationships. The positive nature of these correlates suggests to leaders that pursuing, recognizing, and standing by the truth will indeed set them free and allow them to flourish. The Saints described in Chapter 2 possess high levels of integrity.

Vitality

The legendary Green Bay Packer coach Vince Lombardi once said, "Fatigue makes cowards of us all." Instead, courageous individuals are perceived to be vigorous, energetic and enthusiastic by others. They approach their existence with excitement and liveliness. They perceive life as an adventure. They also put "all that they've got" into their activities.

Vitality has been linked to good physical and mental health. However, physical illness, disability and immunological dysfunction are related to lower vitality. Experienced autonomy (a sense of being in control), effectiveness, and relatedness to others represent positive psychological correlates of vitality.

Of all the character strengths, vitality appears to be the most strongly associated with life satisfaction.[21] No wonder why some leaders seem to glow with an inner strength that draws on something more than extrinsic rewards. It's the leader's vitality that deeply inspires followers to achieve excellence that can bring a sense of shared satisfaction.

Humanity

Recognizing and appreciating what it means to be human is a core virtue that Peterson and Seligman called *humanity*. This virtue represents interpersonal strengths that care for and befriend others in our work and personal lives (see Figure 3.5). For many years, leadership scholars have highlighted the virtue of humanity when discussing the consideration (people-oriented) aspect of leadership behavior. According to Peterson and Seligman, there are three character strengths that reflect the virtue of humanity: love, kindness, and social intelligence.

Figure 3.5.   *Our First Introduction to Humanity Is Through the Family.* Early life experiences in the family help to shape humanitarian and developmental values that leaders often introduce into their organizational cultures.

Love

To love an individual is to be close to them in a caring and emotional way. Peterson and Seligman define love as "valuing close relationships with others, in particular those in which sharing and caring are reciprocated."[22] Research indicates that love is linked to a variety of positive outcomes for adults including less deterioration of trust and intimacy in initial phases of relationships, fewer psychosomatic symptoms in response to stress, using compromise rather than destructive strategies of conflict resolution, higher self-esteem, and less depression and less likelihood of divorce. Together these correlates suggest that those who show love form relationships that are enduring and satisfying.

To be human is to love and need to be loved. Leaders, as humans, need to experience and demonstrate love since they work everyday with human followers. Love also is an important pre-requisite for leaders to provide highly committed and long-lasting coaching and mentoring efforts for follower development. As Sanaya Roman once said, "What you love is a sign from your higher self of what you are to do." You are to lead—by developing and loving others. Unfortunately, the Used-Car Salesman described in Chapter 2 is not capable of displaying such leadership.

Kindness

Individuals who value humanity demonstrate generosity, nurturance, compassion and altruistic love. They do favors and good deeds for others, take care of them and help them. Kindness has been linked to a variety of helping behaviors including volunteerism and its correlates of mental and physical health (including longer life). The ancient Chinese philosopher Lao Tzu said: "Kindness in words creates confidence, kindness in thinking creates profoundness, and kindness in feeling creates love." Leadership is all about building confidence, wisdom and camaraderie in followers. The Saint described in Chapter 2 can easily show kindness to her followers.

Social Intelligence

Individuals who value humanity possess intelligence to recognize and control emotions and to engage in positive interpersonal interactions with others. They know what motivates other people. They know how to fit into a variety of social situations. They are aware of their own motives and feelings, and those of other people. Social or emotional intelligence has been linked to slightly better life judgments and smoother social functioning, more adaptive defense styles, lower levels of aggression with peers, and better provision of customer service. Leaders need to be socially intelligent since leadership is about influencing followers and others in a social setting.

Justice

Fair dealings and righteousness is a core virtue that Peterson and Seligman called *justice.* This virtue represents a set of civic strengths that underlie healthy community life. Leadership scholars have highlighted the virtue of justice when discussing the relationship of leadership to promoting organizational citizenship behavior and procedural justice (see Figure 3.6). According to Peterson and Seligman, there are three character strengths that reflect the virtue of justice: citizenship, fairness, and leadership.

Citizenship

The just individual demonstrates a sense of loyalty, social responsibility, and values teamwork. Peterson and Seligman described this aspect of justice as "working well as a member of a group or team; being loyal to the group; doing one's share."[23] Citizenship has been linked to higher levels of social trust, increased understanding of politics, and more positive views on human nature. These positive correlates help make life easier for leaders. Leaders need to show loyalty to their followers in order to receive loyalty from them. Leaders need to be socially responsible to the communities in

Figure 3.6.   *The Old County Court House Is a Symbol of Justice.* Followers expect their leaders to be just in their interactions with others and in their participation in both local and global affairs.

which they work. Leaders also need to build teams to accomplish organizational objectives. To be a good leader requires demonstrating citizenship.

Fairness

The just individual also "treats all people the same according to notions of fairness and justice; *not* letting personal feelings bias decisions about others."[24] Fairness has been linked to the development of a strong moral identity where being a "nice person" becomes part of the self-concept. Fairness is also related to elevated self-esteem, enhanced perspective-taking capacity, self-reflection and its byproducts of enhanced self-awareness/knowledge, improved relational problem-solving, increased pro-social/caring/helping behavior and decreased antisocial behavior, reduced immoral behavior, and more liberal attitudes. Leaders need to be fair in order to be trusted by their followers. Without trust, there can be no real (or effective) leadership. I'm sure that Bill Clinton and Richard Nixon would have agreed.

Leadership

The broad concept of leadership is considered to be a reflection of the just individual. Building upon the classic work of the Ohio State leadership studies of the 1950s and its distinction between initiation of structure (task-orientation) and consideration (relationship-orientation),[25] Peterson and Seligman defined the leadership character strength as "encouraging a group, of which one is a member, to get things done and at the same time maintain good relations within the group." Leadership has been linked to a wide variety of organizational, group/team, and individual performance and attitudes.[26] Relating transformational leadership (the set of behaviors) to Peterson and Seligman's notion of leadership (the character strength) would be redundant. Therefore I do not attempt to relate these two concepts in this book.

Temperance

Being able to place reasonable boundaries or limitations on personal desires and aspirations is a core virtue that Peterson and Seligman called *temperance*. This virtue is reflected in strengths that protect against excess. Indeed, notions of temperance or self-control have been discussed by philosophers and religious thinkers over the centuries as important for overcoming the human tendency to become self-centered. As shown in Figure 3.7, this virtue is also gaining prominence in contemporary society and organizations. According to Peterson and Seligman, there are four character strengths that reflect the virtue of temperance: forgiveness and mercy, humility/modesty, prudence, and self-regulation/control.

Forgiveness and Mercy

Temperate individuals understand the imperfections that mark human nature and avoid being vengeful. They pardon those who have done them wrong. Forgiveness has been linked to slightly lower levels of anger, anxiety, depression and hostility. Leaders and their followers are human. They make mistakes in their work and in their relationships with associates and other people. Leaders who forgive followers are able to sustain long-lasting associations and build productive and satisfying relationships with them. Rather than ruining relationships and "burning bridges," authentic transformational leaders work to help followers to overcome their weaknesses.

Figure 3.7.   *Instant Karma.* The interconnectedness of mind, body, and spirit is being recognized in a growing number of organizations through various wellness programs.

The same should hold true for followers forgiving leaders. Followers are often quick to idolize leaders for their success, and sometimes quicker to crucify them for their faults and failings. Perhaps we need to rethink our basic assumptions about leader-follower relationships by recognizing their inherent limitations associated with being human. As Alexander Pope once said, "To err is human, to forgive divine."

Humility/Modesty

Temperate individuals are humble when it comes to their achievements. They let their performance speak for themselves and do not seek the spotlight.[27] Humble individuals are less likely to take risks and make foolish decisions, are freer from self-preoccupation, and are more likely to work toward self-improvement goals. They also are rated as excellent mentors.[28] Leaders need to maintain a degree of humility since they, like their followers, are prone to making mistakes. After all, the Western culture and its media like to point out and glorify successful high profile leaders. But it also loves to vilify those same leaders when they make mistakes.

Prudence

Temperate individuals are careful about the choices they make in what they say or do. They avoid undue risks. Prudent individuals are considered to be conscientious, and as such to possess positive personality traits (e.g., agreeableness, extroversion, emotional stability), good physical health, and to be superior performers at work.[29] Leaders need to be very careful in the many choices they make. Their choices have very important effects on the reputations and lives of their associates and the organization.

Self-regulation/Control

Temperate individuals exercise self-control in their interactions with others. This character strength involves "regulating what one feels and does; being disciplined; controlling one's appetites and emotions."[30] Individuals with high self-control have better relationships with others, and are seen as more trustworthy, fairer and more consistent. They report better family cohesion and empathy, higher levels of self-esteem and self-acceptance, less interpersonal conflict, and less pathological symptoms, such as anxiety and anger. Leaders need to present themselves as being calm, collected and in control. Followers gain a sense of comfort and confidence when their leader possesses self-control. Leaders who cannot control their appetites and emotions lose the trust of their followers, and then their leadership vanishes.

Transcendence

Looking beyond oneself for relations with others in this world and in the spiritual realm is a core virtue that Peterson and Seligman called *transcendence*. This virtue is reflected in strengths that provide connections to the larger universe and provide meaning for life. Some people develop these strengths in spiritual or religious services as shown in Figure 3.8. According to Peterson and Seligman, there are five character strengths that reflect the virtue of transcendence: appreciation of beauty and excellence, gratitude, hope, humor, and spirituality.

Appreciation of Beauty and Excellence

Transcendent individuals are often filled with a sense of awe, wonder, and elevation of spirit when they recognize extraordinary people or things. They tend to notice and appreciate beauty and excellence, or skilled performances in various domains of life.[31] Studies suggest that individuals who appreciate beauty and excellence may experience important outcomes such as motivating self-improvement, personal change, altruistic actions and dedication to others and the community. Leaders highlight the importance of attaining the highest standards of performance. An appreciation of beauty and excellence provides leaders with ideas for setting their lofty goals and rewarding their people for achieving outstanding levels of performance.

Figure 3.8.   *One Way Some Leaders Transcend Their Challenges Is by Participating in Religious Services.* Such rituals can provide personal meaning in times of crisis, clarify important values, and sustain cultures by providing continuity between the past, present and future.

Gratitude

Transcendent individuals are able to "count their blessings." They are aware of and are thankful for the good things that happen to them. They also take the time to express thanks to those who have been good to them or have helped them. Gracious individuals report positive attitudes (e.g., optimism, life satisfaction), psychological states (e.g., enthusiasm, energy, determination), better physical health, and longer life. They are also seen as displaying supportive behaviors. Gratitude allows leaders to recognize the fact that their leadership outcomes are accomplished through their followers. Recognition of the help of others can be a highly valued and motivational force in leader-follower relationships.

Hope

Transcendent individuals are optimistic and look to the future with a vision of a situation that is much better than the status quo. They expect the best in the future and possess a positive expectation that they can work to shape it. Hopeful individuals are high achievers in the academic, athletic, military, political, and workplace domains. They are also future-oriented, and attentive to sources of information needed for active problem solving.[32] Hope is an intrinsically satisfying motivational force that encourages leaders and their followers to work hard to overcome challenges and to achieve difficult missions. As Napoleon Bonaparte once said "Leaders are dealers in hope."

Humor

Transcendent individuals use humor in the form of comic relief and playfulness to encourage creativity or to take the edge off of stressful situations. Humor involves "liking to laugh and tease; bringing smiles to other people; seeing the lighter side; making… jokes."[33] Studies indicate that benevolent, self-deprecating and positive forms of humor can promote creativity, provide a buffer against stress, improve physical health, and promote good moods. Humor can allow leaders and followers to better cope with daily difficulties, mundane work, and the imperfections of human beings.

Spirituality

Transcendent individuals possess faith, a strong purpose in their lives, and/or are religious. Spirituality can be defined as "having coherent beliefs about the higher purpose and meaning of the universe; knowing where one fits in within the larger scheme; having beliefs about the meaning of life that shape conduct and provide comfort."[34] Research indicates that religiousness/spirituality has positive effects on interpersonal relationships (e.g., marital quality), promotes pro-social values and behaviors and psychological and physical well-being, and enhances community well-being. However, it also may promote prejudice and play a role in the progression of severe psychopathology in some individuals. Despite these potential pitfalls, spirituality can help leaders to find meaning in their lives and provide meaning for followers to inspire high levels of performance.

Congratulations! You are now familiar with the concepts of authentic transformational leadership and the High Six Virtues and Character Strengths. You are now ready to learn how each of the character strengths can be used to display authentic transformational leadership. In the chapters that follow, I will provide you with 25 cases of leaders who have put their character strengths into action to display outstanding leadership. Building upon these examples, I explain how these character strengths relate to authentic transformational leadership. Twenty-three leadership principles are offered for becoming an authentic transformational leader through character development. I also explain how you can live the leadership principles by fully leveraging the character strengths you actively possess and those that lay dormant in you.

NOTES

1. Interview with John C. Bogle, conducted November 2004 by Michael Imburgia, Joseph McCabe, and Jason McKenna.

2. Jones, J.M. (2004, December 16). Different influences found for Bush, Kerry voters: Fact that Kerry "was not Bush" figured prominently in Kerry vote. *Gallup Management Journal.* Retrieved October 4, 2005 from www.gallup.com.

3. House, R.J. (1977). A 1976 theory of charismatic leadership. In J.G. Hunt & L.L. Larson (Eds.), *Leadership: The cutting edge* (pp. 189–207). Carbondale, IL: Southern Illinois University Press.

4. Sosik, J.J. (2005). The role of personal values in the charismatic leadership of corporate managers: A model and preliminary field study. *The Leadership Quarterly, 16,* 221–244; and Weigel, G. (1999). *Witness to hope: The biography of Pope John Paul II.* New York: Cliff Street Books.

5. http://www.ncpublicschools.org/nccep/lp/lp12.html. Retrieved October 4, 2005.

6. Robbins, S. (2005). *Organizational behavior* (11th edition). Upper Saddle River, NJ: Prentice Hall.

7. Fredrickson, B. L., & Losada, M. F. (2005). Positive affect and the complex dynamics of human flourishing. *American Psychologist, 60*(7), 678–686.

8. Fredrickson & Losada (2005) as cited in Note 7.

9. Csikszentmihalyi, M. (1990). *Flow: The psychology of optimal experience.* New York: Harper Perennial.

10. Fredrickson & Losada (2005) as cited in Note 7.

11. Mullen, B., & Cooper, C. (1994). The relation between group cohesiveness and performance: An integration. *Psychological Bulletin, 115,* 210–227.

12. Luthans, F., & Youssef, C.M. (2004). Human, social, and now positive psychological capital management: Investing in people for competitive advantage. *Organizational Dynamics, 33*(2), 143–160.

13. Peterson, C., & Seligman, M.E.P. (2004). *Character strengths and virtues: A handbook and classification.* New York: Oxford/American Psychological Association.

14. Peterson & Seligman (2004, p. 29) as cited in Note 13.

15. Peterson & Seligman (2004, p. 29) as cited in Note 13.

16. Peterson & Seligman (2004, p. 29) as cited in Note 13.

17. Peterson & Seligman (2004, p. 29) as cited in Note 13.

18. Peterson & Seligman (2004, p. 29) as cited in Note 13.

19. Peterson & Seligman (2004, p. 29) as cited in Note 13.

20. Peterson & Seligman (2004, p. 29) as cited in Note 13.

21. Park, N., Peterson, C., & Seligman, M.E. (2004). Strengths of character and well-being. *Journal of Social and Clinical Psychology, 23*(5), 603–619.

22. Peterson & Seligman (2004, p. 29) as cited in Note 13.

23. Peterson & Seligman (2004, p. 30) as cited in Note 13.

24. Peterson & Seligman (2004, p. 30) as cited in Note 13.

25. Stodgill, R.M., & Coons, A.E. (1951). *Leader behavior: Its description and measurement. Research Monograph No. 88.* Columbus, OH: Ohio State University, Bureau of Business Research.

26. For comprehensive reviews of the leadership literature, see Bass, B.M. (1990). *Bass and Stodgill's handbook of leadership: Theory, research and managerial applications.* New York: Free Press; and Yukl, G. (2002). *Leadership in organizations* (5th ed.). Englewood Cliffs, NJ: Prentice Hall.

27. Peterson & Seligman (2004, p. 30) as cited in Note 13.

28. For details see, Godshalk, V.M., & Sosik, J.J. (2000). Does mentor-protégé agreement on mentor leadership behavior influence the quality of mentoring relationships? *Group & Organization Management, 25*(3), 291–317; and Sosik, J.J., & Godshalk, V.M. (2004). Self-other rating agreement in mentoring: Meeting protégé expectations for development and career advancement. *Group & Organization Management, 29*(4), 442–469.

29. Peterson & Seligman (2004, p. 30) as cited in Note 13.

30. Peterson & Seligman (2004, p. 30) as cited in Note 13.

31. Peterson & Seligman (2004, p. 30) as cited in Note 13.

32. Peterson & Seligman (2004, p. 30) as cited in Note 13.

33. Peterson & Seligman (2004, p. 30) as cited in Note 13.

34. Peterson & Seligman (2004, p. 30) as cited in Note 13.

CHAPTER 4

WISDOM AND KNOWLEDGE

Strengths for Stimulating Vision and Ideas

Life is the only real counselor. Wisdom unfiltered through personal experience does not become a part of the moral tissue.

—Edith Wharton

In this chapter I will present the first of six virtues, introduced in Chapter 3, necessary for becoming an authentic transformational leader: wisdom and knowledge. It was Lin Yutang, a noted Chinese writer, who once said that "Besides the noble art of getting things done, there is the noble art of leaving things undone. The wisdom of life consists in the elimination of non-essentials." To this we might add that persons who are chosen as leaders tend to be those who know how to get things done.[1] Authentic transformational leaders know what requires attention and what can be ignored. They get their followers to focus on what is really important and motivate them to perform beyond their wildest dreams.

Authentic transformational leaders get things done in ways that exceed expectations because they possess the wisdom and knowledge needed to influence followers to act. *Knowledge* is the process of collecting facts. *Wisdom* is the process of applying the facts in an efficient and effective way to solve life's problems. When we use our accumulated facts to make good

Leading with Character, pages 57–77

57

Figure 4.1. *Wisdom of the Ancients.* Not all wisdom comes from accumulated life experiences. Much comes from introspective learning, being sensitive to the social needs and problems of others, recognizing your role in organizations and society, dealing effectively with ambiguous problems, and possessing a keen intuition.

leadership decisions, we reflect the virtue of wisdom and knowledge (see Figure 4.1).

WISE AND KNOWLEDGEABLE LEADERS

Given the importance of getting a variety of things done in today's hectic and multi-tasked workplaces, let's begin with our examination of the virtue of wisdom and knowledge from multiple leadership perspectives. To illustrate this virtue, five leaders from different walks of life are highlighted who exemplify the character strengths associated with wisdom and knowledge (see Figure 4.2).

The Cerebral Stateswoman

When you think of the most powerful and influential women in the world today, chances are Dr. Condoleezza Rice comes to mind. At the time of this writing, Rice was the current U.S. Secretary of State and only the second

Figure 4.2.   *Wise and Knowledgeable Leaders.* Condoleezza Rice, John F. Kennedy, Maya Angelou, Bill Gates, and Brian Wilson.

such woman (along with Madeline Albright) to hold that prestigious position. Charming, polished and intelligent, Rice is constantly hounded by her admirers to run for president. Some supporters even imagine an all-female showdown against Senator Hillary Clinton in 2008. Rice's popularity is based on her knowledge base and proven track record in academia and the federal government.

The pursuit of wisdom and knowledge were two very important virtues instilled in Rice by her father and mother. Her father was a Presbyterian minister and her mother was a music teacher. Both of Rice's parents were very much devoted to her success. No wonder why Rice developed the character strength of love of learning over her life. By the ripe "old" age of three, she could read music! After initially aiming at becoming a concert pianist, she ended up earning bachelors (Phi Beta Kappa), masters, and doctoral degrees. She also learned to speak three languages besides English.

Rice's education prepared her very well for an exceptional academic career at Stanford University. There she became a tenured Professor of Political Science and then served as Stanford's Provost, a top administrative position in the university. This academic setting allowed her to continue to display her love of learning, as she published several books on

U.S. foreign policy and also served on the boards of several major corporations and universities.

Always a firm believer of putting theory into practice, Rice then moved her career into the international affairs arena. She became President George H. W. Bush's expert on the Soviet Union, and National Security Advisor for President George W. Bush from 2001 until 2005, when she was appointed to replace Colin Powell as Secretary of State.[2] All of these accomplishments were made possible by Dr. Condoleezza Rice's never-ending quest for information, her love of learning, and her wise application of knowledge to tough situations.

Most of us in the business world face similar challenges such as keeping up with ever-changing trends in our industry, advances in technology, and current events and their effects on business. Dr. Condoleezza Rice's story shows that keeping up with these changes requires leaders and their followers to constantly learn—and share their learning with others. That is why possessing a love of learning is important. For leaders to add to their knowledge base and make wise decisions, they need to enjoy the process of learning and instill that attitude in their followers. How passionate are you about learning and continuous personal improvement?

Our Most "Interested" President

When I give talks on leadership, I ask audience members to name some charismatic leaders who come to mind. Almost every time, people shout back: JFK! It never fails. When asked why they chose President John F. Kennedy, they explain that "he is an American icon," "he led an exciting life," or "he was interesting." I respond by noting that the reason why he was "interesting" is because he seemed to always be *interested* in many things and experiences. Whether it was a novel situation, a challenge, or a rendezvous, JFK was always open to new experiences. Because JFK suffered from many physical infirmities (Addison's Disease, jaundice, colitis, osteoporosis, chronic back problems, etc.), he seemed to want to get the most out of every minute of his life. He was a man of curiosity, and he certainly lived life to the fullest. Though he was born privileged, it was his curiosity and courage which helped him to overcome many personal and political obstacles.

In his early life, JFK's curiosity manifested itself in his keen interest in English and history classes. As well as in the many pranks he pulled on his family members and school mates. Such monkey business was encouraged at school through his membership in The Mucker's Club, a group of mischievous students whose mission was amusing themselves at the expense of school administrators. At one point, the young JFK was reported to have stolen a life-size figurine of movie star Mae West and placed her in his bed in his dorm room. He was curious to see other people's reactions to his high jinks. Imagine the look on the faces of the school's maids when they found Mae West in his bed! However, JFK was never a standout student academically. His wisdom and knowledge came from his ability to learn from his life experiences and those of the Kennedy clan.

With the mentoring and support of his father, JFK used life as his teacher. He soaked up as many experiences as he could between his many bouts with illnesses. He studied at the London School of Economics for a year and then at Princeton. He graduated from Harvard and published (with the help of his father's business connections) his thesis entitled *Why England Slept*. After graduation, JFK was accepted by the U.S. Navy. His courageous leadership aboard PT-109 after being rammed by a Japanese destroyer is well-known. Despite being thrown across the deck and injuring his back, JFK was able to tow a man three miles across the ocean to an island. He then helped his crew to be rescued. JFK's heroic behavior was awarded with Navy and Marine Corps Medals and the Purple Heart, among other military honors.

After a whirlwind rise to the top of Massachusetts' politics, JFK was elected president of the United States in 1960. At 43, he was the youngest of any American presidents. His presidency was marked by many noteworthy foreign and domestic policy events. Regarding foreign policy, JFK was embarrassed by the Bay of Pigs fiasco. In this scheme, CIA-trained Cuban exiles were trained to overthrown Fidel Castro, the communist dictator of Cuba. The plot failed miserably. JFK took full responsibility for the debacle. More importantly, he learned to collect much more information from multiple sources before making important strategic decisions.

JFK's bitter taste of defeat with the Bay of Pigs taught him the need to remain curious yet cautious. Following the erection of the Berlin Wall by the Communists in 1961, JFK faced another significant challenge—the Cuban Missile crisis. In October, 1962, a U.S. spy plane identified a Soviet intermediate range ballistic missile site under construction in Cuba. The Cuban missile crisis brought the U.S. to the brink of a nuclear war with the Russians. During the tense hours of deciding on a course of action, JFK relied on his strength of curiosity. He met with as many generals, politicians, and historians as possible to absorb as many facts as he could. JFK used his analytic abilities to sort through vast amounts of conflicting information. Instead of succumbing to groupthink as he did during the Bay of Pigs fiasco, JFK relied on his objective and analytic decision-making skills and his deep knowledge of history to decide on a blockade of Cuba. After a week of tense standoff, the Russians backed down and an apocalyptic catastrophe was averted.[3]

JFK's desire to accumulate knowledge and put it into practice is also evident with his development of the Peace Corps, his support for racial integration and civil rights, and support of the space program. The Peace Corps was an avenue for Americans to provide service to underdeveloped nations through volunteering to help with education, farming, economic development, healthcare and construction. The knowledge that Peace Corps volunteers share with underdeveloped nations is exchanged for once-in-a-lifetime global experiences for Americans. In terms of domestic policy, JFK sent the Civil Rights Act to Congress in June of 1963. JFK also intellectually stimulated the nation's scientists and engineers at NASA to work to put a man on the moon by the end of the 1960s. Man had always been curious regarding reaching the moon. It was JFK's leadership and interest that helped us to realize that dream.

Despite his extra-marital affairs and untimely assassination in 1963, JFK is considered by the public to be one of America's greatest presidents. Perhaps that is because JFK embodied a youthful exuberance for curiosity and learning. His presidency was marked by the initiation of many hopeful and optimistic programs aimed at benefiting not only the United States but also the global community.[4] As mentioned in Chapter 3, hope and optimism can be powerful sources of motivation that give people meaning and purpose in life. What are you doing in your organization to ignite a sense of hope, optimism and love of learning?

A Poet with Perspective

Wisdom and knowledge can often be found in the writings of our great poets. One such poet who has touched and inspired countless people is Maya Angelou. Her ability to inspire others, including Oprah Winfrey and Coretta Scott King, comes from her vast knowledge of what it means to be human. This knowledge does not come from formal education, but from the "school of life." Angelou's brilliance stems from her ability to see life from multiple perspectives, various domains, and the many roles she has played in her life. She has used her roles and experiences in life to encourage others to overcome their own personal challenges.

Angelou describes herself as an African-American poet, memoirist, actress and civil rights activist. She has been a successful director, producer, and author. She has displayed many of her talents on the stage, television and in the movies. But her success did not come easy. As an unwed mother, Angelou was forced to make ends meet by doing whatever it took to put bread on the table. She was a night club dancer. She worked as a cable car conductor. She cooked and served up food at a Cajun café. She toiled in an automobile shop, scraping the paint off of cars. She even worked as a madam and prostitute in a San Diego brothel.

But deep down, Angelou knew that there was something much better in her. She shifted her focus to work less toward satisfying her own lower order and immediate needs. Instead, she set her sights on working for a greater cause—working for Dr. Martin Luther King's Southern Christian Leadership Conference and civil rights movement in the 1960s. She also developed her writing skills by editing several African newspapers. After returning to the U.S., she worked for several federal government commissions under Presidents Gerald Ford and Jimmy Carter. Angelou went on to become a Professor of American Studies at Wake Forest University. President Bill Clinton invited her to read her poem *On the Pulse of Morning* at his inauguration in 1993. Angelou has published numerous books of poems including *I Know Why the Caged Bird Sings* (1969) and the Pulitzer prize nominated collection entitled *Just Give Me a Cool Drink of Water 'Fore I Die* (1971).[5]

Maya Angelou's story illustrates the importance of perspective-taking capacity in leadership. To fully understand followers, leaders need to understand the many economic, ethical, spiritual and social challenges that followers face. As the saying goes, "They need to walk a mile in followers' shoes." Then, they need to find a common ground that provides the best solution for all the key players in a situation. Maya Angelou has lived her life by experiencing many different situations—some good, some bad. But that variety of experiences has allowed her to gain perspective by truly understanding the realities of life and realizing the potential of bringing out the best in herself and in the many people she has influenced through her work. Are you able to look at situations from multiple perspectives and find the common ground that makes the unity of different stakeholders possible?

The Computer Nerd

How would you describe the richest man in the world? Yes, I am talking about Bill Gates, co-founder, chairman and Chief Architect of Microsoft. Which of the four leadership types described in Chapter 2 would you use to classify the man who has created the largest software company in the world? I expect that some of you might classify Bill Gates as an Abrasive/Egotistical Hero. If you did, your classification would probably be based on images of Gates you derived from popular culture. "Super-intelligent nerd with immense power," "tyrant," or "evil genius" are labels that the media have placed on Gates due to his clashes with the government over Microsoft's aggressive business practices and their seemingly monopolistic presence in organizations' technology systems.

However, I don't think this classification is fair. Consider Gates' tremendous amount of philanthropy. Gates and his wife, Melinda, have generously funded over $7 billion to numerous causes including underrepresented minority college scholarships, AIDS research, and prevention of diseases that strike mainly in the Third World. With almost $29 billion endowed in the Bill and Melinda Gates Foundation, Gates is well positioned to continue his future philanthropic contributions for years to come. Despite these noble actions, perhaps it is more appropriate to focus on Gate's tremendous amount of industry-specific wisdom and knowledge. (Notice that I am practicing what I preach by accentuating the positive aspects of Bill Gate's character.)

Many people agree that Bill Gate's success is due, in part, to his never-ending desire to learn. Even if he is considered one of the busiest people in the world (he allegedly receives two million emails everyday), he is well-known for his bi-annual, one-week long, retreat to a mountain-side cabin. There he goes through several dozens of reports from his managers and reads many books to formulate strategic direction for Microsoft. These intellectually stimulating behaviors reflect his strong commitment for continuous learning, and perhaps the phenomenal success that Microsoft has generated during the past three decades.

When it comes to the computer industry, there is probably no one who possesses as much knowledge of its history, its status quo and its future as Bill Gates. Over the years, Gate's open-mindedness has allowed him to opportunistically reap the benefits just at the right time. While at Harvard, Gates teamed up with Steve Ballmer, Paul Allen and Monte Davidoff to identify the potential of developing software for the nascent personal computer industry. Gates was open to partnering with IBM to launch the MS-DOS operating system and then to licensing its operating system to non-IBM PC clones. Gates and his developers then were open to mimicking the Apple graphical user-interface with the introduction of MS Windows in 1990. Through constant innovation and hiring very smart and dedicated people, Gates has built Microsoft into the corporate behemoth that it is today.[6] How open are you to continually re-inventing your organization with highly talented people?

The Creative Composer

Picture yourself driving along the Pacific Coast Highway or walking along a beautiful California beach like La Jolla near San Diego. Nice image! Chances are the soundtrack to your vision would include a Beach Boys' tune such as "Surfin' USA," "California Girls," or "Good Vibrations." The creative genius and main producer, composer, arranger and visionary group leader of the Beach Boys was Brian Wilson. While with the Beach Boys, Wilson wrote and produced an amazing string of international hits and popular music classics. The zenith of Wilson's achievements was the release of the *Pets Sounds* album in 1966, which many experts consider to be one of the greatest pop albums ever recorded.

Wilson's celebrated status as a leader in popular music stems from his creative genius. His innovative use of layered harmonies, unusual instruments, spiritual lyrics and perfectionism in his production are legendary. Wilson showed musical talent at an early age and worked very hard to develop his musical talents into strengths. What is more impressive is that he was able to develop his strengths even though he suffered physically from total deafness in his right ear, and psychologically from his abusive and domineering father. Wilson's high level of creativity may be the result of his need to over-compensate for his disability. His incessant drive for perfection may stem from his need to satisfy his father who constantly criticized Wilson. Unfortunately, these issues may have caused Wilson's descent into depression and drug addiction in the late 1960s and 1970s.

After successfully battling his demons, Wilson re-emerged as a musical force in the late 1980s. His re-birth ignited a flurry of creative output including six albums plus the triumphant completion of the *SMILE* album, his magnum opus. After finally completing this critically acclaimed album in 2004 (which took 30 years to make), Wilson is enjoying a successful solo career. Today, he is widely recognized as one of the most important and innovative popular music composers of the 20th century.[7]

When it comes to creativity, those of us who work outside of the music business can learn much from Brian Wilson. His prolific songwriting comes from a deep conviction that what he does is very important. He truly loves his work and is driven to perfection because he feels that he is on a mission to create "spiritual" music. As leaders, when we deeply love what we do and feel that it is our purpose in life to share that purpose with our followers, then we too can create "music" with our followers through our transformational leadership.

HOW WISDOM AND KNOWLEDGE BENEFIT TRANSFORMATIONAL LEADERS

Character strengths that reflect wisdom and knowledge can enable leaders to display several aspects of transformational leadership. Below are five leadership principles to help you put these virtues into action as a transformational leader.

Recall from Chapter 2 that transformational leaders challenge their followers' ways of thinking through intellectual stimulation. This requires leaders to challenge old ways of doing things, question the status quo, and examine problems from different perspectives. They provide a vision that gives meaning and purpose to their followers through inspirational motivation. To inspirationally motivate followers, leaders develop and articulate a new and evocative vision that is different from the status quo. They develop followers through individualized consideration by coaching and mentoring them as well as recognizing each person's unique skills, abilities and knowledge. Your ability to display each of these transformational behaviors depends upon the extent to which you can tap into the character strengths associated with wisdom and knowledge.

Creativity

Creativity is a character strength that provides a solid foundation for displaying intellectual stimulation and inspirational motivation. Creativity is associated with non-conformity to standards and norms, flexibility in perceiving and thinking, and unconventional and risk-taking behavior. These approaches to living and problem solving are often used by inspiring leaders. Brian Wilson's inspirational story of overcoming adversity to impact others through his music over such a long period of time illustrates many aspects of creative thinking. In fact, Wilson's infusion of rich harmonies and lush production into basic rock and roll music defined the West Coast sound. To be inspirational, you need to deviate from what is generally acceptable in order to challenge the status quo. You need to be flexible in your thinking in order to propose appealing alternatives when you craft and articulate your image of the future for your team or organization. Therefore, you need to be creative in order to inspire your followers by presenting them with an evocative vision.

Creativity may also help leaders intellectually stimulate their followers. Such was the case for Brian Wilson in 1966. He challenged the other members of the Beach Boys to move away from their formula for hit records (the traditional "Beach Boy's sound") toward the innovative, beautiful, harmonious and spiritual sound of *Pet Sounds* with its "teenage symphony to God." Like Brian Wilson, creative leaders possess the cognitive and behavioral flexibility to produce innovative products by challenging the basic assumptions of followers. When a leader demonstrates creativity, chances are that his followers will follow suit and role model this behavior. This creates organizational cultures that value change. This makes innovation possible.

PRINCIPLE 1

Creativity allows you and your organization to challenge the status quo and identify opportunities. Your creativity fuels the inspirational motivation and intellectual stimulation of your followers.

Curiosity

Curiosity is another character strength reflecting the virtue of wisdom and knowledge. John F. Kennedy's thirst for information on topics of interest helped him to tap into his curiosity and use it to his advantage in critical leadership situations. Like JFK, transformational leaders possess a strong desire to collect information about all kinds of people, processes and things (see Figure 4.3). Similar to creativity, curiosity may encourage leaders to display both inspirational motivation and intellectual stimulation. People who are curious challenge stereotypes and the many assumptions people commonly take for granted. They engage themselves in greater learning than less curious people. They are more enthralled with their work and as a result perform better than less curious people. They also possess positive moods and attitudes. They see life as worth living because each new day brings on exciting new challenges and opportunities that define their vision.

 PRINCIPLE 2 | Curiosity makes you a more adaptive leader and your company a more learning-oriented organization. Curiosity is a powerful source of inspirational motivation and intellectual stimulation that can energize your associates to be more innovative.

Figure 4.3. *The Internet is a Popular Forum for the Curious Leader.* Those who seek new ways to grow their organizations enjoy exploring and discovering information that they can use to intellectually stimulate their followers.

Open-Mindedness

Closely related to the character strength of curiosity is open-mindedness. Curious leaders collect information and facts about events throughout their life; they are open to and able to see things from different points of view. This makes *open-mindedness* another important character strength for transformational leaders and places them at higher stages of moral development than other leaders.[8] Their greater perspective-taking ability makes them more effective problem solvers by considering and integrating multiple points of view. Like Maya Angelou, they are able to abandon previous beliefs and practices that no longer make sense, and make drastic positive changes in their lives. They take into consideration evidence that goes against their beliefs and habits. This, along with the willingness to revise beliefs and practices when appropriate, allows these leaders to make such changes possible. In essence, they are able to intellectually stimulate themselves and others.

Open-mindedness may help leaders to build a collective vision that satisfies the requirements of a wide range of diverse followers. Think about the wide array of constituents who are inspired by the visionary blueprints for the future of the computer industry drawn by Bill Gates. In fact, open-mindedness is likely to promote the display of inspirational motivation because envisioning the future requires being open to the perspectives of different stakeholders as possible avenues for achieving success. By collecting software performance information from customers, Bill Gates is including Microsoft's customers in his company's leadership system and organizational vision.

In addition, when leaders are open to and appreciate the unique talents, strengths, viewpoints and needs of followers, they demonstrate individualized consideration. These open-minded leaders gain valuable insights from a wider range of followers and associates, especially when the view points and strengths of their followers are very different from their own. This approach is what Lou Gerstner used when he spent his first days at IBM visiting key customers and listening to their opinions of what IBM needed to do to better serve them.

| PRINCIPLE **3** | A leaders' open-mindedness is the key for followers to participate and develop a sense of ownership. Participation and ownership in organizational initiatives are built by displaying inspirational motivation, intellectual stimulation and individualized consideration. |

Love of Learning

One reason why some leaders are more open to ideas and new experiences than others is that their flexibility allows them to *learn* about new things. In my research, I have found that mentors who are more oriented towards learning goals are rated by their protégés as displaying transformational leadership more frequently than mentors who are less learning goal-oriented.[9] Individuals driven by learning goals, such as Dr. Condoleezza Rice, possess a love of learning that is associated with positive feelings about learning and its possible implications. They may develop this character strength early in life like the boy shown in Figure 4.4. As they progress through life, they find models for successful performance of tasks, and experience life as an enjoyable challenge.

A true love of learning may enable leaders to display inspirational motivation, which requires them to clarify their positive vision and teach others about how to reach that future state. Leaders who love to learn display intellectual stimulation which encourages others to value the intellect, use imagination and carefully re-think through solutions to problems. It also helps leaders display the individualized considerate behaviors associated with the

Figure 4.4.   *This Young Boy is Beginning a Life-Long Love Affair with Learning.* This character strength can help him in future leadership positions where the collection and application of information and knowledge can contribute to his company's success.

coaching and mentoring. If we are to serve as a coach and mentor (display individualized consideration), then we must assume the role of a teacher who first masters the subject material and then passes it on to our followers.

PRINCIPLE 4	Love of learning is an important foundation for leaders to identify new trends in the business environment and develop effective strategies for a new set of challenges. Through a love of learning, a leader can demonstrate inspirational motivation, intellectual stimulation and individually considerate behavior, so that followers can face the future more confidently and successfully.

Perspective-Taking

Thomas Jefferson once said "I cannot live without books." Jefferson had an unquenchable desire to learn so that he could accumulate knowledge and build wisdom. Wisdom involves the discovery and accumulation of basic truths as one moves through life. Wisdom is a function of intellectual and temperamental aspects of character including *perspective.* Individuals who possess wisdom or perspective realize larger patterns of meaning or relationships and can see to the heart of important problems.[10]

Perspective or wisdom is often required to display transformational leadership that helps followers see what goal or vision they should focus on achieving. Perspective helps leaders to articulate a vision that has broad appeal or "reach" to many followers. This reach is often based on very sensory language that appeals to the emotions of followers. The emotional content to Maya Angelou's poems has given many people new perspectives on life and inspired many to re-think their basic assumptions about life as well.

Wise individuals have wider perspectives to problem solving and bring both feelings and rationality to problems. Anyone who has listened to JFK's inspiring and intellectually stimulating inauguration address cannot help but hear a call for wider perspective-taking. Such perspective is important for leaders to stimulate intellectual engagement among followers. The more perspectives you have, the more flexible you can be in trying new approaches to solving problems. Greater perspective-taking capability also allows you to be more rational in your approach to problem solving. In this way, you can show that you value the intellect of your followers by encouraging them to think and re-think their ideas thoroughly. Such approaches also show that you are individually considerate of the unique perspectives that your followers and associates possess. By recognizing and appreciating their diverse opinions and knowledge bases, you demonstrate the strength of perspective-taking.

PRINCIPLE 5	Perspective-taking allows leaders to consider both sides of many paradoxes they have to face in today's business environment. The ability to understand these paradoxes through a broader perspective also allows you to show inspirational motivation, intellectual stimulation and individualized consideration to your followers. These transformational behaviors energize your followers to perform beyond expectations.

LIVING THE PRINCIPLES

Here are several guidelines that you can follow to put these principles into practice on a daily basis. Although they are inherently interdependent, these principles can help you build your leadership character more successfully.

Practicing Principle One: Creativity

Being creative helps you to inspire and intellectually stimulate your followers. Creativity can be developed in almost anyone through specific practices and by providing an environment that encourages people to be creative and practice the first principle. Here are a few helpful hints relevant to this principle.

- Work to identify and eliminate any stumbling blocks to creativity. These may come from the organization, your boss, your followers, and (most commonly) yourself. You must change cultures that focus on "making no mistakes" into those that learn and grow through mistakes. Just don't make too many mistakes! Provide examples of successful creative initiatives to win over your boss. Intellectually stimulate your followers to help them to be more creative.
- Give yourself and others autonomy or freedom to choose as many relevant and interesting work tasks as possible. People typically choose what they are interested in and therefore exert more effort on tasks they enjoy. Freedom of choice is a powerful way to intellectually stimulate and inspire your followers.
- Support and reward yourself and your people for creative initiatives. Be open and informal in meetings. A supportive and open environment that recognizes small creative successes goes a long way in fostering authentic forms of leadership.

- Use brainstorming sessions to separate idea generation from idea evaluation. The rules of brainstorming include: (a) the more ideas, the better; (b) the wilder the ideas, the better; (c) piggyback your ideas on the ideas of others; and (d) do not allow ideas to be criticized or evaluated during the brainstorming session. Also, consider using electronic brainstorming technologies such as Ventana Corporation's *GroupSystems.* In my research, I have found that such advanced forms of information technology enhance the positive effects of goal setting and inspirational motivation on team members' creativity.[11]

Practicing Principle Two: Curiosity

Being curious also helps you to inspire and intellectually stimulate your followers. We are born to be curious. From a very young age, children are often preoccupied with the question "Why?" As adults, our curiosity continues to grow as we search for truth and meaning from the world around us. Here are a few helpful hints relevant to the second principle.

- Give yourself and your associates freedom (autonomy) at work. Autonomy allows us to be curious about our tasks, situations and fields of interest. If, as a leader, you want to be inspired or inspiring to others, you must become obsessively curious about your organization's mission, systems, structures, and people.
- Identify gaps between what is currently known about an organizational or personal issue and what is unknown. The difference between what you know and what you *need* to know often increases your level of curiosity because most people want to eliminate the gap. This will allow you to formulate a compelling vision of where your organization currently is (the unacceptable status quo) and where it needs to go (the ideal state for your organization).
- Consider life to be one big adventure with plenty of opportunities to meet new people, or experience new things. Some experiences will be good. Some will be bad. But, in the end, they all will add to your knowledge base. Some might even get you to enjoy being curious. Life experiences are often the best means for authentic leadership development.
- Get "in the zone." In other words, do things that you find fascinating at both work and at home. These optimal experiences are exciting and intrinsically motivating. They put you "in flow" because your perceived challenges match your perceived skills.[12] These experiences should make you curious to learn more. Such curiosity and intrinsic

motivation are the powerful motivational forces behind inspirational motivation and intellectual stimulation.

Practicing Principle Three: Open-Mindedness

Being open-minded helps you to inspire, intellectually stimulate and develop your followers. This is a difficult principle to practice given our tendency over time to become set in our ways or limited in our thinking. As leaders, we need to be deep and critical thinkers whose open-mindedness supports our transformational leadership. Here are a few helpful hints relevant to this principle.

- When thinking about or debating an issue, make a list of all the arguments and pieces of evidence that support your position. Then go the extra mile by listing counter-points to every point you have on your list. Better yet—try to list more arguments *against* your position than you listed *for* your position. This exercise not only prepares you to follow up with compelling responses, it also intellectually stimulates (exercises) your mind so you can be a leader who is mentally sharp.
- Take a university course on negotiation strategies. Most of these courses are excellent ways to become open-minded since they force you to consider your opponents' point of view. Leaders need to take the perspectives of their constituents into consideration to build consensus or to formulate visions that have a broad reach.
- Consider the issue you are struggling with to be of the utmost importance. Research indicates that high quality thinking processes that consider multiple perspectives occur when the decision is considered to be important.[13] Leaders who are inspiring point out what is truly important for their followers so that they can put extra effort into their work.
- Construct picture puzzles or complete crossword puzzles. These mental exercises force you to consider "what fits" and "what does not fit" when solving problems. When solving these problems, think about why a solution meets the requirements and why another does not. Such deep thinking is necessary to influence followers why they need to perform some tasks they really don't want to perform.

Practicing Principle Four: Love of Learning

A love for learning new ideas and concepts helps you to inspire, intellectually stimulate and develop your followers. Today we live in the information age—a time when knowledge is power. You must never grow tired of learning new things because the world is constantly changing. Ignoring change puts you and your organization at a big disadvantage. Here are a few helpful hints relevant to the fourth principle:

- Establish a culture that values learning and sharing information. I have worked with several clients in the health care field to establish "communities of learning." These learning communities include small group meetings, updates on new information, and problem solving sessions. Information systems that act as knowledge repositories and means for communicating and sharing information are also very helpful. Such social and technical systems are very effective means to intellectually stimulate and develop your followers.

- Consider learning as an opportunity for personal development. Identify and explain to your followers the reason why learning is important. What will each of them get out of the learning process? What is the payoff or value-added? Often, the payoff is intrinsic satisfaction. If so, point this out. Otherwise, identify the extrinsic reasons why learning is important, such as career advancement, salary increases, or promotions. Learning is perceived as important when it adds value both personally and organizationally. It is the transformational leader's job to point out both the intrinsic and extrinsic value added for followers and their organization.

- Make learning fun. This approach converts your (and your followers') perception of work into a perception of play. Just think of all the extra minutes or even hours of overtime people may be willing to put in if they consider their work to be "play." Such approaches to fostering a love of learning makes inspirational motivation and intellectual stimulation easy to display.

- Consider learning as an opportunity to make new friends or social connections. Learning as part of a group is beneficial since group members can bond over common interests or the joint development of skills. As a transformational leader, it is your duty to connect people to others who can bring out the best in each other. Such connections often arise out of opportunities to coach or mentor others and inspire communities who share a passion for an important cause or mission.

Practicing Principle Five: Perspective-Taking

Having perspective helps you to inspire, intellectually stimulate and develop your followers. Perspective is often reflected in wisdom, not necessarily associated with chronological age, but from accumulated life experiences integrated into a sound set of principles for dealing with life and leadership issues. Here are a few helpful hints relevant to the fifth principle.

- Be a mentor and/or be mentored. Sharing your own personal life experiences and career lessons with junior or less advanced individuals helps you to gain wisdom. Mentoring others is a great way to display individualized consideration. In addition, learning from others who can share their life and professional wisdom with you is an excellent way to develop perspective. Being mentored by the right person can be an effective way to become intellectually stimulated and inspired. The leadership lessons you learn can be passed onto others. That's how strong transformational cultures are built.

- Reflect upon and learn from your life experiences. Set aside a few minutes at the end of each day to "debrief" yourself regarding what you have experienced during the past day. Answer the following questions. What good did you accomplish for yourself and others? Where did you fall short on your aspirations? What and how can you do better? What lessons did you learn from the moments you spent interacting with others? Taking the time to conduct this inner dialogue can help you to realize larger patterns of meaning or relationships between events in your life. You can then better identify your purpose-in-life which you can present to your associates in an inspirational and intellectually stimulating story.

- Read the classic works of literature or philosophy to learn the "wisdom of the ancients" as well as more modern sages. My personal favorites include the works of Plato, Socrates, Saint Augustine, William Shakespeare, Mahatma Gandhi, and Benjamin Franklin's *Poor Richard's Almanac*. Reflecting on the ideas of the great thinkers can give you insights into how to deal with some of the timeless challenges associated with being human. Many of the great quotes from literature and history can be quite inspiring and intellectually stimulating.

- Re-visit the history lessons of your youth from non-traditional perspectives. For example, find and read books about the discovery and colonization of America written by Native Americans. Or read the Declaration of Independence, the Preamble of U.S. Constitution and the Bill of Rights. Do all Americans share in what is proposed in these documents? Such readings and thoughtful reflection can infuse perspective into your thinking. A broader perspective can help you to see beyond deeply engrained biases, habits and narrow ways of thinking. These vices are stumbling blocks to idealized influence, inspirational motivation and intellectual stimulation. Work to remove these stumbling blocks by looking at issues from as many perspectives as possible. This will help you to formulate an inspirational

vision that will have broad appeal. To craft an appealing and evocative vision takes wisdom, but to articulate it in way that is compelling
takes courage, which is described in the next chapter.

NOTES

1.   Bass, B.M. (1990). *Bass and Stodgill's handbook of leadership: Theory, research and managerial applications.* New York: Free Press, p. 65.

2.   Felix, A. (2005). *Condi: The Condoleezza Rice story.* New York: Newmarket Press; Hawkins, D.B. (2005) *Condoleezza Rice: A woman of faith.* New York: Penguin Group; and Morris, D., & McGann, E. (2005). *Condi vs. Hillary: The next great presidential race.* New York: Regan Books.

3.   Barnes, J.A. (2005) *John F. Kennedy on leadership: The lessons and legacy of a president.* New York: AMACOM; and Editors (2002, January 14). The secret skills of leaders. *U.S. News and World Report,* p.8.

4.   Burns, J.M. (1961). *John Kennedy: A political profile.* New York: Hartcourt; Dallek, R. (2003). *An unfinished life: John F. Kennedy, 1917–1963.* New York: Little, Brown & Company; and O'Brien, M. (2005). *John F. Kennedy: A biography.* New York: Thomas Dunne Books/St. Martin's Press.

5.   Angelou, M. (2004) *The Collected Autobiographies of Maya Angelou.* New York, NY: Modern Library; Bloom, H. (2001). *Maya Angelou.* New York: Chelsea House Publishers; Courtney-Clarke, M. (1999) *Maya Angelou: The poetry of living.* New York: Clarkson Potter; and Kite, L.P. (1999). *Maya Angelou.* Minneapolis, MN: Lerner Publications.

6.   Gatlin, J. (1999) *Bill Gates: The path to the future.* New York: Harper; Lesinski, J.M. (2000). *Bill Gates.* Minneapolis, MN: Lerner Publications; Schultz, S. (2005, October 31). For a healthier globe. *U.S. News & World Report, 139* (16), 76; and Wallace, J., & Erickson, J. (1993). *Hard drive: Bill Gates and the making of the Microsoft empire.* New York: Collins.

7.   Carlin, P.A. (2006) *Catch a Wave: The rise, fall and redemption of the Beach Boys' Brian Wilson.* Emmaus, PA: Rodale Books; Kottler, J.A. (2006). *Devine madness: Ten stories of creative struggle.* San Francisco: Jossey-Bass; Priore, D. (2005). *Smile: The story of Brian Wilson's lost masterpiece.* London: Santuary Press; and White, T. (1994). *The nearest faraway place: Brian Wilson, the Beach Boys, and the southern California experience.* New York: Henry Holt & Co.

8.   Kuhnert, K.W., & Lewis, P. (1987). Transactional and transformational leadership: A constructive developmental analysis. *Academy of Management Review, 12,* 648–657.

9.   Sosik, J.J., Godshalk, V.M., & Yammarino, F.J. (2004). Transformational leadership, learning goal orientation, and expectations for career success in mentor-protégé relationships: A multiple levels of analysis perspective. *The Leadership Quarterly, 15,* 241–261.

10.   For interesting discussions on wisdom and perspective, see DiTomaso, N. (1993). Weber's social history and Etzioni's structural theory of charisma in organizations: Implications for thinking about charismatic leadership. *The Leadership Quarterly, 4,* 257–275; Hinterhuber, H.H. (1996). Commentary: Oriental wisdom and western leadership. *International Executive, 38,*

287–302; and Peterson, C., & Seligman, M.E.P. (2004). *Character strengths and virtues: A handbook and classification.* New York: Oxford/American Psychological Association.

11. For information on e-leadership in computer-assisted work teams, see, for example, Sosik, J.J., Avolio, B.J., & Kahai, S.S. (1997). Effects of leadership style and anonymity on group potency and effectiveness in a group decision support system environment. *Journal of Applied Psychology, 82,* 89–103.

12. Csikszentmihalyi, M. (1990). *Flow: The psychology of optimal experience.* New York: Harper Perennial.

13. Peterson & Seligman (2004) as cited in Note 10.

CHAPTER 5

COURAGE

Strengths for Weaving Moral Fiber

Abraham Lincoln did not go to Gettysburg having commissioned a poll to find out what would sell in Gettysburg. There were no people with percentages for him, cautioning him about this group or that group or what they found in exit polls a year earlier. When will we have the courage of Lincoln?

—Robert Coles

The quest for personal courage is a lifelong journey. During your childhood days, you may have watched the classic movie entitled *The Wizard of Oz* (1939). The movie's creative plot is an excellent portrayal of the development of character strengths. Along with Dorothy, the heartless Tin Woodsman, and the brainless Scarecrow, the cowardly Lion ventures to the Emerald City in search of courage. During your days in high school, you might have read *Profiles in Courage* (1957), President John F. Kennedy's Pulitzer Prize winning biography of eight U.S. Senators who risked their careers by standing up for their personal beliefs. You might also be familiar with the courage of Socrates. Standing up to an Athenian court, Socrates refused to be silenced in his tireless critique of the assumptions of Ancient Greek society. In his defense, Socrates promised only to continue his role as critic, knowing he had sealed his death sentence. He stood up for his principles and was true to himself to the bitter end.

Leading with Character, pages 79–99
Copyright © 2006 by Information Age Publishing
All rights of reproduction in any form reserved.

Those who possess the courage of Socrates and Lincoln are more common than we realize. Consider the cases of corporate whistleblowers whose stories emerge in popular press and media now and then. These courageous individuals often put their economic and social futures on the line by challenging corporations engaged in corrupt and unethical practices.

Such authentic transformational leaders possess the psychological, physical and moral courage to stand up for what they believe is right. Their ability to act in ways that are true to themselves and true to what they expect of others is based on different forms of courage as shown in Figure 5.1. *Psychological courage* involves motivating yourself to carry on and persist in your beliefs despite setbacks, failures, attacks from critics, and even the loss of

Figure 5.1.   *Let's Get On With It.* Courage in the workplace takes many forms. Leaders inspire their followers to persist with difficult tasks by showing them how their work helps to achieve the organization's mission and their own personal development as well.

support from others. *Physical courage* involves bravely putting yourself in harm's way and fighting for your cherished values. *Moral courage* involves letting others know what you stand for (and what you will not stand for). As Jesse Jackson once said, morally courageous leaders don't simply go along to get along; they meet the moral challenge of the day. When we dare to display these forms of fortitude, we reflect the virtue of courage.

COURAGEOUS LEADERS

When most people think of the virtue of courage, they frequently describe brave soldiers who stoically face battle with a keen sense of self-determination and purpose. But courage is evident in many more life situations. Consider the many missionaries who put their lives in danger for their religious beliefs. Another example is the terminally-ill cancer patient living her last days in a hospice. Yet another is the brave wife who must rear her children after the untimely death of her husband. Based on your life experiences, you can probably think of many more examples. Take the next 3–5 minutes to add to this list of examples and reflect on how your examples illustrate courage.

Now that you have some personal examples of courage in mind, notice that courage is more prevalent than you might think. Given the wide range of situations where courage is required for outstanding leadership, let's examine the virtue of courage from multiple leadership perspectives. To illustrate this virtue, four leaders are highlighted from different walks of life who exemplify the character strengths associated with courage (see Figure 5.2).

The First Lady of Civil Rights

Rosa Parks passed away at the time of this writing. I had just discussed Parks' grassroots approach to transformational leadership with a group of aspiring leaders the night before she died. Her example of idealized influence goes to show that you do not have to be the "world-class" type of leader, like CEOs or presidents, to be transformational. Ordinary people, just like you and me, can do extraordinary things. But the secret to success for idealized leadership is exercising integrity—a simple yet difficult task.

When it comes to integrity, Rosa McCauley Parks was considered by most people, including Dr. Martin Luther King, Jr., to personify the character strength. Born in Tuskegee, Alabama, Parks grew up on a farm where she began her lifelong membership in the African Methodist Episcopal Church. Living on a farm and continually growing in her faith throughout her life taught her patience, optimism, and hopefulness. At the same time,

Figure 5.2.   *Courageous Leaders.* Rosa Parks, Martin Luther King, Jr., Joe Namath, and Pat Tillman.

Parks' schooling during the days of the Jim Crow laws showed her that there was a very separate "Negro world" and "White world." Park's righteous anger toward segregation, shared by her husband Raymond Parks, prompted her to join the Montgomery chapter of the National Association for the Advancement of Colored People (NAACP) in 1943. She was soon elected secretary to its president and was a tireless worker for the NAACP.

At the time, the legally mandated segregated seating on public buses in the South was the epitome of inequity. In many cases, the law required Negroes to relinquish their seats and/or leave the bus. Such was the case for Parks on a rainy day in 1943, when she was forced off the bus. The bus driver then quickly sped away. Parks walked home for five miles *in the rain.* Ironically, it was the same bus driver who was driving on that famous day (December 1, 1955) when she refused to move from her seat and was subsequently arrested. She refused because of her firm convictions, her strong determination, and clear belief that the bus seating law was a violation of her constitutional rights. Parks did *not* refuse to move from her seat because she was tired. She was simply tired of giving in.

Parks became the perfect symbol and test case for the Civil Rights Movement's leadership because of her upstanding character. By nature, she was a very quiet and serene person. She was highly intelligent and held strong convictions. She was married, had a relatively good job, and had an aura of quiet confidence about her, which stemmed from her involvement in the NAACP. As a result of her arrest and the publicity of her case, Dr. King and the Civil Rights leaders initiated the Montgomery Bus Boycott. This form of nonviolent resistance was effective in lifting the law requiring segregation on public buses. It also helped to bring national attention to the Civil Rights Movement. According to Jesse Jackson, the entire Civil Rights Movement stands on the shoulders of Rosa Parks.[1]

The ultimate validation of this statement came, following Rosa Park's death, when the U.S. Senate passed a resolution to honor Parks by allowing her body to "lie in state" in the U.S. Capitol Rotunda. She was the first woman and first American not previously in government to lie in state. While living she earned many prestigious awards from the NAACP, the Presidential Medal of Freedom, the Congressional Gold Medal, among others. Her status as an American icon and influential leader of integrity stems from her ability to behave in a way that was consistent with her ideals—equality and justice. She publicly stood up for her moral convictions when she sat down on that bus in 1955 and refused to give up her seat. Her life was guided by her strong faith and value system. Parks was an authentic leader who emphasized the importance of being yourself. Indeed, Rosa Parks is a fine example of the Saint in our leader typology.

The Beautiful Dreamer

Baptist minister. Peacemaker. Quintessential charismatic leader. Hero. American Nobel Laureate. Martyr for the Civil Rights movement. These are just some of the many important roles Dr. Martin Luther King, Jr. played in his lifetime. But perhaps the most important role that King ever played was the part of a brave visionary leader. That's because he forever inspired us with his most beautiful dream for mankind:

> When we let freedom ring, when we let it ring from every village and every hamlet, from every state and every city, we will be able to speed up that day when all of God's children, black men and white men, Jews and Gentiles, Protestants and Catholics, will be able to join hands and sing in the words of the old Negro spiritual, "Free at last! Free at last! Thank God Almighty, we are free at last!"[2]

King's vision of unity, cooperation and equality is the product of his life-long belief that an authentic person has to do more than preach about ideals. The authentic person, in King's opinion, must also act upon his ideals to promote positive change. It is by fostering interdependence, not divisiveness and segregation, that transformational leadership works to facilitate such change. And to ignite the spark for that change, it takes only one extraordinary life.

King's stream of life events flowed in a way that enabled him to live by his ideals and work toward his vision. The influence of his mother and father (also a Baptist minister), his education from Morehouse College, Crozer Theological Seminary, and Ph.D. from Boston University helped forge his strong faith, rock solid values, and vision quest. At the time of the Montgomery Bus Boycott, King was the pastor of the Dexter Avenue Baptist Church. As a result of his involvement in the leadership of the boycott, his house was bombed.

This act of violence did not deter King's civil rights activism. He bravely carried on by founding the Southern Christian Leadership Conference in 1957. He organized and led marches for blacks' right to vote, desegregation of schools and busing, fair employment practices and other civil rights. During these events, King modeled his protest strategies after Gandhi's approach of non-violent resistance. However, many of the events did turn violent and involved police, fire hoses, and canine units. King and his family were also the victims of numerous death threats, harassing phone calls, and other forms of intimidation. The police brutality against civil rights marchers near Selma, Alabama on "Bloody Sunday" March 7, 1965 was horrendous. Fortunate for the cause, the violence was caught on tape and televised to a generally appalled nation.

Despite the violence, King continued to exercise his bravery and depended upon God to guide him. After several setbacks, he was finally able to lead the famous March on Washington on March 25, 1965. More than 250,000 people attended this great event and were mesmerized and incited by King's "I Have a Dream" speech. In addition to being inspirational, King made specific demands for meaningful civil rights legislation. After the success of the March on Washington, King set his sights on helping the Negro situation in the North. In Chicago, he established a chapter of his organization and left it in the hands of Jesse Jackson, then a young Civil Rights activist.[3]

By 1967, King expanded his own activism by speaking out against the Vietnam War. This seemed to irk people in Washington. For example, J. Edgar Hoover, director of the FBI, had despised King all the way back to 1961. The FBI wire-tapped King's home, bugged his hotel rooms, and had its agents follow King as he traveled across the country. Despite these and other forms of threats and intimidation, King showed valor in consistently proclaiming his message and working toward his vision. He was brave because he carried on fully knowing what the future might hold. He expressed these thoughts in a speech he delivered the night before he was gunned down in Memphis:

> Some began to...talk about the threats that were out— what would happen to me from some of our sick white brothers...Like anybody, I would like to live a long life. Longevity has its place, but I'm not concerned about that now. I just want to do God's will. And He's allowed me to go up to the mountain. And I've looked over, and I've seen the Promised Land. I may not get there with you. But I want you to know tonight, that we as a people, will get to the Promised Land. And I'm happy tonight. I'm not worried about anything. I'm not fearing any man. Mine eyes have seen the glory of the coming of the Lord.[4]

What a powerful message! His words exemplify bravery. What do these words mean to you and the world we live in today? Take a few moments to reflect on the source for Dr. Martin Luther King, Jr.'s bravery.

Why was King so brave? Perhaps it was his strong faith that sustained him in the face of danger. Or he may have "confidently pursued his vision for social change and civil rights, at great personal risk to himself and his followers, with a low need to seek the approval of the vast majority of Americans who condoned, either actively or passively, racial inequality."[5] In other words, bravery requires that the action is voluntary. No one ever forced King to initiate and persist in his mission. To be brave also involves understanding the risks that are involved in pursuing a course of action. King's final speech, excerpted above, shows that he knew the great risks that he and his family were up against. Bravery also must occur in the presence of danger, loss or injury. The fire bombings of his house, the death threats, intimidating phone calls, wire-tapping, and FBI surveillance serve as evidence of the sense of danger King must have felt.

King's bravery earned him the Nobel Peace Prize and American Liberties Medallion. It has also been the basis for comparisons to Abraham Lincoln and the courage he showed in uniting a nation divided over the slavery issue.

Broadway Joe

The quest to achieve victory by uniting diverse groups was also valued by Joseph William (Willie) Namath. A product of the working class Pittsburgh, Pennsylvania suburb of Beaver Falls, Namath was raised on the values of hard work, trust, collaboration, and the Golden Rule (treat others as you would have them treat you). Beaver Falls was a melting pot of different ethnic and racial groups including: Hungarian, Italian, Polish, Irish, Lithuanian, German, and African American. From this setting, Namath learned how to get along with many different types of people and integrate their unique differences to build effective teams. Namath's knowledge of how to leverage the power of diversity served him well in his professional football career.

While in high school, Namath excelled in three sports—football, basketball and baseball. He turned down offers from six Major League Baseball teams and many other college football programs to join Bear Bryant's Crimson Tide from the University of Alabama. Bryant considered Namath to be the best quarterback and athlete he had ever coached. Bryant's opinion was based on Namath's amazing ability to throw highly accurate passes with blazing speed. Namath's talent was all the more remarkable since he accomplished this feat while suffering from a bad knee that limited his mobility as a quarterback. Unfortunately, he suffered a serious knee injury requiring surgery in his senior year at Alabama. Despite these setbacks, Namath courageously lead Alabama to two number one national rankings. He accomplished this feat with his fierce competitive drive, "never-give-up" attitude, maverick personality, and genuine commitment to his teammates.

Namath's collegiate successes set him up in 1965 as the number one draft pick by the New York Jets of the fledgling American Football League (AFL). Namath's long hair, white shoes and charismatic flamboyance was a perfect fit for the AFL with its wide-open and creative style of play. It made for a marked contrast with the traditional and rigid style of the established National Football League (NFL). While in the AFL and later with the Rams in the NFL, Namath suffered additional knee injuries requiring surgeries. His knees were so bad that they frequently swelled up with fluids and required draining even during games. Despite these physical hardships over his career, Namath has been recognized by the AFL and NFL numerous times in his career as an all-star, Pro Bowler, and NFL Hall of Fame member.

The most spectacular highlight of Namath's career came in 1969's Super Bowl III when he led the Jets to an unexpected victory over the highly favored Baltimore Colts. Prior to the game and in response to a heckler, Namath *guaranteed* that the Jets would win. This was not a display of cockiness. Namath simply stated a true belief based on his team's collective sense of confidence. Their confidence came from their review of films revealing that the Jets' strengths could perfectly exploit the Colt's weaknesses. In addition, Namath's ability to bond with both his black and white team members strengthened their trust levels and heightened their level of expectations for success. That's because he was a true role model on the field. He was the first player to arrive at practice and the last to leave. And unlike Terrell Owens, he never badmouthed any of his team mates.[6]

Figure 5.3.   Joe Namath signing autographs for young fans (circa 1973).

When I was 11 years old, my Uncle Ed arranged for my cousins and me to meet Joe Namath at the Tampa International airport. We had a picture taken of us with Namath signing his autograph as he boarded an Eastern Airlines flight (see Figure 5.3). Namath was our idol. Our meeting with him was somewhat of a letdown since he appeared to us to be very aloof. Over time, I have learned more about Namath's inner struggles with his need for attention, his involvement in the "Bachelors III" scandal, and a televised ESPN fiasco where the inebriated Namath stated twice that he wanted to kiss Suzy Kolber, a female interviewer. Namath's complex personality shows that in every leader (and every person) there is a constant struggle between other-oriented and self-serving behavior. As John Lennon once said, "We're all Christ and we're all Hitler... We want Christ to win."[7]

In retrospect, Joe Namath represents more than simply a charismatic quarterback. His courageous leadership of the Jets to victory in Super Bowl III added legitimacy to the AFL. With his white shoes, Fu Manchu mustache, playboy image, and full-length fur coat or velvet pants that he wore on the sidelines, Namath symbolized rugged individualism. He bravely stood out and expressed who he truly was. This is the essence of authentic leadership. Amazingly, as an individualist, he still was able to stand up against locker room racial bigotry directed at his black teammates. He united players from different races and ethnic backgrounds. He also persistently battled his chronic knee problems and played to the bitter end when it was evident that his knees could no longer sustain him as an effective quarterback in the NFL. Based on his perseverance on the field, Namath is considered by many to be a patron saint of underdogs. Whether Namath is a Saint or an Abrasive/Egotistical Hero in our leader typology is open to debate. But he certainly was an authentic charismatic leader.

Man of a Higher Calling

Carpe diem is Latin for "seize the day." This phrase may very well have been the mantra of Pat Tillman. This NFL Arizona Cardinals' football star, in response to the events of September 11, 2001, turned down a $3.6 million NFL contract and enlisted in the U.S. Army. Tillman rejected wealth and fame to serve his country. After serving as an Army Ranger in Iraq, Tillman had the opportunity for an "early out" from service. Instead, he chose to complete his three-year service requirement in Afghanistan, where he was said to have been killed by friendly fire in April 2004.

Tillman always made the most of every moment of his life. The words of Senator Edward M. Kennedy describing his slain brother Robert F. Kennedy are equally applicable for portraying Tillman: "*He loved life completely and he lived it intensely.*" He would do things that most people would talk about, but not actually do. And what Tillman did, he did with all of his heart and at full throttle. As a child, he would climb and swing from tree to tree—like Tarzan, but without a net below to catch him if he fell. Although Tillman was considered too small to play college football, he was voted PAC-10 defensive player of the year while at Arizona State University in 1996. While at ASU, he befriended a student with Downs Syndrome, read on a wide range of subjects, climbed the 200-foot tall light towers at Sun Devil stadium, and graduated with a 3.84 GPA in three and one-half years. Tillman never was one who could stand still; he believed that there always was another experience for him to live to the fullest.

After completing a 70 mile triathlon and being drafted by the Arizona Cardinals in 1998, Tillman worked hard to play safety on defense. Tillman's ferocious play on the field and true commitment to his team was recognized by the St. Louis Rams, who offered him a $1.8 million contract. Guided by his value of loyalty, he turned it down for his $500,000 contract with the Cardinals. Even with that modest NFL salary, Tillman felt that he was living the good and easy life.

But everything changed on September 11, 2001. Tillman felt compelled to do something meaningful by serving his country and fighting for the American way of life. Compared to his grandfather who fought at Pearl

Harbor and other family members who served in the military, Tillman felt his role as an NFL player was insignificant. So he, with his brother Kevin, enlisted in the Army and became part of the elite Army Rangers. This was Tillman's higher calling or purpose in life. Ultimately, his zeal for working toward achieving meaningful missions was extinguished forever during a confusing ambush and the friendly fire it drew.[8]

Throughout his entire life, Pat Tillman possessed a fierce drive to live life to its fullest. He gave all of himself for what he believed to be a noble cause. Many Americans, including former Vietnam War hero Senator John McCain of Arizona, were touched not only by Tillman's magnificent sacrifice, but also by his zest for life. It is ironic that Tillman never actively sought out to be a leader. Instead, he was rather humble and unassuming. Yet his vigorous behavior exemplified charismatic leadership and his many accomplishments in life reflected the extraordinary achievements associated with such leadership. By serving as a positive role model, Tillman gained many more loyal followers after his death than some leaders today have during their life. That's what is truly meant by idealized influence.

HOW COURAGE BENEFITS
TRANSFORMATIONAL LEADERS

Character strengths that reflect courage enable leaders to display several aspects of transformational leadership. Below are four leadership principles to help you put these virtues into action by displaying transformational leadership.

Bravery

To be a charismatic or transformational leader requires hardiness and self-confidence. For example, Dr. Martin Luther King Jr. faced many death threats that shook his confidence in his ability to lead. Despite these threats, he always regained confidence in himself by deciding that he needed to carry on by "walking in faith, not in fear."[9] Like King, leaders need to be resilient and bounce back from many public and private setbacks that they face. These personality traits are often reflected in acts of bravery—a key character strength reflecting the virtue of courage.

Brave leaders demonstrate courage by taking appropriate risks. For example, fire-fighters take risks every time they battle a blaze. But the risks they take are appropriate due to the training, planning and preparation they put into their jobs. Likewise, brave leaders are likely to understand these risks and accept the consequences of their actions.[10] These are the qualities we see in idealized leaders who take calculated risks, assume full responsibility for their actions, and address crises head on. Bravery may also help inspiring leaders to demonstrate self-determination and commitment to reaching goals while facing difficult situations. Leaders who show high levels of personal determination and commitment can inspire others to join the noble cause. That's because their actions are symbolic of cherished organizational or cultural values.[11]

Brave leaders do not exist only in political and sport settings mentioned above. There have been many "grassroots" leaders who showed incredible bravery despite the challenges they faced in order to make a more ethical decision or prove that their personal values could not be compromised. Two such leaders have been the subject of popular motion pictures. Without a bachelor's degree or training as a lawyer, Erin Brokovich courageously helped to bring down the mighty P G & E Corporation for its unethical poisoning of the water supply of Hinkley, California. Likewise, Karen Silkwood was a union activist who was concerned with health and safety issues at the Kerr-McGee plutonium processing plant. In her whistleblower role, Silkwood bravely stood up against her employer regarding these troubling issues. She died in a suspicious automobile accident on her way to deliver important company documents to a newspaper reporter in 1974.[12] The bravery of these two leaders should serve as an inspiration for all of us to be true to ourselves and our cause.

Bravery not only inspires but can also intellectually stimulate followers. By bravely standing up for his principles, Socrates intellectually stimulated those present and future generations who have read about his courage in the Athenian court. He argued that every human being must think for himself and that the unexamined life is a waste. The fact that you are reading this book to develop your character pays tribute to Socrates' vision of continuous improvement throughout life. These examples lead to the sixth principle concerning using one's valor to role model for and inspire others to achieve their own greatness.

PRINCIPLE 6

Bravery will demonstrate your willingness to act consistently with your values and beliefs. You can inspire the people in your organization by bravely acting on your most passionate beliefs. In essence, your bravery fuels your ability to inspirationally motivate and intellectually stimulate your followers.

Persistence

The planning and preparation that enables bravery is also important for developing the character strength of persistence. During the September

11, 2001 terrorist attacks, former New York City Mayor Rudolph Giuliani made decisions based on existing plans that the city had in place for hazardous materials, riots, fires and other emergency situations. The relentless preparation of the city government and emergency crews to anticipate and rehearse responses to these situations proved to be invaluable as the 9/11 attacks unfolded.[13] Winston Churchill's admonition to the British people to "never give up" during the Nazi blitz of England illustrates the power of persistence. Like Churchill, transformational leaders need to demonstrate a high level of perseverance to stand up to and fight against injustices, powerful enemies, or simply to influence people and organizations to change.

These examples show that by persevering in their preparation, transformational leaders can build the character strength of persistence. Persistence is often noted as an outcome of self-efficacious and iron-willed individuals.[14] Transformational leaders are self-efficacious and hold strong convictions about their beliefs, purpose and vision. Their persistence is often reflected in their charismatic messages and symbolic behaviors that reflect the leader's personal values.[15]

Joe Namath shared a vision of winning Super Bowl III with the New York Jets. To help achieve this vision, he built up his teammates' confidence levels by working hard at practice. He acted as a positive role model by overcoming many physical injuries over his career. He also emphasized the importance of teamwork and showed respect for all his teammates. Namath often talked about his values to his teammates. His actions on the field reflected the values of hard work, teamwork and appreciating people for their unique talents, skills and personal styles.

Like Joe Namath, persistent leaders are determined to get followers to work together toward their vision. They create a sense of joint mission and ownership, and demonstrate commitment to reaching difficult goals. These attitudes, formed in followers, are associated with a leader's display of idealized influence and inspirational motivation. Role modeling persistence shows followers how to be hardy and tough-minded. Persisting through struggles, with visions of success in mind, can be very inspirational.

There are examples of business leaders who showed a high level of persistence for what they believed to be the right thing to do. William Donaldson, the former chairman of the Securities and Exchange Commission demonstrated what persistence is all about. Although he was a Republican, he repeatedly sided with the SEC's two Democratic members in 3–2 votes in favor of tougher rules on business and increased investor protection despite harsh attacks from business and his own political party. His persistence was based on his determination in "doing what was right rather than what was politically expedient."[16] Therefore, the seventh principle, working industriously and never giving up, is a means to role model a work ethic needed to achieve a meaningful and inspiring mission.

| PRINCIPLE 7 | Persistence will allow you to win trust and loyalty from your followers. Persistent behaviors demonstrate your determination to practice your values and beliefs. Doing so allows you to display idealized influence and inspirational motivation to your followers. |

Integrity

When a leader persistently displays idealized behavior over time, despite challenges from others, she demonstrates consistency between her values/attitudes/beliefs and her behavior. More importantly, she demonstrates self-consistency over time which shows others that her character is forged on a "rock-solid" foundation of wholeness, soundness and strength. This personal characteristic represents the notion of integrity.[17]

Integrity is central to the meaning of the phrase *"When what you say is what you do, and you are true to yourself, then you are an authentic leader."* Rosa Parks truly believed in the cause of the NAACP and the Civil Rights Movement. By her one modest act of defiance, she put her values into action and was true to herself. Idealized leaders, like Rosa Parks, present themselves in a genuine way and act in a straightforward manner. They demonstrate integrity because they set high moral standards for themselves and others, and serve as a role model whose behavior is consistent with the espoused standards. By practicing what they preach, idealized leaders demonstrate authentic leadership, with integrity at its core.[18]

Integrity involves telling the truth, being guided by a code of socially accepted values, and following through on commitments. It also includes being authentic by being true to oneself, genuine with others, and being open and honest about one's feelings.[19] Being authentic allows you to be whole and sound as suggested by the phrase "the truth will set you free." Integrity provides the foundation for displaying idealized influence.

Integrity is increasingly becoming the most important and fundamental requirement for leadership due to the several corporate scandals discussed in the previous chapters. People expect their business leaders to fight for justice, the truth, and the betterment of their organization, community, and the world. Integrity was what motivated Michael Capellas, the new President and CEO of MCI (formerly WorldCom), to hire MCI's first ethics officer and launch an anonymous hotline for employees to report code-of-conduct violations.[20] Let's now move to our next principle, which is being true to yourself, honest and open with others.

PRINCIPLE 8

Integrity will make you a more confident leader because you know you are doing the right thing. Being true to yourself is the essential aspect of an authentic leader and integrity is the foundation of such leadership. To be an authentic, idealized, leader in the eyes of your followers is to possess integrity.

Vitality

Leaders who seek to maintain a sense of integrity must value mental and physical vigor. The notion of being full of zest, enthusiasm, and contagious energy is one way to explain the character strength of vitality.[21] Vitality is what Tom Peters referred to as "tons of animal energy" and is an important element of what makes a successful leader. Consider former New York Jets' head coach Weeb Eubank of Super Bowl III fame. Coach Eubank is said to have told his running backs to "run the ball every time like it is your last chance to run the ball." He wanted to motivate his players to not do things halfhearted or halfway, but with much vigor and vitality. Like Eubank, transformational leaders are full of positive energy and enthusiasm. Their zeal stems from their need for ascendancy and power and their strong convictions. These characteristics cause them to be perceived by others as charismatic and inspirational.

Charisma (idealized influence) involves a strong emotional connection between the leader and the follower. This connection causes followers to identify with and desire to be like the leader. It also has several other important effects on followers. Followers become emotionally attracted to the leader. They desire to achieve to show support for the leader. They are willing to trust the leader. And they exert extra effort in their work for the leader.[22] The tremendous outpouring of emotion, awe and respect shown for Pat Tillman after his death illustrates how positively people can respond to vitality that is used for the greater good.

These powerful effects on followers seem to come from the inspirational nature of charisma. To inspire literally means to breath into, to energize others, or to share one's charismatic energy with others. When shared, charisma turns into a "raging fire", with its contagious, emotional energy manifesting in the leader and having a stronger effect on followers, and in turn, on the organization. Extroverted leaders, such as Pat Tillman, who live life with a great deal of zest and aspire to make their mark in the world display idealized and inspirational behaviors. Therefore, vitality may be required for leaders to display idealized influence and inspirational motivation. This brings us to our ninth principle, which involves living life as an adventure at 100% full throttle.

PRINCIPLE **9** | Vitality will make you a more dynamic leader with followers who feed from your contagious energy to produce extraordinary results. Vitality is the source of fuel for displaying idealized influence and inspirational motivation to your followers.

LIVING THE PRINCIPLES

The rest of this chapter offers suggestions on how to put these four principles into practice. Living these principles can build your leadership character by developing the important character strengths of courage.

Practicing Principle Six: Bravery

Being brave helps you to inspire and role model for your followers. But learning how to be brave is not easy. Nevertheless, bravery can be developed in some individuals who possess "the right stuff" through specific practices and by providing an environment that encourages people to be brave and practice the sixth principle. Here are a few helpful hints relevant to this principle:

- Take time to reflect on your purpose-in-life (PIL), value system, and behavior. What are you here for? What is your most important leadership goal or PIL? Make sure that your PIL is very clear to you. Then, note what values are most important for you to possess in order to accomplish your purpose. Make sure it is other-directed and not self-serving. Behaving in ways that are consistent with your values and PIL makes it relatively easy to be brave. That's because by being true to yourself, you will feel confident that you are doing the right thing. This exercise establishes your personal constitution or compact of understanding that shows you and others what you stand for. Such an understanding is essential for displaying idealized influence and inspirational motivation.
- Learn to develop and possess Positive Psychological Capital described in Chapter 3. Be thankful for what you have, instead of wishing for what you don't have. Think about all of your successes and work hard to turn your talents into strengths. Individuals who are brave are also optimistic, hopeful, and self-confident. These traits are essential to the authentic display of inspirational motivation. Brave people also have a strong value system that guides their behav-

ior. Behaving in ways that align with your values makes you an authentic and idealized leader.

- Learn bravery from co-workers, family members or other significant others. By reflecting upon what other brave individuals have accomplished, you can build your own sense of confidence to carry on in the face of danger. Imagining all of those who support you in your initiative can give you confidence that you have social support backing you. That can be a very powerful source of inspirational motivation. At the same time, you should reciprocate such support by encouraging them to become more courageous as well.

- Practice bravery through moral habit. Make it a point to try to do the right thing every time, even when no one is watching. Look for opportunities to stick up for the underdog or the down-trodden when justice is not being served.

- Provide strong leadership that backs up your followers. Reinforce the importance of their mission through speeches or messages. Continually clarify organizational values and the importance of telling the truth for your followers. Such actions can help followers to see that they are connected to a larger community working together to accomplish a noble mission. This builds bravery through a sense of strength in numbers. It also is quite inspiring to others who are interested in demonstrating valor.

Practicing Principle Seven: Persistence

Persevering also helps you to inspire and role model for your followers. The character strength of persistence is a matter of mental toughness and putting the time in to do what it takes to be successful. Here are a few helpful hints relevant to the seventh principle:

- Encourage yourself to put extra effort into staying with a task. Do this by rewarding yourself for raising the bar and then meeting your own self-imposed elevated goal. Elevating expectations is a form of inspirational motivation. Also, try to find others who are working on tasks similar to yours and provide social support to each other. That is, if you are really committed to working hard on the goal.

- If, at first, you don't succeed try, try again. Don't tell yourself that you don't have the ability to perform the task. Instead, attribute your initial failures to an inadequate amount of effort. When you put more effort into a task, you will find yourself trying harder and persisting. This approach has worked for my colleagues and me several times in our "battles" with journal article reviewers over initial critiques of our academic papers. In the end, our work was much improved and we felt good about convincing other experts who were gate-keeping what gets published in the scholarly literature on leadership.

- Take personal responsibility for failure, but remember to attribute your failure to insufficient effort. Simply put, you need to work harder. This means learning how to improve your skills or fine-tuning your behaviors. There are no short cuts in life. Hard work is the only authentic and idealized pathway to persistence and eventual success.

Practicing Principle Eight: Integrity

Acting with integrity is the foundation for serving as a role model for your followers. Being truthful with others (and true to yourself) can be very difficult given our extremely fast-paced and competitive world. But this character strength is essential for authentic transformational leadership because all others stem from it. How can you exercise vitality when you really don't believe in what you are doing? How can you develop a love of learning if you cheat through school or training sessions? Even though "the truth may hurt," it is what it is. It simply must be dealt with to the best of your ability. Here are a few helpful hints for dealing with being truthful that are relevant to the eighth principle:

- Recognize the truth as a moral imperative. If you view the truth as a source of enlightenment and empowerment, then you and your followers can gain from it. If the truth reflects well on you, then you should celebrate your success. If the truth reflects poorly on you, then you should work to correct your problems and enhance your knowledge, skills and abilities. This should help you in your future endeavors.
- Practice prayer, meditation, reflection and yoga. These techniques are ways to integrate your thinking, feeling, and acting. As a result, you may begin to understand who you really are, and what you possibly can become. It is much easier to become your true self rather than to become someone else. Understanding who you really are is required for role modeling idealized leadership.
- Reflect on your hoped-for and feared possible selves. Hoped-for possible selves reflect what you would like to become. Feared possible selves reflect what you are afraid of becoming. This exercise allows you to clearly define your self-concept and detect your purpose-in-life. Try to behave in ways that are true to what you hope to become. Avoid behaving in ways that will make you become what you fear.

Doing so allows you to exercise idealized influence because your possible selves reflect images or roles you need to play as a transformational leader.[23]

Practicing Principle Nine: Vitality

Demonstrating vitality or zest for life helps you to serve as a role model
for and an inspiration to your followers. While some of this depends on
your general physical condition, an important part of it is based on possessing a positive mental attitude. As leaders, we need to demonstrate high levels of energy and enthusiasm so that our followers come to desire our
positive psychological states as well. Here are a few helpful hints relevant to
Principle Nine:

- Get up, get out, and do something physical—like exercising, working
  out, jogging or walking. Enjoy nature. Join sports teams. These
  "change of pace" activities give you a break from your mental exercises at work. They refresh your mind, body and spirit. They also can
  help you to see the bigger picture about things. Seeing the bigger
  picture and what is truly important in life is a key form of inspirational motivation.
- Howard Powell was a senior trainer at the Center for Leadership
  Studies at SUNY–Binghamton back in my graduate school days.
  Despite his advanced age, Howard was one of the most positive and
  vigorous people I ever met. He'd come to work each morning greet-
  ing each of us with a heartfelt "*Good morning! What a beautiful day.*"
  Given Binghamton's notorious reputation for generally cold and
  cloudy weather, his comment was difficult for me to understand at
  the time. But Howard wasn't talking about the weather. He was talking about the fact that each day offers us unbounded opportunity to
  learn and socialize with other people. That was his source of energy.
  Let it also be your source of energy. To be a transformational leader,
  you need to be like Howard—seize the day, smile, and be well.
- Get involved in activities that you enjoy doing. Whether it is reading
  a good book, listening to your favorite music, or going on a vacation,
  any activity that raises the spirit can promote your vim and vigor. To
  help your followers, you need to match their talents and strengths
  with appropriate tasks and projects that they find interesting. By
  doing this, your inspirational motivation can rub off on them.
- Consider every new day a gift. Live each day as if it were your last. We
  really don't know when our time will come to pass from this earth.
  That's why it's so important to try to enjoy as much as we can every day.

As individuals, we have very different interests and ideas on what we enjoy doing. But the world has so much to offer. Most of us have the freedom to choose what we will experience. We also have the responsibility to choose wisely and, as inspirational leaders, to share our passion for the choice we make with others. As we learned from Pat Tillman, life is not a read-through. Life is meant to be lived actively and passionately. To hold such an attitude toward life takes courage, but getting your people to also adopt this attitude takes understanding humanity, which is described in the next chapter.

NOTES

1. Brinkley, D. (2000). *Rosa Parks*. New York: Viking; Edwards, P.D. (2005). *The bus ride that changed history: The story of Rosa Parks*. Boston: Houghton Mifflin; Kohl, H.R. (2005) *She would not be moved: How we tell the story of Rosa Parks and the Montgomery bus boycott*. New York: New Press; and Shamir, B., Arthur, M.B., & House, R.J. (1994). The rhetoric of charismatic leadership: A theoretical extension, a case study, and implications for research. *The Leadership Quarterly, 5*, 25–42.

2. Excerpt from King's "March on Washington" speech, March 25, 1965, http://www.historychannel.com/speeches/ra/970828.ram.   Retrieved November 11, 2005.

3. Deats, R.L. (2003). *Martin Luther King, Jr.: Spirit-led prophet*. Hyde Park: New City Press.; Garrow, D. (1981). *The FBI and Martin Luther King, Jr.* New York: Penguin Books; and George, B., Buhrman, R., & McLean, A.N. (2005). *Martin Luther King, Jr.: A young minister confronts the challenges of Montgomery*. Harvard Business School case 9-406-016, Boston, MA: Harvard Business School Publishing.

4. Excerpt from King's "I've Been to the Mountaintop" speech, April 3, 1968, http://www.americanrhetoric.com/speeches/mlkivebeentothemountaintop.htm. Retrieved November 11, 2005.

5. Sosik, J.J., & Dinger, S.L. (in press). Relationships between leadership style and vision content: The moderating role of need for social approval, self-monitoring and need for social power. *The Leadership Quarterly.*

6. Kriegel, M. (2004). *Namath: A biography*. New York: Penguin Books; and Sanford, W.R., & Green, C.R. (1993). *Joe Namath*. New York: Crestwood House.

7. Lennon, J.W.O. (1986). *John Lennon: Live in New York City* (liner notes) [LP]. Hollywood, CA: Capitol Records.

8. McCain, J., & Salter, M. (2005). *Character is destiny: Inspiring stories every young person should know and every adult should remember*. New York: Random House; Smith, G. (2004, May 3). Code of honor. *Sports Illustrated, 100*(18), 40–46; and Towle, M. (2004) *I've got things to do with my life: Pat Tillman and the making of an American hero*. Chicago: Triumph Books.

9. George et al. (2005) as cited in Note 3.

10. Peterson, C., & Seligman, M.E.P. (2004). *Character strengths and virtues: A handbook and classification.* New York: Oxford/American Psychological Association.

11. Bass, B.M, & Riggio, R.E. (2006). *Transformational leadership* (2nd ed.). Mahwah, NJ: Lawrence Erlbaum Associates.

12. Brockavich, E., & Eliot, M. (2001). *Take it from me: Life's a struggle but you can win.* New York: McGraw-Hill; and Rashke, R. (2000). *The killing of Karen Silkwood: The story behind the Kerr-McGee plutonium case* (2nd ed.). Ithaca, NY: Cornell University Press.

13. Giuliani, R.W. (2002). *Leadership.* New York: Hyperion.

14. Schyns, B. (2004). The influence of occupational self-efficacy on the relationship of leadership behavior and preparedness for occupational change. *Journal of Career Development, 30*(4), 247–261.

15. Sosik, J.J. (2005). The role of personal values in the charismatic leadership of corporate managers: A model and preliminary field study. *The Leadership Quarterly, 16,* 221–244.

16. Anonymous (2005, September). The courageous few. *Fast Company, 98,* 54.

17. Peterson & Seligman (2004) as cited in Note 10.

18. Gardner, W.L., Avolio, B.J., Luthans, F., May, D.R., & Walumbwa, F. (2005). "Can you see the real me?" A self-based model of authentic leader and follower development. *The Leadership Quarterly, 16,* 343–372.

19. Park, N., Peterson, C., & Seligman, M.E. (2004). Strengths of character and well-being. *Journal of Social and Clinical Psychology, 23*(5), 603–619.

20. Anonymous (2005, September) as cited in Note 16.

21. Peterson & Seligman (2004) as cited in Note 10.

22. Bass & Riggio (2006) as cited in Note 11.

23. Sosik, J.J., Avolio, B.J., & Jung, D.I. (2002). Beneath the mask: Examining the relationship of self-presentation attributes and impression management to charismatic leadership. *The Leadership Quarterly, 13,* 217–242.

CHAPTER 6

HUMANITY

Strengths for Developing Others

Business! Mankind was my business. The common welfare was my business; charity, mercy, forbearance, benevolence, were all my business. The dealings of my trade were but a drop of water in the comprehensive ocean of my business![1]

—The Ghost of Jacob Marley to Ebenezer Scrooge

Most everyone is familiar with Charles Dicken's timeless classic entitled *A Christmas Carol* (1843). This heartwarming story about the amazing moral transformation of Ebenezer Scrooge raises some important leadership issues about the role of business in society, self-knowledge, human nature, and the ties that bind people together. At one point in the story, Jacob Marley's ghost attempts to teach Scrooge that a businessman's goal is not to simply accumulate wealth. Rather, it is also to improve the lives of others and to use business as a means for elevating associates to higher levels of economic, professional and moral development. Scrooge's visions of ghosts point to the need for leaders to take a closer look inwards, so they can evaluate their behavior towards others. Such self-reflection is required for us to periodically adjust our course in life by questioning the selves we have become and determining what larger purpose our lives serve.

Dickens' story also illustrates a self-centered tendency in all of us that questions: What, if anything, do we in business owe to the poor, and what

---

good charitable acts do for society? How we answer these questions depends on the degree of compassion we have for others, our humanity, and our view of ourselves as either independent or interdependent. Scrooge certainly lacked a sense of compassion, and was terribly isolated from the people in his community as well. This is because he worshipped an idol—greed—and lost touch with all who were once close to him. Scrooge had forgotten what it meant to be human. As a result, he didn't care for people because he didn't really understand them anymore.

Few leaders become so utterly lost and isolated from humanity and yet many leaders come face to face with the demons that lead to their downfall. For example, Michael Milken, the financier extraordinaire and father of the junk bond, was charged in 1989 with 98 counts of racketeering and fraud. For this widely publicized scandal, Milken was indicted by a federal grand jury and spent 22 months in jail. While serving time in prison, Milken realized that business leaders must be much more socially responsible than what Milton Friedman suggested. Milken's new-found attitude toward social responsibility and his bouts with prostate cancer have led to his donating significant amounts of his fortune in charitable contributions. He also has worked to establish numerous foundations to further research in economics, education and medicine.[2] Sometimes a leader's self system must be shocked for him to become more humane.

Today's leaders do not need to be visited by spirits or shocked by critical life events in order to be transformed into more humane and socially responsible individuals. Instead, they must be willing to look at their own behaviors objectively and with an open heart instead of merely looking out for their own self-interests and blindly fitting in with organizational, industry or societal norms. Is your organizational culture making you something that you have not normally been in the past or really do not want to become? What has your career advancement cost you in terms of who you are as a person today? Have you lost your positive sense of self, your ability to show genuine concern for others, or your connection with the larger family we call humanity?

Humanness and genuine concern for others are not traits people are born with, but instead are learned through our experiences and self-revelation. Authentic transformational leaders do not gauge success by the money they acquire through life, but by the number of people they have positively influenced through their leadership. Given the complexity of business today and the countless difficult choices facing us each day, we have a responsibility to make an effort to evolve into leaders of humanity so we can maximize the positive impact we can have on society.

HUMANITARIAN LEADERS

Leadership is a social influence process that is accomplished through human relationships. This process is embedded in a larger social system comprised of the world and its people. To successfully exercise any form of leadership requires an understanding of one basic truth: *effective leadership rests on interdependency among people.* In other words, we must truly understand what it means to be human. We must love and be kind to others. We must understand what makes people (including ourselves) tick. And we must understand how to navigate through the often turbulent social and political waters of organizations. Doing so makes us more human.

Given the difficulty of truly understanding what it takes to show love, be kind, and demonstrate social intelligence, let's examine the virtue of humanity from multiple leadership perspectives. To illustrate this virtue, four very different leaders who exemplify the character strengths associated with humanity are highlighted next (see Figure 6.1).

Figure 6.1.   *Humanitarian Leaders.* Shirley Chisholm, Mother Teresa, Princess Diana, and Pope John Paul II.

The Catalyst of Change

Most Washington insiders laughed when the feisty Shirley Chisholm ran for president of the United States in 1972. But Chisholm, the first African American and first woman to make a serious run for the presidency, got the last laugh. Through her ethnically diverse voter base and support from the National Organization for Women, she was able to capture enough electoral votes to influence the 1972 Democratic platform and swayed Democratic nominee George McGovern on several important social issues. Chisholm's passion to assert her constitutional right to run for president, in spite of hopeless odds, was fueled by her genuine concern for improving the welfare of others. She was strong enough to sustain this motivation even though she faced both racial and gender prejudice throughout her life.

Chisholm was born in 1924 in Brooklyn, New York. Her mother decided to move the family to Barbados so that they could own a home and give all four children a proper education in a British-run school. Intellectual pursuits were encouraged within the Chisholm household by her father, who was an avid reader and admirer of Marcus Garvey and Franklin D. Roosevelt. After moving back to Brooklyn, Chisholm's family discussed important political and social issues and movements. This intellectually-stimulating environment helped to shape Chisholm's genuine concern for people.

After earning bachelor's and master's degrees relevant to her work as a teacher, Chisholm went on to direct and consult for child day care centers. She realized that the vision she had for using education to help poor children better themselves could only be achieved through political means. So, she aimed her sights at state politics and in 1964 ran and was elected to the New York State Legislature. She went on to serve in the federal government in 1968. Only four years later, when Chisholm was a junior Democratic member of the House of Representatives, serving New York's 12th District, she decided to embark on her crusade to shake up the country by running for president.

The late 1960s/early 1970s was a turbulent period in American history. Demonstrations against the war in Vietnam, racial unrest, civil rights, questioning of authority, abuses of power in government, and other troubling social and economic problems created a context that was ripe for change. Throughout her career, Chisholm was a leader motivated by strong willpower and her refusal to accept the status quo. She was a champion for giving workers a right to a minimum wage, improving opportunities for inner-city residents, increasing spending on education, healthcare and other social services. She opposed the draft and voted for reductions in military spending. After retiring from politics in 1983, Chisholm came full circle by returning to academia; she taught for four years at Mount Holyoke College in South Hadley, Massachusetts.[3]

In retrospect, Shirley Chisholm was a humane and authentic leader for several reasons. In no way did she behave as a typical "politician." Her sense of integrity allowed her to conduct herself in a brutally honest and honorable way that sought to expose the truths about the conditions of the American people and American politics. She once pointed out that the American political system is not democracy in the truest sense of the word. Rather, she felt that it is tainted by backroom deal-making and transactional exchanges. Her insider's view of politics troubled her enough to speak out about it in numerous interviews. As a politician, educator and author, Chisholm was a woman who was true to her principles of maintaining integrity and serving the needs of others. She did what she said and she said what she did. Because she possessed a true love for people and principles of honor, she dared to be a catalyst for change by exposing what was wrong in American society and its system of democracy.

The Compassionate Caregiver

Love and kindness are integral elements of the leadership of Mother Teresa of Calcutta (Agnes Gonxha Bojaxhiu), the Albanian nun who founded the Missionaries of Charity. Her vision to care for the poorest of the poor in Calcutta, India expanded into a world-wide religious order and social services organization. Mother Theresa's global work of care-giving earned her numerous awards including the 1979 Nobel Peace Prize. Her writings on Christian spirituality, prayer, and social work earned her global fame and a reputation as a "living saint" during her life. After passing away in September 1997, she was beatified by Pope John Paul II in October 2003, opening the way for her to be eventually recognized as a saint in the Catholic Church. But there certainly is no need to wait to classify her as the "Saint" in the leadership typology outlined in Chapter 2.

At the age of 12, Mother Teresa felt a calling to serve God by helping the very poor. She joined the Sisters of Loreto and began her missionary work in India. In 1950, she started her own order of nuns, the Missionaries of Charity, whose purpose was to serve "the hungry, the naked, the homeless, the crippled, the blind, the lepers, all those people who feel unwanted, unloved, uncared for throughout society, people that have become a burden to society and are shunned by everyone."[4] After expanding her work to other countries beginning in the 1960s, she had accomplished an amazing feat of leading a global organization in 123 countries staffed by over 4,000 sisters, 300 brothers, and more than 100,000 lay volunteers by 1997. Over the years, her Missionaries of Charity has established hospices, shelters, soup kitchens, orphanages, schools and family counseling programs. Her organization has also worked to combat serious social and medical issues including homelessness, leprosy and AIDS. She also has helped many financially rich but spiritually poor individuals find greater happiness and peace in her message of selfless service.[5]

Mother Teresa accomplished so much in her 87 years on this earth. We can learn not only from her deeds, but also from her words. In her writings and speeches, she encouraged people to get involved and take action to bring about the social and spiritual changes that the world needs desperately. She advocated a grassroots approach to community leadership when she said *"Do not wait for leaders; do it alone, person to person."* She championed authentic leadership (before we knew what the term meant) as she encouraged people to let their actions speak for them with words such as *"There should be less talk; a preaching point is not a meeting point. What do you do then? Take a broom and clean someone's house. That says enough."* But, most essentially, she taught us how to display love in its simplest form when she said *"Love begins at home, and it is not how much we do... but how much love we put in that action."* In Mother Teresa's words we find true wisdom. Stop and reflect upon what these words mean to you, and how they can help you to demonstrate your own authentic transformational leadership.

Sometimes we mistake the meaning of the word "poor." Poverty denotes being without something essential. Who are the people in your organization who are impoverished of leadership and purpose? What else do they lack that a humane and compassionate leader could give? How would their lives change if such an authentic transformational leader provided them with the care and love that Mother Teresa so freely gave to others?

The Candle in the Wind

At one point she was probably the most famous woman on earth. Her elegant image graced the covers of countless magazines and newspapers. Television reporters and photographers followed her everywhere. Her pioneering charity work with the poor, AIDS babies, and landmine survivors demonstrated that she was beautiful both inside and out. At her funeral, her close friend Sir Elton John re-wrote and performed his song "Candle in the Wind" as a tribute to her. She had truly become "England's Rose." She was Diana Frances Mountbatten-Windsor (Spencer), Princess of Wales.

To her admirers, Diana was a role model who showed high levels of kindness to the less fortunate. Her idealized influence, however, did not stem from exemplary early years, but grew over the course of her life as she put her values of kindness and compassion into action. Diana was an academically below-average student who suffered from self-esteem issues that plagued her throughout her life. Yet, she was able to overcome these issues by re-focusing her efforts on activities that were a better match for her inborn talents in music, sports, ballet, and charity work.

Throughout her life, Diana was a generally kind individual, whose radiance charmed most everyone she came in contact with, including Prince Charles. They were married in July 1981 with over 1 billion people watching via television. Diana's failed marriage to Prince Charles produced two sons, William and Harry. Rather than remaining in the plush, opulent and protected environment of the Royal Family, Diana dared to make a difference in the world. Her inherent kindness motivated her to partner with Mother Teresa on projects involving the care of the poor and AIDS babies. At a time when people were afraid to touch AIDS patients, Diana held the hand of a man with AIDS in a hospital. As Bill Clinton noted, "...She showed the world that people with AIDS deserved not isolation, but compassion..."[6] She also worked with the International Red Cross to help raise awareness of the land mine problem that was plaguing areas of Africa and Eastern Europe. Her concern was largely based on the fact that such mines caused injuries to many children worldwide. Her influence initiated the signing of the Ottawa Treaty by several governments which banned the use of anti-personnel landmines.[7]

At her funeral, Diana's idealized influence was reflected upon her by an extraordinary amount of public grief. All over the world, even in India where Mother Teresa had died the day before Diana, there was a sense of tragic loss. I recall driving in my car and listening to news reports of public reactions to the deaths of these two icons of leadership. What struck me most was how two women from very different backgrounds and life paths could do similar good, be criticized by adversaries in their lives, and then be lionized in death. How shallow and self-centered are we who cannot recognize exemplars of humanity while we are graced with their presence!

The People's Pope

When it comes to understanding what it means to be human, Pope John Paul II (Karol Jozef Wojtyla) was certainly one of the most socially intelligent, loving and beloved leaders of our time. John Paul II was born in 1920 in southern Poland. Throughout his life, he experienced the best and the worst of humanity. After his mother died when he was only nine years old, John Paul II was raised by his father, who instilled in him a strong faith and work ethic, along with a devotion to the Polish culture. As a child and an adult, John Paul II was well-rounded and likeable. He possessed a love for athletics, theater, and language. Each of these interests involved the formation and coordination of human relationships. As a result, John Paul II had friends of many different ethnic backgrounds and social statuses. These friendships provided him with a keen understanding of the inherent good in people.

Over the course of his life, however, John Paul II faced challenges from three evil social systems. The first challenge came when Nazi Germany invaded his native Poland in September 1939. The Nazis rounded up Jews, Gypsies, Catholic priests, and university professors and placed them in concentration (i.e., death) camps such as Auschwitz. John Paul II was deeply affected by the internment and extermination of his many Jewish friends. As a non-Jewish Polish male, he was forced to work in a limestone quarry. John Paul II learned much about human wants and needs as he forged friendships with the common laborers.

The Nazis also placed severe limitations on Catholic religious services. They sought to ultimately eliminate any form of Polish tradition or identity. They wanted to replace it with Nazi ideology and culture. In response, John Paul II and his friends took the advice of their Polish priests and fought the Nazis with their most powerful weapon: *their intellect.* They outsmarted the Nazis by going underground in an effort to sustain the Polish culture through secret meetings. In these gatherings, they attended Mass, studied philosophy and theology in an underground seminary, read and performed Polish literature and plays, and devised ways to help their Jewish friends hide from the Nazis. While working to sustain their culture, their culture helped to sustain them.

The second challenge facing John Paul II came immediately after the end of World War II. Instead of liberating the devastated Polish nation, Stalin and his Soviet Red Army imposed their brutality and dark ideology on Poland. Individualism was to be replaced with Communism. Religion was to be replaced with atheism. The rights and dignity of human beings were to be replaced with the supreme importance of the Communist Party. Any form of Polish culture and tradition was banned from practice.

It was during these very difficult times that John Paul II was ordained a priest, earned two doctorate degrees, and became the youngest bishop in Poland. Throughout the 1950s until the mid-1970s, he led the Polish community by adeptly and cunningly outwitting the Soviet occupiers and Communist Polish government puppets. His life experiences, friendships, connections with the elite in Poland, and ability to comprehend people made him a socially intelligent leader, who used the Polish culture as a weapon to combat the Communists. These small and steady victories made life more bearable for the Polish people.[8]

Suffering builds character. Character builds faith. And in the end, faith will not disappoint. On October 16, 1978, at the age of 58, John Paul II was elected Pope. I vividly remember the day he was elected. There was a sense of sheer elation, an overpowering amount of pride and emotion overflowing from Polish communities all over the world. In particular, I recall my mother, standing in the driveway of my childhood home in Wilkes-Barre, Pennsylvania, calling out to my uncle "Joe, we have a Polish Pope!" And time has proven that her joy and pride were not unwarranted. For John Paul II's deeds as Pope have earned him references as "John Paul the Great."

But greatness and goodness are often seen as threats by others. The third challenge facing John Paul II was an assassination attempt made on his life by Mehmet Ali Agca, a far-right Turkish militant of fundamental Islamic and Soviet influence. Miraculously, John Paul II survived the handgun shot from close range. Even more astonishing is the fact that John Paul II visited and forgave his attacker. Despite the malice shown toward him, John Paul II became a good friend to the would-be assassin's family. How many of us have a hard time forgiving people who have wronged us with non-life threatening attacks such as slander, adultery, lies, or deceit? How many of us can forgive to the level that John Paul II was capable of?

As pope, John Paul II demonstrated what it means to be a humane leader. His teachings clarified the interdependencies within and between God and His people, highlighted the dignity of women and the family, and presented lessons on numerous moral issues including murder, euthanasia and abortion. He taught that no human being should ever be used as a means to an end. In his writings, he warned against a culture of death, rampant materialism and injustice that seems to pervade society today. He also was a pilgrim pope who sought out to be a bridge between peoples, traveling more than 725,000 miles while making 104 foreign trips. As a bridge-builder, he sought to improve relations among the Catholic Church, the Eastern Orthodox Churches, several Protestant churches, and the Jewish people. He sought unity for a fragmented religion. He also apologized to several groups that had been wronged by the Church over the centuries.

In essence, John Paul II was a pope for people of all ages. Both children and adults loved him. Record-breaking crowds greeted him during World Youth Days. Millions of people attended his masses when he visited countries all over the world. At these gatherings, people would chant "*John Paul II, we love you*," and he would reply "*No. John Paul II, he loves YOU*." He was able to make a connection with people from all over the world because he understood the essence of what it means to be human: to love and to be loved.

Perhaps the greatest validation of the world's love for John Paul II was the attendance at his funeral in 2005, which may have been the largest attended funeral of all time. Two million people within the Vatican, more than 2 billion Catholics world-wide, and many non-Catholics mourned the death of John Paul II.[9] In the end, his legacy is one of human rights and dignity, social responsibility, and showing compassion and kindness to others, while maintaining a keen awareness of and fearless battle against the forces that seek to destroy humanity and social order.

HOW HUMANITY BENEFITS TRANSFORMATIONAL LEADERS

Character strengths that reflect humanity can enable leaders to display several aspects of transformational leadership. Ironically, two most unlikely leaders of our time mentioned love as part of their leadership style. The hyper-competitive NFL coaching legend Vince Lombardi is often associated with the saying "Winning isn't everything. It's the only thing." However, sports historians agree that Lombardi borrowed that quote from a college football coach from the 1930s. In a speech to corporate and government managers on teamwork, Lombardi actually did say "Love is loyalty. Love is teamwork. Love respects the dignity of the individual. Heartpower is the strength of your corporation." Similarly, Rudolph Giuliani, formerly known for his cold and distant approach to leadership, has told audience members during his post 9/11 speeches to love what you do, and love the people around you.

These ideas have not been lost on leadership scholars. For example, Bernard Bass has suggested that love may be quite relevant to outstanding leadership. Bass identified sociability, nurturing, femininity, and more feeling than thinking as personality traits that correlate with charismatic/transformational leadership. These personality traits are also reflected in measures of love to the extent that they involve forming and maintaining a warm, developmental and caring relationship between the leader and the follower.[10]

Love

We can best understand what it means to love by examining its component parts. Love is composed of three elements: attachment, caring, and intimacy.[11]

Attachment

Attachment is the powerful desire to be in another's presence, to be approved by another, and to be cared for (see Figure 6.2). Attachment of the follower to the leader is part of the identification process activated with idealized influence behaviors and attributes. When a follower sees her leader as idealized, she shares common values, beliefs and aspirations with the leader. These similarities enable the follower to bond with the leader in deep emotional and sometimes even spiritual ways. This kind of strong

Figure 6.2. *Mother and Child Union.* The love and compassion that this child learns from her mother may shape the way the child interacts with employees, customers and suppliers when she becomes an adult and runs her own business.

bonding based on love was evident in the special relationship John Paul II had with Catholic youth, who saw him as a hero, a role model and their idealized leader.

Caring

Caring involves the willingness to sacrifice oneself for the sake of the other person. Authentic transformational leaders sacrifice their own personal interests for the good of their followers and therefore demonstrate idealized influence behaviors. They also show they care when they recognize and appreciate their followers' unique talents, strengths and skill sets, and when they spend time coaching and mentoring their followers who may be suffering from difficult work or home-related problems. John Paul II demonstrated this form of care when he admonished priests in Nicaragua for getting involved with the Sandinista government, or when he provided spiritual guidance to participants at the World Youth Days. The purpose of providing such care to followers is to bring them closer to the vision, norms and expectations shared by the organizational community.

Intimacy

Intimacy can also be viewed as a strong bond between leaders and followers. This bonding often involves agreement between the leader and follower on important beliefs and guideposts for behavior—what scholars call *value congruence*. When leaders and followers share values and beliefs, they are likely to form very close relationships similar to those between siblings, romantic partners, or other loving relationships. Most of us spend a great deal of our time at work building relationships with our associates who become our "surrogate family" members. Why not model our working relationships after our plutonic loving relationships?

When most people think of love, they think of romantic forms of love with its passionate desire for physical and emotional closeness. To the extent that leaders and followers may not possess the same amount of power in the organization, such forms of love are likely to produce unhealthy or dysfunctional outcomes. However, compassionate (rather than passionate) forms of love *can* and do exist in leader-follower relationships. This happens when followers feel that the leader accepts the follower for who he is, and helps and supports the follower to achieve his full potential. These perceptions and behaviors reflect individualized consideration and are often found in mentoring relationships in organizations.[12]

Love also can exist when the follower feels safe and content being with the leader, hates to be away from the leader, feels passionate about the leader and his vision, or would do almost anything for the leader. These attitudes and viewpoints reflect idealized influence in healthy and positive authentic transformational leader-follower relationships. Unfortunately, they also can show up in dysfunctional and negative pseudo-transformational leader-follower relationships. The challenge for followers is to identify situations when they are being taken advantage of by such leaders who use their power for their own welfare at the cost of others. These inauthentic leaders must be confronted and brought down with the same passion and conviction that followers put into their efforts to build up and sustain authentic transformational leaders. This brings us to the tenth principle, which involves forming compassionate relationships with followers.

PRINCIPLE 10 — When you love your followers, you show real compassion for them as human beings. Showing compassion proves that you care for them as persons and not as things to be used to achieve some purpose. Love is the foundation for close relationships in which leaders and followers show trust, loyalty and commitment to each other, and followers go the extra mile for the leader.

Another form of love is what some theologians, philosophers and psychologists consider to be the noblest form of love—an unconditional, selfless, and altruistic type of love called *agape*. The origin of this idea goes back to the New Testament of the Bible with the words of Saint Paul:

> *Love is patient, love is kind. It does not envy, it does not boast, it is not proud. It is not rude, it is not self-seeking, it is not easily angered, it keeps no record of wrongs. Love does not delight in evil but rejoices with the truth. It always protects, always trusts, always hopes, always perseveres.* (1 Corinthians 13:3–10)

Kindness

This form of love is as an orientation away from the self and toward others. People show it by being generous, nurturing, caring and compassionate as you can see in Figure 6.3. In everyday terms, we call it "kindness."[13] Leaders, like Diane, Princess of Wales, who display idealized influence towards their followers show their kindness when they sacrifice self-gain for the gain of others. Leaders who display individualized consideration towards their followers show their kindness when they shower care, concern and empathy towards them. They also demonstrate kindness through individualized consideration when they pay attention to followers who are ignored or neglected by others.

Figure 6.3.   *Bringing Sunshine.* Volunteering at assisted living centers is a form of kindness. Such community service is often a prerequisite for career advancement to executive-level and political leadership positions.

We see kindness in leaders when their genuine concern for others is expressed through helping behaviors and when their words match their deeds. Shirley Chisholm's example of authentic transformational leadership illustrates this point. Chisholm recognized that the essence of humanity is degraded by racial or gender prejudices. Her realization did not deter her from pursuing her vision of improving social and economic conditions in America. Instead, it strengthened her convictions to work harder to attempt to wash away the ills of labor abuse, poverty, illiteracy, ignorance, and want. And she was never afraid to challenge her colleagues in Washington on these issues, as she did in a speech she delivered August 10, 1970:

> ...*artificial distinctions between persons must be wiped out of the law. Legal discrimination between the sexes is, in almost every instance, founded on outmoded views of society and the pre-scientific beliefs about psychology and physiology. It is time to sweep away these relics of the past and set further generations free of them.*[14]

We also see kindness in the work of Mother Teresa. Her life-long dedication to the care of the hopeless, the destitute, and the sick should encourage all of us to demonstrate acts of kindness with our associates. All the people you work with are prone to human suffering, be it struggles or hardships, such as illness, disease, family problems, divorce, or grieving over a death in the family. Therefore, the eleventh principle involves a leader's moral responsibility to engage in kindhearted and charitable acts and to treat all people with dignity and compassion.

PRINCIPLE **11**	By showing kindness to your followers, you make a very important statement to them: They are more important than the tasks that you require of them. The tasks will always be there, but your people may not. The genuine kindness that you show to your followers sets a very positive example for them to follow (idealized influence), and shows that you recognize and appreciate their unique talents and skills (individualized consideration).

Social Intelligence

In order to show kindness, leaders need to understand their own feelings, and relate well and empathize with their followers and associates. In fact, leaders need to be intelligent enough to carry out abstract thinking about similarities and differences among people, realize relationships within and between people and situations, and recognize patterns of behavior in others and what effects these patterns can have on them in the future.

This type of intelligence can be broadly classified as social intelligence, which also includes emotional intelligence and personal intelligence.[15] Social intelligence deals with relationships among individuals and groups and understanding the implications of any political alliances. Like John Paul II, a socially intelligent leader is able to identify key individuals in political pecking orders, use historical information on friendships and personality types to get followers to work in partnership, or simply act appropriate to the situation (i.e., self-monitor one's behavior).[16]

Emotional Intelligence

Emotional intelligence involves recognizing, understanding, and controlling one's own emotions and the emotions of others. An emotionally intelligent leader uses emotional information to stimulate appropriate thinking and behavior. For example, instead of lashing out at others when angry, she would pause, take a deep breath, and use the emotion to think through an appropriate response.[17] This response is extremely important to all leaders who are in the public eye (see Figure 6.4). When presented with racial and gender slurs during her life, Shirley Chisholm showed amazing calm and conviction, as she logically argued against her detractors.

Personal Intelligence

Personal intelligence refers to knowledge of how well one performs tasks, understands one's own thought processes, reacts to a variety of feedback, and develops a self concept or identity that is different from others.[18] John Paul II showed extraordinary levels of personal intelligence in his negotiations with the Polish and Soviet Communist authorities. He knew how to read the signals given by the communists. He knew when to encourage the Solidarity movement to stand up for their rights, and when to sit back and show patience with the communists. Through his keen understanding of history and human nature, John Paul II formed a unique identity of being a leader who used spiritual, peaceful and intelligent methods to help bring down the Soviet empire, which was known for using brute force and violence to achieve its ends.

Social and emotional intelligences represent personal traits helpful in displaying transformational leadership. Research suggests a link between social intelligence and transformational leadership.[19] These studies demonstrate that leaders (even information technology managers!), who can understand their own emotions and the emotions of their followers, are seen by their followers as displaying high levels of transformational leadership. Aspects of social intelligence provide transformational leaders with the ability to engage in impression management and image building required to influence followers to perform beyond the call of duty. We often see these forms of influence used by the Politicians/Well-Meaning

Figure 6.4.   *Here's How it Works.* Emotionally intelligent leaders are effective com-
municators. Influencing followers requires the ability to monitor your own and others' feelings and emotions, to understand differences among them, and to use this
information to guide your thinking, speech, and actions.

Chameleons in our leadership typology, but they are also used strategically
by the Saints, such as John Paul II.

Research also suggests that leaders who are rated highly on transformational leadership by followers possess high levels of emotional control
while interacting with others. Like Shirley Chisholm, leaders who view
themselves as transformational have a strong purpose-in-life, are confident
in their ability to accomplish their tasks, possess emotional control and are
self-confident in social situations. These traits are all aspects of emotional
intelligence.[20]

Personal intelligence also may be helpful to transformational leaders. It can help them to be more self-aware of the way they present themselves to followers. Followers often provide feedback to leaders based on their observations regarding the leader's behavior and performance. As with John Paul II and Shirley Chisholm, personal intelligence helps individuals to interpret feedback and understand their thought processes. Leaders who possess personal intelligence may be better equipped to present themselves appropriately as an idealized, inspirational and individually considerate leader. Thus, social, emotional, and personal intelligence appear to be important to a transformational leader's ability to attract, inspire and build developmental relationships with followers. This brings us to our twelfth principle.

| PRINCIPLE 12 | Leadership is a social influence process. To effectively influence followers, leaders must be keenly "tuned in" to their own emotions, motives, actions, and concerns, and those of their followers. In addition, understanding the dynamics of organizational social systems helps leaders to act as an appropriate role model for followers (idealized influence), inspire followers to work harder (inspirational motivation), and identify and develop followers' talents (individualized consideration). |

LIVING THE PRINCIPLES

The remainder of this chapter describes what you need to do to put these three principles into practice. By living these principles, you can further develop your leadership character by being more humane.

Practicing Principle 10: Love

Tina Turner once sang "What's love got to do with it?" You may be asking a similar question: "What's love got to do with leadership?" The answer, quite simply, is a lot. Leaders need to love and accept themselves in order to be confident and courageous. Leaders need to love change and learning so they can continually improve themselves and their followers. Leaders also need to love and accept their followers for who they are. That's because followers have unique talents, strengths and developmental needs that require transformational leadership to bring out "the diamonds in the rough." Here are a few helpful hints to form more loving relationships with your followers:

- Look for the good in every person—and love it! Yes, all of us have our own agendas, idiosyncrasies, weaknesses, and failings. All of us have been taken advantage of at some point in our lives. But we have survived. We've survived because we are able to take a negative event, refrain from being bitter and unforgiving, and see the mirror image of what *good* has come from the event. Change patterns of negative interactions into patterns of positive interactions that foster bonding experiences. Sensitivity training, such as executive programs offered by professional consulting firms, can transform troubled relationships into healthy and satisfying ones. These programs are one way you can create cultures of idealized influence.
- Spend more time in spiritual and/or religious activities. Such activities often force us to reflect upon what true plutonic love is and how we can show it to others. Use the examples you learn about in your spiritual/religious activities to act as a role model (idealized leader) for what you can do at work.
- Communicate to your people that you are all connected to each other in important ways and that your collective success depends on your relationships with each other. By forming loving relationships, we elevate trust and motivation levels that provide the foundation for authentic transformational leadership.
- Examine your conscience. Isn't it funny how each of us has this little voice inside that seems to judge our past behavior? No matter how we try to justify our actions, deep down, we know what is wrong and right. Use this force within you to judge whether you are creating loving (developmental) or spiteful (destructive) relationships with your followers. Adjust your behavior appropriately.

Practicing Principle 11: Kindness

Kindness is the gift that keeps on giving—and it also gives back! Kindness helps you to role model what is expected from your followers and shows that you are willing to help them achieve their full potential, so they can help your organization achieve its potential. Here are a few helpful hints relevant to the eleventh principle:

- Make your organization a haven of charity. Get involved with your people in United Way programs, volunteer agencies, church or synagogue groups, Big Brothers/Big Sisters, or other forms of community outreach. Doing so builds a strong reputation of social responsibility for your organization. It develops the character strength of kindness in your people as well.

- Establish work-related, topic interest groups that share information and provide assistance to others working on similar tasks. Experiment and find topics that work for you, such as leadership, ethics, innovation, communication, the latest technology gizmos, or family support groups. Doing so gives people the opportunity to show they are good organizational citizens because they help others who are struggling with difficult work or life issues.
- Implement training sessions that highlight the individual and cultural diversity within and between the business units of your organization. By engaging in this form of individualized consideration, you teach your followers to recognize and appreciate the many differences within today's workforce. More importantly, you show them how to harness the wide breadth of knowledge, skills, abilities, and expertise that people accumulate over their lives and can share to help the lives of others.

Practicing Principle 12: Social Influence

Demonstrating the forms of social intelligence allows you to understand the context for exercising your leadership. Leadership doesn't exist in a vacuum. It is embedded in social contexts that set boundaries on how you must inspire, be a role model, and develop your followers. As leaders, we need to understand the politics, resource availability and constraints, and constituent needs of our organization. Since the leader-follower relationship in transformational leadership is largely based on an emotional connection, we need to possess an awareness and regulation of our own emotions and those of our followers as well. Here are a few helpful hints relevant to the twelfth principle:

- Spend time talking to *all* key players in your organization and industry. By asking them questions about their perceptions of what is going on in the organization and industry, you can collect valuable information. This information can tell you a lot about alliances, rifts in relationships, resource bases, and historical events that have shaped how the organization operates. Lunches, golf outings or other social occasions provide convenient means to display individually considerate behavior aimed at really getting to know the movers and shakers in your organization and industry.
- Participate in and learn from 360-degree feedback assessments of your leadership behavior. The degree of agreement between how you view your own leadership behavior and how others view it is a measure of self-awareness, which is one form of emotional intelli-

gence. Whether you over-estimate, under-estimate, or are in-agree-ment (good or poor) with your raters determines your ability to elicit and show trust, produce developmental relationships, and perform effectively as a transformational leader.[21] Based on your results, write a development plan that addresses what you need to work on, and what strengths you can build upon in the future. Then go out and live the words you put down on paper!

- Take a university or training course on developing your emotional intelligence skills. Courses, such as those offered by the Institute for Health and Human Potential, help you to identify emotions in your-self and others, what they mean, and how you can work to control the effects they have on your behavior and followers. Since emotion is such a potent form of influence in transformational leadership, use the time in these classes to develop more inspiring and developmen-tal habits of speech. Instead of using negative forms of influence such as yelling, nagging or being sarcastic, words of faith, inspiration, encouragement and support will be a better response. Remember: Positive emotions can result in tremendously *constructive* results—but negative emotions produce monumentally destructive results for peo-ple and their organizations. Stay positive about people and prosper!

NOTES

1. Dickens, C. (1843, p. 219). A Christmas carol. In M. Hendricks (Ed.), *A trea-sury of Christmas stories and poems* (pp. 209–245). Norwalk, CN: Easton Press.

2. Stewart, J.B. (1991). *Den of thieves.* New York: Simon & Schuster.

3. Chisholm, C. (1970). *Unbought and unbossed.* New York: Houghlin Mifflin; and Chisholm, C. (1973). *The good fight.* New York: Harper and Row.

4. Spink, C. (1998). *Mother Teresa: A complete authorized biography.* San Francisco: Harper.

5. Mother Teresa. (1997). *Mother Teresa: In my own words.* San Francisco, CA: Harper; and Wright, P.A. (2006). *Mother Teresa's prescription: Finding happiness and peace in service.* Notre Dame, IN: Ave Maria Press.

6. Smith, S.B. (1998). *Diana in search of herself: Portrait of a troubled princess. New York: Times Books.*

7. Denney, C. (2005). *Representing Diana, Princess of Wales: Cultural memory and fairy tales revisited.* Madison, NJ: Fairleigh Dickinson University Press.

8. http://www.vatican.va/holy_father/john_paul_ii/biography/index.htm (Accessed December 14, 2005); and Weigel, G. (1999). *Witness to hope: The biography of Pope John Paul II.* New York: Cliff Street Books.

9. O'Connor, G. (2005). *Universal father: A life of John Paul II.* New York: Bloomsbury USA.

10. Interesting discussions of humanity, love and leadership can be found in Bass, B.M., & Riggio, R.E. (2006). *Transformational leadership* (2nd ed.). Mah-

wah, NJ: Lawrence Erlbaum Associates; and Peterson, C., & Seligman, M.E.P. (2004). *Character strengths and virtues: A handbook and classification.* New York: Oxford/American Psychological Association.

11. Rubin, Z. (1973). *Liking and loving: An invitation to social psychology.* New York: Holt, Rinehart, and Winston.

12. Sosik, J.J., & Godshalk, V.M. (2004). Self-other rating agreement in mentoring: Meeting protégé expectations for development and career advancement. *Group & Organization Management, 29*(4), 442–469.

13. Peterson & Seligman (2004) as cited in Note 10.

14. http://americanrhetoric.com/speeches/shirleychisholmequalrights.htm (Accessed December 12, 2005).

15. Peterson & Seligman (2004) as cited in Note 10.

16. Kihlstrom, J.F., & Cantor, N. (2000). Social intelligence. In R.J. Sternberg (Eds.), *Handbook of intelligence* (pp. 359–379). Cambridge, England: Cambridge University Press.

17. For interesting discussions of emotional intelligence, see Goleman, D. (1995). *Emotional intelligence.* New York: Bantam; and Salovey, P., Mayer, J.D., & Caruso, D.R. (2002). The positive psychology of emotional intelligence. In C.R. Snyder & S.J. Lopez (Eds.), *The handbook of positive psychology* (pp. 159–171). New York: Oxford University Press.

18. Gardner, H. (1993). *Frames of mind: The theory of multiple intelligences.* New York: Basic Books.

19. Research linking social intelligence to transformational leadership includes Bass, B.M. (2002). Cognitive, social and emotional intelligence of transformational leaders. In R.E. Riggio, S.E. Murphy et al. (Eds.) *Multiple intelligences and leadership* (pp. 105–118). Mahwah, NJ: Erlbaum; and Bass & Riggio (2006) as cited in Note 10; and Sosik, J.J., Potosky, D., & Jung, D.I. (2002). Adaptive self-regulation: Meeting others' expectations for leadership and performance. *Journal of Social Psychology, 142,* 211–232.

20. Mandell, B., & Pherwani, S. (2003). Relationship between emotional intelligence and transformational leadership style: A gender comparison. *Journal of Business and Psychology, 17,* 387–404; and Sosik, J.J., & Megerian, L.E. (1999). Understanding leader emotional intelligence and performance: The role of self-other agreement on transformational leadership perceptions. *Group & Organization Management, 25,* 291–317.

21. Sosik & Godshalk (2004) as cited in Note 12.

CHAPTER 7

JUSTICE

Strengths for Role Modeling

Justice is conscience, not a personal conscience but the conscience of the whole of humanity. Those who clearly recognize the voice of their own conscience usually recognize also the voice of justice.

—Alexander Solzhenitsyn

If there is one virtue that people have demanded of their leaders over the ages, it is justice. Whether it is human rights, civil rights, women's rights, religious freedom, labor privileges, etc., we have always fought for a sense of justice to ensure the rights and obligations of all members of our society. As one of Aristotle's cardinal virtues, justice serves to regulate social order. For example, while detained in a gulag as a dissident of the Soviet Union, Alexander Solzhenitsyn realized that an injustice to one person or social group cannot go unnoticed, and is eventually corrected because of the interdependence of people. The idea of interdependence among people is even more prevalent today because the forces of globalization and technologies such as the Internet connect us in increasingly more ways.

In ancient days when today's technology was absent, the Buddhists recognized that interdependence among people was the crucible of justice. Tu-Shun used the metaphor of the *Net of Indra* to explain how people need

Leading with Character, pages 123–141
Copyright © 2006 by Information Age Publishing
All rights of reproduction in any form reserved.

to possess a sense of interdependence and obligation to the common good to achieve fairness and civil order. To understand the Net of Indra, imagine a vast net whose sections are connected by a multitude of jewels. Each jewel reflects all other jewels in the net. Each jewel represents a human being. Through the net, each jewel is connected to all the others. When one jewel changes, it is reflected in all other jewels. If we place a dot on one jewel, the dot shows up on all of the jewels. Therefore, we know that the multitude of jewels in the net is really one.[1]

The lesson that Indra's Net teaches us is that whatever socially responsible, compassionate, just or constructive behavior a leader displays often cascades within and between organizational units, industries or even societies, and eventually can produce beneficial outcomes throughout the world. At the same time, leaders who display socially irresponsible, heartless, unjust or destructive behavior, even to only one person or social group, produce a cascading effect of destruction throughout the world. Think about the cascading *constructive* effects that leaders like Pope John Paul II, Mother Teresa, Rosa Parks and Bill Gates have produced. Then think about the cascading *destructive* effects that leaders like Joseph Stalin, Adolph Hitler, Saddam Hussein or Ken Lay have produced. Yes, leadership is certainly one of the most awesome human forces for promoting justice or injustice in the world.

Today's leaders must take responsibility and get involved in the affairs of their organizations, towns, cities, nation and world. They are called to give some of their time to work for the good of others. They are called to make the world a better place for future generations. They are also called to do what is morally right, be kind and respectful to everyone, and be responsible for their own behavior. Are these behaviors important to who you are as a person? By displaying these behaviors of justice, you can serve as a positive role model for your associates and help to create a healthy organizational culture and a virtuous society.

LEADERS OF JUSTICE

Transformational leadership is about adaptation. It is embedded within a larger social system comprised of communities, nations, and the world, all of which are constantly changing. Unfortunately, social systems, like all systems, are often unstable and dysfunctional. It is naïve to believe that all social systems or institutions are good for society over time. Like home heating systems, they need constant monitoring and adjustments to fine tune their operation and adapt to their environment. These ideas about adaptation originated from Robert K. Merton, a sociologist who coined the term "role model." Merton's *theory of deviance* proposed that similarity between cultural goals and institutionalized means for achieving those goals determines the modes of adaptation that an organization and its leaders choose.

When cultural goals are achieved through institutionalized or traditional means, there is little need for transformational leadership since *conformity* is the modus operandi for adaptation. Dwight Eisenhower's leadership of the U.S. during the 1950s illustrates a time when society valued conformity. When cultural goals are achieved in ways that deviate from tradition, transformational leadership is needed to develop new ways to achieve these goals. *Innovation* is the means to this end. John F. Kennedy's leadership in the early 1960s illustrates a time when society started to value innovation. When cultural goals and means are rejected and a substitution of other goals and means are desired, there also is a need for transformational leadership since *rebellion* becomes the modus operandi for adaptation. The wide-spread social unrest of the late-1960s and early 1970s, marked by the leadership of Malcolm X and Betty Friedan, illustrates a time when society valued rebellion. It is in times of innovation and rebellion that the character strengths of citizenship and fairness come to the forefront of leadership processes.[2]

Today, more than ever before, we are witnessing social, political and economic conditions that call for innovation and rebellion. Forces such as increased diversity in our communities, ethical scandals in our corporations and churches, rapid changes in technology, political instability, and global terrorism are forcing us to question the basic assumptions of our organizations, institutions, and social order. Retreating to past practices or relying on tried and true rituals are not acceptable alternatives for us. Instead, we need to increase our efforts to demonstrate citizenship, be socially responsible and fair, so we can rebuild our troubled organizations, communities, and industries. Doing so allows us to role model aspects of justice.

To better understand what it takes to demonstrate citizenship, loyalty, teamwork and fairness, let's examine the virtue of justice from multiple leadership perspectives. To illustrate this virtue, four unique leaders are highlighted who exemplify the character strengths associated with justice (see Figure 7.1).

The Queen of Talk

She went from living in poverty in Mississippi and Tennessee to living in "The Promised Land," a $50 million 42-acre ocean-view estate in Montecito, California. She went from being called "the Sack Girl" who, as a child, wore dresses made from potato sacks, to being one of the most fashionable celebrities of her day. She went from living in desperately poor economic condi-

Figure 7.1.   *Leaders of Justice.* Oprah Winfrey, Andy Griffith, Margaret Thatcher, and Governor James Hunt.

tions to being worth an estimated $1.4 billion. She is the phenomenally successful TV talk show hostess and entrepreneur Oprah Winfrey. Her life story is full of leadership lessons about citizenship and fairness.

Based on her early childhood experiences, Winfrey's rise to the pinnacle of success was highly unlikely. Besides being economically disadvantaged, she was the unfortunate victim of repeated sexual abuse. When she was 14 years old, she became pregnant and gave birth to a premature, stillborn boy. What do experiences like these do to a person? They certainly could embitter, demotivate, or completely destroy someone who lacked strength of character. But, not Oprah Winfrey! Instead, Winfrey used these negative events to tap into her innate intelligence and talent for being "on stage." Building upon her talents, she made education a priority in her life. She won a full scholarship to Tennessee State University and studied speech and performing arts. Her education helped her to advance her career, as she gained a reputation for being a first-rate news anchor and talk show host in both Nashville and Chicago. She launched *The Oprah Winfrey Show* in 1986, and today her talk show is seen by over 21 million viewers a week in 150 countries.[3]

Unlike most of today's daytime talk shows that feature lowbrow and sensational content, Winfrey uses her show to address social, psychological and spiritual issues that she thinks are very important for women. Whether the issue is poverty, crime, illiteracy, child abuse, or sexual abuse, she presents these topics in a way that empowers people through greater understanding and confidence building. Winfrey has used her popularity to influence what others should read through a segment of her television show called "Oprah's Book Club." She has pointed out the perils of eating beef and its associated Mad Cow disease, much to the dismay of the U.S. beef industry. She also has created *The Angel Network* which collects millions of dollars each year for various charities.

Winfrey is a good example of the "Politician/Well-Meaning Chameleon" in this book's leadership typology since she has used her acting ability to benefit herself and others. Winfrey's ability to perform in many roles has enabled her to build up a large amount of business connections or "social capital" throughout her career. Her success has enabled her to appear in ten movies including *The Color Purple,* and act in or produce 13 TV shows. Each of these achievements is driven by her need to help others who are in difficulty, and work to correct social and economic inequalities.

Oprah Winfrey's most recent crusade is rewarding people on her TV show for identifying sexual predators or offenders who are fugitives from the law. That's what negative life experiences can do to some people, like Winfrey, who possess the character strength to overcome hardship and eventually become champions for justice. They say life isn't fair. Maybe it isn't, but transformational leaders like Oprah are working hard to bring justice to all.

Sheriff Without a Gun

One of the most popular and enduring TV shows of all time was the brainchild of a country boy from Mount Airy, North Carolina. If you ever get the chance to travel south on Interstate 77 through Virginia into North Carolina, take it! You will experience the same breath-taking mountain views and rich culture that Andy Griffith did as a child. Although Griffith's original goal was to work as a minister, he found work in the theater to make ends meet. He began his career as a comedian, stage actor, and movie star after earning a bachelor's degree in music from the University of North Carolina—Chapel Hill. His initial success in the entertainment field propelled him into the world of television where he acted in and/or produced six TV series, including *The Andy Griffith Show* and *Matlock*, five TV miniseries, 19 made-for-TV movies, and numerous films.

Of all these accomplishments, perhaps none is more significant than Griffith's involvement with *The Andy Griffith Show*. Airing from 1960–68, the show was an instant hit. Today, it is even more popular than ever as it continues on in seemingly perpetual reruns on TV-Land and other stations. Why? Each show was purposely written with a moral message. The characters were generally lovable individuals who exemplified both the strengths and shortcomings of humanity.[4] In fact, the show illustrated many of the basic character strengths discussed in this book such as integrity, citizenship, fairness, hope, humor, and spirituality.

In the show, Griffith portrayed Sheriff Andy Taylor, a role that the Museum of Broadcast Communications described as "Lincolnesque...a character more appropriate to the role of single-parent father, and by extension, father to the small town of Mayberry."[5] Taylor epitomized the character strength of citizenship, with its emphasis on social responsibility, loyalty and teamwork. As a single-parent father raising his son Opie and serving as sheriff of Mayberry, Sheriff Talyor possessed much folk wisdom about life and people. In a down-to-earth way, he looked out for the best interests of the citizens of Mayberry, often putting his self-interests aside in favor of the interests of others. He could do this because he knew what made people tick, what their fears and foibles were, and how to make them feel better about themselves as people. But he did not take advantage of this knowledge. Instead, he used these skills altruistically to form positive emotional and caring relationships with the citizens of Mayberry. The ability to use knowledge in a benevolent way is essential to helping others when there is nothing to be gained from them.

Griffith used his life experiences of growing up in rural North Carolina to write episodes where character development could occur alongside humor. For example, an episode entitled "Citizen's Arrest" concerned the value of friendship and the dangers that we assume when we fall victim to self-aggrandizement. In this episode, the ineptly nervous Barney Fife (Don Knotts) eventually sees the folly of his pride after he quits his job as deputy because he was apprehended by Gomer Pyle for making an illegal u-turn. Andy helped Barney realize that a quick temper and a sharp tongue can often destroy good friendships. Barney learned that rules and regulations apply to all people and two wrongs don't make a right. Indeed, the beauty of the show stems from its characters, such as Fife, in whom we can sometimes see ourselves, as we strive to overcome our own character flaws by working toward the ideals described in this book.

It is refreshing to know that *The Andy Griffith Show* has inspired a number of continuing education and inspirational study courses on character development across the U.S. Visit http://www.barneyfife.com and you will find a website devoted to an entire course developed by Joey Fann, a software engineer from Huntsville, Alabama. The site includes lesson plans, handouts and class outlines for character development, video clip images and humorous quotes from the show, and references to scripture. For those of us who have always enjoyed the show, it is nice to know that the moral points that Andy Griffith intended for his show are being highlighted on the Internet in ways that can be passed on to future generations. Issues of character development are timeless and that's why Andy Griffith's moral leadership carries on.

The Grounded Governor

James B. Hunt, Jr. is a nationally recognized leader in education. As three-term Governor of North Carolina (1977–1985; 1993–2001), Hunt has been at the forefront of education reform not only in his state, but across the U.S. as well. *"Education is our future—it's everything. We must not settle for anything short of excellence in our schools."* Hunt's inspiring words point to a major purpose in his life: promoting education excellence for all of our children. Driven by his vision of excellence in education, Hunt has championed North Carolina Public School System's introduction of character development programs into the curriculum. He has also served on the Carnegie Task Force, which created the National Board for Professional Teaching Standards. As an education innovator, Hunt has lead several national conferences on education and public policy. In recognition of his work, Hunt has received over 15 national awards including the National State Boards of Education "Policy Leader of the Year Award," and the Columbia University Teachers College Medal for Distinguished Service.

Hunt's passion for elevating teaching standards and sharing opportunities for education with all children come from his belief that every child should get his fair share. His strong belief about fairness was instilled in him by his strict father, who was a farmer/soil conservationist. Hunt still lives in Wilson, North Carolina, only 75 yards away from the farmhouse where he grew up. He begins and ends almost every day on his North Carolina farm, while currently working as a "rainmaker" (an executive who uses his wide professional network of connections to bring in new corporate clients) for Womble Carlyle, North Carolina's largest law firm.[6]

Hunt's elaborate professional network is the product of his many years as a major player in public policy and educational think tanks. He has influenced the likes of Bill Clinton and several state governors regarding educational issues. Hunt has always worked with a passion and enjoys putting in long and hard days. He believes that "we are all in this together" and that we need to work together to correct social and economic inequalities. Hunt's drive is grounded in his rural North Carolina roots and his Presbyterian emphasis on social responsibility and equality. In an interview with Rob Christensen, staff writer for North Carolina's *The News & Observer,* Hunt talked about his progressive concern for the poor and minorities:

> I want to see things better. I drove up here from Wilson County this morning where I live on a farm. Every day, I see poor people. I see uneducated people. I see Hispanic people and their children. I see a community that doesn't have enough jobs…I go to my Presbyterian church on Sunday and go to Sunday school. I think about what God wants us to do and what kind of people we ought to be. That helps drive me to make things better.[7]

Authentic transformational leaders, like James Hunt, take it upon themselves to work towards making things better for the community. They also take the time to reflect upon the kind of people they should be while striving toward their goal. More importantly, they take responsibility for their own actions and make sure that they are behaving in ways that truly reflect who they think they ought to be. Who is the leader that *you* ought to be? Are you acting the way you think a leader should act? Are you working hard, each and every day, to make things better for your organization and community? Think about it, and then do something about it.

The Iron Lady

A life of politics and public service was not what Margaret Thatcher had in mind when she attended Oxford University. Her keen analytic mind, steadfastness, and conscientiousness were well-suited for her choice of chemistry as her first career. Thatcher first worked as a research chemist for two British companies. Interestingly, she was a member of the team that developed the first soft ice cream. But Thatcher was never a "softy" when it came to her convictions, and she soon found her chosen profession to lack personal meaning. So she decided to follow her father's lead and, with the financial assistance of her husband Denis, she became involved in national politics after studying for and then qualifying as a Barrister in 1953. Throughout the 1950s and 1960s, Thatcher gained prominence in the House of Commons because of her expertise in tax policy and labor issues, and her strong stances against the abolition of capital punishment and communism.

After successful stints as Secretary of State for Education and Science in the Heath administration and leader of the Conservative opposition party, Thatcher was elected Prime Minister. She became the first and only woman yet in Great Britain's history to attain that position. Her coat of arms read "Cherish Freedom." In many of her staunchly conservative speeches, she branded the Soviet Union as a morally-corrupt imperial nation bent on world domination. This prompted the Soviet press to label her as the "Iron Lady." She shared many of her convictions with Ronald Reagan, who became a sort of political soul mate and protégé. This special relationship carried on to the day of Reagan's funeral in June 2004 when Thatcher paid her last respects to her close friend and colleague.

Through her political philosophy of "Thatcherism," she sought to restore the glory of Britain's rich past. Thatcher stood firm against the Argentinean invasion of the Falkland Islands in 1982 and quickly ousted the invaders with a dramatic show of force. She took hard stands against labor unions by reducing their power. She lessened the influence of government in business ventures and promoted a culture of entrepreneurship throughout Britain. She also worked to expand the amount of real estate investment and home ownership in her country. Many of the political agenda items that defined Thatcherism such as reduced public spending, lower income taxes, de-regulation, and privatization of government-owned industries, paralleled those of Reaganomics from the 1980s. Thatcher's supporters claim that her policies led to a period of sustained improvement in Great Britain's economy.[8]

Like all charismatic leaders, Margaret Thatcher was a controversial figure who brought out strong emotional reactions from individuals. Her supporters loved her as a tough agent of change, while her detractors detested her as an abrasive and inflexible egomaniac. Nevertheless, she played one of the most significant roles in the 20th century when she partnered with Reagan to influence reformist Soviet leader Mikhail Gorbachev to bring the Cold War to an end in 1989. Through her intransigence, strong convictions, and dedication to serving the people of Great Britain and other supporters of democracy, Thatcher personified what it means for a leader to demonstrate citizenship. She emphasized the importance of the family and individuals as the priceless raw material in the social fabric of her country. Her ideals and political philosophy made her who she was and determined how she behaved. And this was what she thought other people should be like. This is what made her truly authentic. Time will tell whether Margaret Thatcher should be classified as a "Saint" or an "Abrasive/Egotistical Hero" in this book's leadership typology. But for now, can you think of a time when your authentic leadership, like Thatcher's, caused you to be labeled as a rigid intransigent? What has Thatcher's story taught you about the cost of being true to yourself?

HOW JUSTICE BENEFITS TRANSFORMATIONAL LEADERS

Character strengths that reflect justice can enable leaders to display several aspects of transformational leadership.

Citizenship

Consider the notion of citizenship, with its emphasis on social responsibility, loyalty and teamwork.[9] Going back to the ancient Greeks and Romans, the notion of citizenship held both rights and responsibilities. Like Margaret Thatcher, leaders who value citizenship see themselves as being part of a larger community—a community that they are responsible for helping to shape. Many successful leaders recognize that the team, organization, community and society have given them rights to exercise their leadership. These rights have helped them to achieve their accomplishments within the community. These rights must be sustained so that others may also reap similar benefits in the future. Consequently, authentic transformational leaders feel that they must give something back to their followers and community.

Some leaders, like Dr. James Goodnight of SAS Institute, Inc., give back by providing community service in their city or town. Some, like the top managers at Ben and Jerry's, help to save our environment from pollution or other forms of abuse. And others, like Stride Rite Chairman Arnold Hiatt, work with other business and political leaders to improve the social and economic conditions of the poor. All of these socially responsible actions reflect citizenship because they involve using one's own time to help others; putting the public good ahead of one's own self-interests. Andy Griffith's portrayal of Sheriff Taylor illustrates the need for leaders to role model exemplary citizenship, often through self-sacrifice, for the sake of helping followers who suffer from problems with their self-esteem (Barney Fife), mentality (Gomer Pyle), addictive personality (Otis Campbell), or interpersonal harmony (Ernest T. Bass).

The notion of citizenship also extends to the workplace. Some leaders, like Lawrence Babbio Jr. of Verizon, work to help the less fortunate among their co-workers. Others, like Frances Hesselbein, former CEO of Girl Scouts of the USA, build teams to improve the conditions within their own organizations (see Figure 7.2). Organizations often expect their members to perform such activities that go above and beyond what is explained in their job description. These *organizational citizenship behaviors* include being a good sport, being altruistic and courteous to others, being conscientious, and identifying with the people in their company or community.[10] Leaders

Figure 7.2.   *Kicking It Around.* Teams are the basic building blocks of organizations today. Leaders who inspire followers to possess team spirit develop good organizational citizens.

and their followers need to be aware of these expectations for citizenship in order to fit in and advance in their organization.

Transformational leaders often place a high value on citizenship since they sacrifice self-gain for the gain of others. When they create a sense of joint mission and ownership, transformational leaders display idealized influence that reflects a sense of citizenship. When leaders such as Oprah Winfrey or James Hunt show followers the benefits of giving back to the community, they set positive examples for followers.[11] These positive examples reflect a virtuous approach of living since they help to shape organizations and communities in a positive way.

Through their exemplary behaviors, transformational leaders create a sense of empowerment in followers as well. A "can-do" positive attitude helps followers to become leaders in their own right and time. Idealized leadership also creates a sense of loyalty and commitment on the part of followers that is required to form highly cohesive teams.[12] James Hunt's relentless advocating of education and excellence in schools has helped him to create teams of educators who share a common passion for improving the future of the children of North Carolina's public school system. Therefore, the 13th principle requires leaders to act as a role model by demonstrating exemplary citizenship in their organizations and community.

PRINCIPLE

Leaders are good citizens of their organization and community. As good citizens, they are granted the right to work toward prosperity, as well as the responsibility to help others, show loyalty to their people, and be a good team player. Valuing citizenship shows your commitment to the common good that builds followers' trust, emotional attachment and dedication to you, and increases the amount of idealized influence your followers attribute to you.

Fairness

Any good citizen recognizes the need for fairness when dealing with others, especially during times of trouble. When the United States had its back up against the wall during the Great Depression, President Franklin D. Roosevelt sensed what the nation needed to get back on track. One thing Roosevelt did was to establish the Works Progress Administration (WPA). The WPA provided jobs for many of the unemployed citizens who put in a fair day's work for a fair day's wage.[13] Likewise, Margaret Thatcher's sense of fairness extended beyond the context of Great Britain to the people behind the Iron Curtain victimized by the Soviet Union. Her outrage over the Soviets' inequitable distribution of resources, disregard for human rights, atheism, and obsession with world domination was a product of her moral judgment.

The notion of fairness is also important for helping you to distinguish between transformational leaders (the Saints and Politicians/Well-Meaning Chameleons in our leadership typology) from the pseudo-transformational leaders (the Abrasive/Egotistical Heroes and Used Car Salesmen), who often rear their ugly head during crises. Although transformational leaders possess a high need for power to exert their influence over others, they refrain from seeking and using power for personal gain. Instead, they, like Andy Griffith, use their power to work towards organizational goals and to empower followers to do the same. Authentic transformational leaders do not view followers as a means to an end. They view followers as ends in themselves. They want their followers to get their fair share of respect, compensation, and personal and professional development.

But it's more complicated with pseudo-transformational leaders. These leaders possess a high need for power, but they are quite deceptive. They may appear to be working for the good of the group or organization. But they can't control their urge to use power for their own personal aggrandizement at the expense of their followers. Pseudo-transformational leaders can't refrain from displaying self-centered behaviors and instead, actively seek opportunities to gain control over followers and conquer adversaries. These self-centered leaders cheat followers out of their right to personal development. They disrespect followers by using them as a means to an end to advance the leader's personal agenda. In their minds, they are the only ones entitled to get their own "fair" share.

They hold such beliefs regarding "fairness" because they operate at low stages of moral development, often associated with criminals punished in our courts of law (see Figure 7.3). Determining what is fair (what's right, what's wrong, and what one should do) often depends on moral judgment. *Moral reasoning abilities* include a person's capability to move beyond a nar-

Figure 7.3.   *Is Justice Blind?* The metaphor of justice, often depicted with a judge and his scale, is at the root of many theories of leadership and moral reasoning. But the scale metaphor is not the only one we might adopt and may be misleading in its strong emphasis on equity at the expense of care and compassion.

row-minded or self-centered perspective to one that considers the multiple viewpoints of others and integrates them into one coherent solution. Perspective-taking capacity ranges from egocentric uncoordinated viewpoints to outlooks that coordinate the views of self and others. Are you capable of looking beyond your self-interests to include the interests of others in the everyday problems you face as a leader?

This capability reflects *integrative complexity* of social reasoning that focuses on cognitive differentiation (understanding how things are dissimilar) and integration (understanding connections between things) of information. Self-centered perspectives are low in integrative complexity and are based on rigid and dogmatic interpretations of events, intolerance of inconsistencies of concepts, and decision-making based on only a few prominent pieces of information. Self-defining (other-oriented) perspectives are high in integrative complexity and are based on multidimensional criteria, openness to new information, and decision-making based on integrating a wide variety of evidence.[14]

Understanding the range of perspective-taking capability can help you to advance to higher levels of moral development. Higher levels of moral reasoning abilities are typical of developmentally-oriented individuals, such as authentic transformational leaders, who have progressed over time from simple (self-centered) to more complex (self-transcendent and self-defining) modes of understanding.[15] Fairness is typically reflected in the more complex modes of understanding, such as those demonstrated by Franklin D. Roosevelt, Oprah Winfrey and other role models described in this book. Role modeling is an essential element of idealized influence, with its emphasis on principled moral reasoning and interdependence among people.

A leader's level of moral development plays an important role in determining whether she has the character necessary to display authentic transformational leadership. Individuals who are at higher stages of moral development, like Sheriff Taylor in *The Andy Griffith Show,* tend to display pro-social, altruistic, friendship, helping, and teaching behavior.[16] Such caring reasoning and behavior adds to the principled moral reasoning by teaching followers that we, as humans, are connected to each other through our relationships. Transformational leaders often teach followers about the importance of interdependence, teamwork, and loyalty by sharing their values, vision, knowledge and expertise.

Being perceived as an ethical, caring and compassionate "teacher" enhances a leader's ability to coach and mentor followers. Such behavior is pro-social, altruistic and caring because it is other-oriented. It shows that the leader is interested in developing the follower to her full potential. Coaching and mentoring are important aspects of individualized consideration, with emphasis on providing equal opportunity for development to all. Through her successful TV talk show, Oprah Winfrey has worked to provide social support to victims of sexual abuse, so that they can overcome their adversity and help to put the perpetrators of such crimes behind bars. This brings us to the 14th principle, which involves being fair by giving balanced and equitable consideration to the legitimate rights of and caring for all members of the organization and society.

| PRINCIPLE 14 | Leaders who value fairness, justice, and principled moral reasoning in their interactions with others become idealized by their followers. Leaders who value an ethics of care for the needs, interests and well-being of others display individualized consideration. Both behaviors build a sense of "oneness" in the organization, where people believe "if the organization succeeds, then I succeed." |

LIVING THE PRINCIPLES

The remainder of this chapter describes what you can do to put these two principles into practice. Living these principles helps you build your leadership character by being just.

Practicing Principle 13: Citizenship

Being a good organizational, community or national citizen allows you to teach your followers about the benefits of being socially responsible. One benefit of being socially responsible, in addition to the satisfaction gained from helping others, is the network of connections with its resources and opportunities that emerges from partnering with others on important social projects. Recall the impressive social capital network that James Hunt created over his many years as Governor of North Carolina and how it is being used by his present employer as a means to develop new business. Like James Hunt, transformational leaders are responsible for creating and expanding social capital for their organization. Here are a few ways you can role model citizenship with your followers and expand your opportunities for success:

- Get involved in regional political groups or local civic organizations such as Rotary International, or Lion's Clubs. Being active in church groups or professional and industry associations also are good ways to connect with other people who share an interest in working for the common good. These activities help you to display idealized influence by role modeling the character strength of citizenship, and at the same time build your professional network and social capital.

- Become a coach or mentor in your community's Big Brothers/Big Sisters programs, or scouting programs, such as Boy Scouts or Girl Scouts. These programs are designed to improve the lives of children through character development and the passing on of important life lessons. Schools, through their Parent Teacher Associations or character education programs, provide another opportunity for you to teach others about the importance of citizenship. By sharing your important leadership values and life experiences, you can demonstrate idealized influence by passing on your ideals to shape the character of our future generations.

- Create a culture within your organization that values and rewards citizenship. Talk to your associates about expectations for performance both in the role of their jobs and beyond what is formally described in their job description. Use training programs to teach your people about the importance of "extra-role" expectations for performance such as showing altruism toward associates, being conscientious, identifying with the company, and valuing interpersonal harmony. Then set up a committee that rewards your people on a quarterly or annual basis for demonstrating such organizational citizenship behavior. These activities foster loyalty, promote team spirit and demonstrate idealized leadership.

Practicing Principle 14: Fairness

The ability to be fair with others stems from your level of moral development. The capacity to see things from other people's perspectives and to formulate solutions that are in everyone's best interest develops as your cognitive abilities grow over time. The character strength of fairness is essential to leadership since the foundation for excellent leadership is a transactional exchange or implied contract between the leader and the follower. The leader provides direction and support to the follower and rewards him for meeting expected levels of performance. In return, the follower is supposed to meet the leader's expectations of performance. Both parties must be fair and follow through on their side of the deal. Otherwise, the deal falls apart, trust is broken and the leadership relationship dissolves.[17]

Fairness is also important for transformational leaders since they work with a wide range of followers, associates, and constituents. Such an array of key players in the leadership system comes with competing values, viewpoints, motives and goals. This hodge-podge of interests poses problems regarding how to satisfy the diversity of interests. Fairness, stemming from just and moral reasoning, helps leaders to come up with solutions to satisfying the diverse interests embedded within these problems. Here are a few ways to develop your ability to be fair with your followers:

- Take James R. Rest's *Defining Issues Test* (DIT).[18] This tool assesses your level of moral development based on how you respond to several interesting ethical dilemmas. The awareness that you gain from knowing whether you make your decisions based on self-centered or other-oriented perspectives can guide your next steps toward moral development. If you score low on the DIT, you can enroll in moral discussion or philosophy classes at your local college or university or join discussion groups in your faith community. Getting involved in democratic decision-making processes in your community or working in team-based organizations, where consensus and participation are valued over authoritarian and directive leadership processes, can also help. These activities help you to see that the whole is greater than the sum of its parts. Remember that in the grand scheme of things, you are a small, but important, part of the universe.
- Increase your level of moral development by becoming more involved in industrial, community, political, national, or global organizations that interest you. When we learn about new things, meet new people, read about new ideas, or visit new places, we increase our perspective-taking capacity. We realize that our worldview can sometimes be quite parochial because our limited life experiences place boundaries on the way we view things. But when we see ourselves within the larger social context of history, geography, and world cultures, and then reflect upon how we fit into an expanded view of things, we can develop pathways that expand our moral reasoning. Sharing what we have learned through these new experiences and reflections with our followers allows us to be seen as an idealized leader.
- Treat yourself to an "out of my comfort zone" experience. Do things, or visit places or organizations that you normally would not feel comfortable in. If you are a Christian, visit a Jewish service in a synagogue. If you are an agnostic or atheist, read the *Confessions of St. Augustine*. If you're a Democrat, attend a Republican fundraising event. If you enjoy hard rock music, start listening to jazz or classical music, or (God forbid) disco music by Donna Summer or the Village People! Or, go to social events you haven't been to. Such experiences can be eye-opening. They can increase your tolerance of difference and appreciation of cultures of others, and help you to become an

individually considerate leader. You may even learn that the people you once distrusted or feared are not really that different from you.

- Talk about moral issues/dilemmas with your children at home and your associates at the office. Stimulating moral discussions at home, work, school, or in your faith community are great ways to teach others to reason in a just and caring way. They also are effective ways to learn how people reason differently over moral issues. As you participate in and lead these discussions, make sure that you use a participatory and interactive style, and be supportive and nurturing to all members of your discussion group. Doing so allows you to role model love of learning, collaboration, and collective reflection, and to create an intellectually stimulating environment that fosters interdependency. To create and sustain the value of interdependency in the minds of followers requires strengths of justice, but to increase its value in their hearts requires strengths of temperance, which I discuss in the next chapter.

NOTES

1. http://www.geocities.com/the_wanderling/awkening101.html (Accessed December 28, 2005).

2. Merton, R.K. (1996). *On social structure and science.* Chicago: University of Chicago Press.

3. Adler, B., & Winfrey, O. (1997). *The uncommon wisdom of Oprah Winfrey: A portrait in her own words.* Seacaucus, NJ: Carol Publishing; Garson, H. S. (2004). *Oprah Winfrey: A biography.* Westport, CN: Greenwood Press; and Mair, G. (1994). *Oprah Winfrey: The real story.* Seacaucus, NJ: Carol Publishing.

4. Collins, T. (1995). *The Andy Griffith story: An illustrated biography.* Mount Airy, NC: Explorer Press; Kelly, R. (1993). *The Andy Griffith Show.* Winston-Salem, NC: John F. Blair; and Robinson, D., & Fernandes, D. (1996). *The definitive Andy Griffith show reference: Episode-by-episode, with cast and production biographies and a guide to collectibles.* Jefferson, NC: McFarland.

5. http://www.museum.tv/archives/etv/G/htmlG/griffithand/griffithand.htm (Accessed December 19, 2005).

6. Grimsley, W. (2003). *James B. Hunt: A North Carolina progressive.* Jefferson, NC: McFarland & Company; and Poff, J.M. (2000). *Addresses and public papers of James Baxter Hunt Jr.—Governor of North Carolina* (Vol.: 1993–1997). Raleigh, NC: North Carolina Dept. Cultural Resources; and http://www.uncg.edu/iss/huntbio.html (Accessed December 19, 2005).

7. http://www.newsobserver.com/102/story/371763.html (Accessed December 19, 2005).

8. Hole, D. (1990). *Margaret Thatcher: Britain's prime minister.* Berkeley Heights, NJ: Enslow Publishers; and Thatcher, M. (2002). *Statecraft: Strategies for changing the world.* New York: HarperCollins.

9.   Peterson, C., & Seligman, M.E.P. (2004). *Character strengths and virtues: A handbook and classification.* New York: Oxford/American Psychological Association.

10. Organ, D.W. (1990). The motivational basis of organizational citizenship behavior. In B.M. Staw & L.L. Cummings (Eds.), *Research in organizational behavior* (Vol. 12, pp. 43–72). Greenwich, CT: JAI Press.

11. Bass, B.M., & Steidlmeier, P. (1999). Ethics, character, and authentic transformational leadership behavior. *The Leadership Quarterly, 10,* 181–217.

12. Jung, D.I., & Sosik, J.J. (2002). Transformational leadership in work groups: The role of empowerment, cohesiveness, and collective-efficacy on perceived group performance. *Small Group Research, 33* (3), 313–336.

13. Alexrod, A. (2004). *Nothing to fear: Lessons in leadership from FDR.* New York: Portfolio.

14. Interesting discussions of moral judgment capacities and systems can be found in Kolhberg, L. (1984). *The psychology of moral development.* San Francisco: Harper & Row; Peterson & Seligman (2004) as cited in Note 9; and Selman, R. (1980). *The growth of interpersonal understanding.* New York: Academic Press; and Tetlock, P.E. (1981). Pre- to postelection shifts in presidential rhetoric: Impression management or cognitive adjustment? *Journal of Personality and Social Psychology, 41,* 207–212.

15. Kuhnert, K.W., & Lewis, P. (1987). Transactional and transformational leadership: A constructive developmental analysis. *Academy of Management Review, 12,* 648–657.

16. Sosik, J.J., & Lee, D.L. (2002). Mentoring in organizations: A social judgment perspective for developing tomorrow's leaders. *Journal of Leadership Studies, 8* (4), 17–32.

17. Bass, B.M. (1985). *Leadership and performance beyond expectations.* New York: Free Press.

18. Rest, J.R. (1979). *Development in judging moral issues.* Minneapolis: University of Minnesota Press.

CHAPTER 8

TEMPERANCE

Strengths for Keeping the Ego in Check

*Educate your children to self-control, to the habit of holding passion and prejudice
and evil tendencies subject to an upright and reasoning will, and you have done much
to abolish misery from their future lives.*

—Daniel Webster

It is New Year's Day as I begin writing this chapter. For people around the
world, one year ends and another begins as we enter the month of January.
The first month of the year is named after the Roman god Janus, who is
often depicted with two-faces, one looking forward and one looking back.
That's why it is common for people to make New Year's resolutions. They
set goals to make positive changes in their lives based on reflections of
what they've achieved in the past year, what they've left undone, and what
they intend to accomplish in the coming year.

Many of the resolutions we make involve temperance or adding discipline to our inner life. Temperance acts like a foundry that forges our
character through a rigorous process of refinement and sometimes pain-
ful molding. It sharpens our mind and disciplines our will to carry on
despite challenges, to set our priorities, and to put things into perspective.
Temperance also softens our hearts and deflates our occasionally unrealis-

Leading with Character, pages 143–167

tic opinions of ourselves. It helps us to better understand what it means to be human.

While delivering a graduation address at Stanford University in June of 2005, Apple Computer CEO, Steve Jobs, spoke of the tempering effect that his bout with pancreatic cancer has had on him. In the past, Jobs was well-known as possessing a big ego and a bad temper, which often drove his employees crazy. Today, his leadership is tempered with more disciplined self-control and understanding of others.[1] Why do we, as leaders, sometimes have to wait for life threatening events to force us to strengthen our minds and soften our hearts?

The discipline that comes from temperance protects us from the excesses that can harm us. To avoid our mistakes of the past, some of us strive to make better life decisions through more careful planning and reflection. Some hope to mend broken relationships with friends, family or co-workers through more frequent and honest communication. Some seek to redirect their lives away from selfishness and towards others through participation in service organizations. Like the tempered eagle shown in Figure 8.1, some learn patience and how to display dignity to all. Others strive to become more self-disciplined and control their excessive

Figure 8.1.   *Limestone Eagle atop Market Street Bridge, Wilkes-Barre, PA.* How much temperance does your leadership character require?

appetites and emotions through exercise, diet, or anger management programs. As human beings, we seem to have unlimited opportunities for self-improvement in areas where we've gone too far or have overly indulged in selfish activities.

Take a few moments to assess areas where you may have fallen victim to excessive self-indulgence in your personal and leadership roles. Carefully review the checklist of "The Ugly Eight Vices of Self-Excess" shown in Table 8.1. Respond *honestly* by checking "True" if the item accurately describes you or "False" if it does not. Then score your responses according to the directions provided to determine which of these vices (hubris, excessive love of praise, anger/impatience, unbelief, deceit, self-will, fear of man, and jealousy) may be haunting you. Any item that you answer as "true" represents an area for self-improvement that left unchecked can have negative long-term effects on relationships with your followers. For each of the items you marked as "true," think about what these harmful effects might be. What can you do this year to protect yourself from the excesses that power, privilege and prosperity can bring to your leadership? Have such excesses turned you into someone you no longer recognize? Might they limit your potential for growth as an authentic leader?

Your potential for growth as an authentic transformational leader depends largely upon seeking the virtue of temperance. Temperance helps us control our tendency to be lustful rascals, seeking power, extravagant wealth, various forms of satisfaction, and attention for ourselves. History is replete with lustful rascals whose excesses ran amuck. Hubris and deceit were the downfall of Richard Nixon, Ken Lay, and "Chainsaw" Al Dunlap. Excessive love of praise and deceit were the downfall of Bill Clinton, Jim Bakker, and Jimmy Swaggert. Self-will and obsessive compulsive behavior, with its excessive worry and repetition, tore down Howard Hughes' enjoyment of the fortune and fame that his brilliance had built for him. Anger, impatience, and jealousy, along with superfluous collections of shoes, tainted the reputations of Leona Helmsley and Imelda Marcos. What greater feats might each of these leaders have achieved if it were not for their lack of temperance!

Temperance also plays an important role in the success of many of today's corporate leaders, especially when they are expected to *serve* rather than *control* in today's management environment. Recently, business and leadership research communities have shifted their emphasis from developing highly charismatic and self-aggrandizing leaders to developing more humble and servant-like leaders. In his best-selling book, *Good to Great*, Jim Collins identified a more humble and modest type of leadership as an important factor in companies that sustained outstanding organizational performance over a 20-year period. For example, several CEOs he labeled as "Level Five leaders," such as Alan F. Wurtzel of Circuit City and Darwin

Table 8.1.　The "Ugly 8" Vices of Self-Excess Checklist

Item		True	False
1	I feel that I am better than others based on my success, position in the organization, or social status.	☐	☐
2	I love to impress and get praise from people who are important in my field of work.	☐	☐
3	I get angry, nervous or impatient with people who don't perform up to my expectations.	☐	☐
4	I worry and complain a lot in times of pressure, opposition or hardship.	☐	☐
5	I resent and get back at people who disapprove or contradict what I say.	☐	☐
6	I feel that I am better than others because of my personal appearance.	☐	☐
7	I love to outdo other people and show my supremacy over them.	☐	☐
8	I am a very important, independent individual.	☐	☐
9	I draw attention to myself in conservations with other people.	☐	☐
10	I have sometimes evaded and covered up the truth.	☐	☐
11	I have a touchy and sensitive spirit.	☐	☐
12	I can sometimes be stubborn and set in my ways.	☐	☐
13	I never avoid my duties and obligations to people of wealth, power or position.	☐	☐
14	I secretly envy people in my company.	☐	☐
15	I can leave a better impression of myself than is really true.	☐	☐
16	I often argue with others.	☐	☐
17	I am afraid that someone will offend and drive a prominent person away from my inner circle.	☐	☐
18	I speak of the faults and failings, rather than the virtues and successes, of people more talented and successful than me.	☐	☐
19	I tend to criticize and pick flaws in others when I feel that I'm not getting the attention I deserve.	☐	☐
20	There are powerful people in my organization or community that I fear.	☐	☐
21	I don't enjoy seeing the success and recognition of others.	☐	☐
22	I lack faith and trust in God.	☐	☐
23	I have sometimes covered up my real faults.	☐	☐
24	I become easily discouraged in times of pressure, pain and discomfort.	☐	☐

Please tally up the number of Trues you checked for the following scales:

Hubris	$[1 + 6 + 8]$	= _____
Excessive love of praise	$[2 + 7 + 9]$	= _____
Anger/impatience	$[3 + 5 + 11]$	= _____
Unbelief	$[4 + 22 + 24]$	= _____
Deceit	$[10 + 15 + 23]$	= _____
Self-will	$[12 + 16 + 19]$	= _____
Fear of man	$[13 + 17 + 20]$	= _____
Jealousy	$[14 + 18 + 21]$	= _____

Smith of Kimberly-Clarke, attributed their sustained success to luck and their employees' efforts rather than to personal charisma and ability.[2] If we follow the examples of these leaders and the four individuals described next, we can learn to work hard in pursuit of noble goals, in a more modest, humane and dignified manner, befitting of an authentic transformational leader.

LEADERS OF TEMPERANCE

Jesse Jackson once said: *"Don't judge me by this campaign, because God is not finished with me yet."* Jackson was making the point that as leaders and human beings, we are works in progress. Our life experiences and willingness to develop ourselves and others forge our character over time. In order to grow as more virtuous leaders, we need to develop the character strengths associated with temperance. As human beings, we are imperfect. We make mistakes. So as leaders, we need to show forgiveness and mercy to followers and others, if we expect to receive the same treatment from others if and when we fall from grace. Heaven knows, we've witnessed enough failures in corporate and government leadership in the past and in recent history.

As leaders, we also need to display humility and modesty if we want to display the Level Five leadership associated with companies that have gone from "good to great." We must be prudent in carefully planning our future realizing that what we do today has important implications for that future and for those in our organizations. Exercising self-control in our interactions with others is paramount since our actions have profound effects on our followers and organization.

Given the wide range of ways that excess can harm us and the difficulty of disciplining our inner life through forgiveness and mercy, humility, prudence and self-control, the virtue of temperance is illustrated with several leadership examples. Four very different leaders are highlighted who exemplify the character strengths associated with temperance (see Figure 8.2).

The World's Greatest Investor

To look at Warren Buffet one wouldn't think that he is the second-richest person in the world, with an estimated net worth of $40 billion. He does not buy his business suits from the finest clothiers or eat at the world's premier restaurants. Instead, Buffet wears baggy suits right off the racks from Sears. He is happier eating hamburgers from Dairy Queen (one of the many companies he owns) than filet mignon steaks from the swank restaurant in the Omaha Marriot. He only collects an annual salary of $100,000 per year, a pit-

Figure 8.2.   *Leaders of Temperance.* Warren Buffet, Andy Grove, Nelson Mandela, and Eleanor Roosevelt.

tance compared to the extravagant salaries of today's top executives (of course, most CEOs other than Bill Gates aren't worth $40 billion dollars). And Buffet still lives in the same modest home in the suburbs of Omaha, Nebraska that he bought almost 50 years ago. All of these idiosyncrasies point to Buffet's well-known frugality, modesty and self-controlled way of life.

This same philosophy of temperance has served Buffet well in his leadership of Berkshire Hathaway, a holding company consisting of investments in organizations such as Geico Insurance, American Express, General Re, The Washington Post, The Coca-Cola Company, and Dairy Queen. All of the diverse companies within the Berkshire Hathaway umbrella have one thing in common—good long-term growth potential.

Through his prudent identification of such investments, Buffet has been able to create more millionaires per square mile in the Lincoln-Omaha Nebraska region than anywhere else in the U.S.

Buffet's philosophy of temperance was forged during his early years growing up in Omaha in the 1930s and 1940s. Buffet's father was a stock broker and his grandfather was a grocery store owner. They encouraged Buffet to be entrepreneurial and to value education. At the age of 13, he delivered *Washington Post* newspapers and filed his first income tax return. His university educational experiences included the Wharton School of the University of Pennsylvania, the University of Nebraska at Lincoln, and Columbia Business School. Over the next several decades, he used his talents for finding and nurturing great investment opportunities to amass an enormous fortune and become one of the most powerful businessmen in the world. In fact, by the age of thirty-one, Buffett had already become a millionaire.[3] Buffet's life shows that intelligence, coupled with personal drive and education, can really pay off, both figuratively and literally.

What is more impressive, from a leadership standpoint, is Buffet's frank criticism of President George W. Bush's tax and economic policies. Buffet has written several editorial columns in newspapers critiquing decisions regarding recent dividend, property and income taxes that, in his view, favor the rich. His columns suggest that class warfare is being waged on the American public and the wealthy are winning. To address these perceived inequities, he has served as an advisor to Democratic candidates such as John Kerry. He also is active in philanthropy through the Buffet Foundation. For example, he has donated large sums of money to the University of Nebraska at Lincoln's business school as well as social organizations. It is refreshing to see a man at Buffet's age and position *not* turn into a Scrooge, but rather speak up for what he feels is right and equitable regarding the economic and social conditions of the U.S.

Warren Buffet represents a fine example of the character strengths of prudence, modesty, and self-control. He is prudent because he focuses on identifying investments with long-term growth sustainability in industries that he understands. He is modest because he lives well beneath his means. He exercises self-control because he refrains from the iniquity that excessive wealth can bring to its holders. By possessing these strengths of character, Buffet has not fallen victim to hubris, self-deceit, or excessive love of praise. It could take only minutes for these vices to destroy Buffet's reputation—a priceless fortune that he has built over the last 30 years.[4]

The Paranoid Strategist

Andy Grove, co-founder of Intel, thinks leaders need to be afraid. But there is one thing that Grove has never been afraid of and that is *change*.

Grove was born in 1936 into a middle-class Jewish family living in Budapest, Hungary. He learned early in his life about the need for change. When Nazi Germany invaded Hungary in 1944, Grove's mother changed his name from Andras Grof to the more Slavic-sounding Andras Malesevics. When the Soviets invaded one year later, he once again became Andras Grof. After escaping into Austria from Hungary during the Hungarian Revolution in 1957, he changed his name to Andrew S. Grove. He was an excellent student and most likely would have been a successful academic in Hungary, had revolution not broken out in 1956. He eventually made his way to the U.S. and changed his field from journalism to chemistry. His ability to embrace change served him well in his career in the semiconductor industry.

Grove went on to earn a bachelor's degree in chemical engineering from City College of New York in 1960, and a Ph.D. from the University of California at Berkley in 1963. After working at Fairchild Semiconductor, he co-founded Intel Corporation, which produces the semiconductors that power many forms of today's computer technology. As CEO, then Chairman and CEO, and finally Chairman of the Board of Intel, Grove has successfully lead Intel's sustained growth over a span of 20 years. He has shared his wisdom on the technology of the semiconductor, and the lessons he taught himself about leadership and strategic management in the five books he has authored, such as *Only the Paranoid Survive* (1996). At the same time, he survived a diagnosis of prostate cancer. Grove was named *Time* magazine's Man of the Year in 1997. Now retired from Intel, he is currently a lecturer at Stanford University's Graduate School of Business.

What do all the changes that a man, such as Grove, goes through in his early life do to his leadership psyche? Such experiences may have made him obsessed with the notion of change. Applying his training in physics and chemical engineering to management dilemmas at Intel, Grove became fascinated with the notion of "strategic inflection points." These critical organizational events determine when to shift from one industry to the next, when to introduce or drop products, or when to replace an executive who had reached his point of incompetence (as described by the Peter Principle). Grove mapped out systems of linear equations to find answers to these questions.[5]

Such careful planning and strategic thinking, with the use of exacting mathematical decision making tools, illustrates Grove's prudent approach to leadership. This approach to leadership demonstrates the foresight needed to carefully examine how today's actions effects tomorrow's results. Grove's prudence has paid off royally in shaping his legacy. He is widely recognized as making significant contributions in both the fields of systems engineering and management.

Statesman of Reconciliation

Do you know a person whose unjust or difficult life experiences have made him jaded or bitter? Maybe you've heard his resentful attitude explained away by others as "It's not his fault; life has made him that way." Nelson Mandela could have easily become such a person based on his early life experiences. But instead of letting life mold him into a prickly cur-mudgeon or vengeful authoritarian, Mandela used his difficult life experiences to temper him in a more positive manner by seeking virtue in his behavior. As a result, he's become one of the modest famous and respected leaders of our time.

Mandela was born in 1918 into a South African tribe where he referred to himself as a prince. As a part of his indoctrination into tribal nobility, he was taught the importance of virtues in shaping character and a guiding force in conducting himself. In his youth, one of his chores was to press the pants of his uncle. The young Mandela performed this task dutifully. Iron-ing was not directly related to his leadership training. However, this task taught him about the importance of duty and accountability. He also took a liking to boxing and running. These sports taught him to have patience. His patience would come in handy later in life in his political activity and imprisonment.

After completing an undergraduate degree at the University of South Africa and a law degree from the University of Witwatersrand, Mandela formed a law partnership with his life-long friend, Oliver Tambo. Their law practice provided free or low-cost representation to many black South Afri-cans who otherwise could not afford such services. Mandela felt sorry for these individuals because of the difficult political, social and economic hand that life had dealt them. He was outraged at the unjust social condi-tions in South Africa and joined the African National Congress (ANC) in 1942 in order to help in the struggle against apartheid.

Throughout the late 1940s and through the early 1960s, Mandela led many of the ANC's attacks against military and government targets. He also raised funds to help with the struggle. In 1962, he was imprisoned for his connections with the ANC and other anti-apartheid groups, which had been banned by the government of South Africa. Mandela spent 27 years in prison, mostly on Robben Island, where he helped to provide leadership for the struggle against apartheid. Mandela's long internment made him a figurehead for the anti-apartheid movement, whose notoriety had spread around the world with slogans and songs calling for his release. Finally, on February 11, 1990, Mandela was released from prison by South African President F.W. de Klerk, who ended the ban on the ANC.

I can recall watching Mandela and his then wife Winnie on television being let out of a government car and walking along a road with thousands of supporters of the ANC and other anti-apartheid groups. I wondered what would happen next in South Africa since other changes of historic proportion were sweeping the world at the time. The Iron Curtain of Communism had just been torn in half as the Berlin Wall was being leveled. Now it seemed that another corrupted political and social system was being brought to justice, as Mandela promised that he would now work to bring peace to South Africa and the right to vote to the blacks of his nation.

His promises came to pass beginning in April of 1994 as Mandela became the first democratically elected President of South Africa. He did not seek vengeance against the former government officials that had unjustly treated him, the ANC and the black South Africans. Instead, Mandela initiated a tempered response of forgiveness and reconciliation. He did not put on Nuremburg-like trials, but offered truth-telling conciliatory trials where pardons were given out in return for telling the true story of what had happened to his people and their country during the days of apartheid. In fact, Mandela formed a Government of National Unity which included de Klerk as his deputy president. For his lifetime work, Mandela was awarded the Nobel Peace Prize in 1993. The progress in social, economic and reconciliatory reforms that he achieved during his years as president (1994–1999) gained him international respect and admiration for achieving some of the racial equality goals that we in the U.S. are still struggling with. Through his life's work, Mandela has become an iconic leader whose actions authentically display his love of freedom, peace, and reconciliation for all people.[6]

Nelson Mandela's life story shows us how the virtue of temperance can lead to very positive effects on society and the world in the long run. Through the tempering forces of reflection and persisting in "fighting the good fight," this ex-boxer's character and authentic transformational leadership was forged and solidified. Mandela's ability to see the importance of self-control, forgiveness, and mercy in shaping a new and racially integrated and interdependent South Africa defines what it means to be a transformational leader. Mandela has shown us how to adapt to the environment through deep self-reflection and thought, value all key political players, forgive those associated with the negative forces of the past, and work collectively to create a positive future of international understanding and peace.

First Lady of the World

How would it feel to have been made fun of as a child, not just by schoolmates, but by your family members as well? What would this do to your self-esteem and self-concept when you are teased and criticized about your exceedingly plain looks and "abnormal" height? How would you respond to being forced by your parents into an arranged marriage to someone who proved unfaithful? How would you deal with your sexual orientation being questioned by detractors and opportunists?

Such life events would have devastating effects on the ordinary person. But Eleanor Roosevelt was far from ordinary. Roosevelt possessed a tempered character that was forged through psychologically challenging life events and polished with the self-control, forgiveness and mercy she showed to others. Despite these challenges, Roosevelt gained acclaim as the longest serving First Lady of the U.S., visitor of troops during World War II, international stateswoman and diplomat, human rights activist, feminist, and educator. She achieved prominence through her activities at a time when women played few leadership roles.

Roosevelt's parents died when she was very young. Consequently, she was raised by her authoritarian and stoic grandmother (on her mother's side). Although she was unloved as a child by most members of her family, she was the favorite niece of Theodore Roosevelt, who admired her mental toughness and excellence in archery and bow hunting.

Eleanor and Franklin D. Roosevelt, who were 5th cousins, were married in 1905 and had six children. Their marriage was generally not happy. Numerous accounts of FDR's extramarital affairs have been written. Eleanor's bitter taste of her husband's adultery and prior emotional wounds from other family members have given rise to allegations made by some authors that she had a lesbian self-identity, although other authors dispute this.[7]

Sexual identity aside, Roosevelt possessed strong convictions about justice and cared deeply about social groups that she perceived to have been wronged. For example, the African-American opera singer Marian Anderson was not allowed to perform at Constitution Hall in Washington in 1939. Roosevelt empathized with the singer's plight and arranged for her to perform on the steps of the Lincoln Memorial to a 70,000 person audience and countless others listening over the radio. She strongly believed that all people should have the opportunity to develop and prosper. She became involved in feminist movements and remained active in Democratic politics for many years. Roosevelt had a unique sensitivity to the world's changing times and worked hard to support change. Perhaps her most significant achievement was her part in formulating and championing the United Nation's Declaration of Human Rights in 1948. Up until her death in 1962, Roosevelt was an outspoken champion for human, civil and women's rights through her world travels, speeches and editorials. Harry S. Truman recognized her achievements in these areas by dubbing her the "First Lady of the World."[8]

It is easy to admire Eleanor Roosevelt because she overcame the ill effects of much disapproval from the people in her life. She was rejected by her grandmother, friends, and family. She was even betrayed by her husband. Instead of letting such experiences bring out the worst in her, Roosevelt looked beyond her pain toward the needy of society and the world. Instead of retiring into her own self-contained world of privilege, she felt mercy for the plight of other sufferers and actively championed their causes. She was able to forgive her family and husband for their misdeeds and heroically went about her public life as if nothing was wrong. While this is not authentic leadership, it does exemplify a heroic type of leadership that many women over the years have had to display because they lacked the economic, social or educational opportunities that are available today.

HOW TEMPERANCE BENEFITS TRANSFORMATIONAL LEADERS

Character strengths that reflect temperance can enable leaders to display several aspects of transformational leadership. One of the most important of these is the ability to forgive and to be merciful towards others.

Forgiveness

When an individual does us harm, it is normal for us to experience a negative shift in our attitude towards the transgressor. Any positive feelings about the person who wronged us sour into negative thoughts. Vengeful images of punishing the transgressor satisfy our desires for justice and equity. Calmness erupts into anger and resentment. Trust erodes into distrust. Since organizations are often reflections of the personality of their top leader,[9] imagine the type of toxic culture that can be created if such attitudes of leaders are left to fester.

Leaders and followers form relationships based on mutual trust and loyalty. This relationship is a type of social exchange—a deal of sorts.[10] The leader's part of the deal is to provide guidance and support regarding what the follower should do to accomplish an objective. The follower's part of the deal is to work to achieve the leader's expectations of performance in an efficient and effective manner.

As discussed in the last chapter, unfortunately leaders and followers don't always follow through on their part of the deal. Leaders may fail to provide the support they promised to followers or act in unethical ways causing followers to question their integrity. Distrust will soon follow. At the same time, followers may neglect to perform. The result of these transgressions can be feelings of betrayal, anger, and disbelief. Such feelings can progress into broken trust, disillusionment, and damaged relationships. Since relationships are the basic building blocks in conducting business, any damaged or dysfunctional relationships may seriously impede organizational effectiveness.

The problem with holding on to grudges, grievances and vengeful attitudes is that they weigh heavy on our psyche and become toxic to us. They make us feel tense and nervous. They put us on the defensive. They sometimes put us on the offensive—when we offend not only the target of our hostility, but also others around us who witness our negative behavior. All of this is quite a heavy burden to bear. Day-in, day-out, month after month, year after year, if we let these feelings linger, we find ourselves being shaped by unfortunate circumstances. We lose control of who we once were, or who we really want to become. If we are smart, we start to understand that all of this negativity is simply a waste of time, energy and self. We realize it is time to rebuild, instead of tear down.

Repairing damaged relationships requires leaders (and followers) to be forgiving and merciful, like Nelson Mandela and Eleanor Roosevelt. It involves a reconciliation or restoration of the broken relationship.[11] Mending relationships requires leaders to get over hurt feelings or disappointments and to shift the negative views of others back to their original positive attitudes. By engaging in these forms of reconciliation, leaders may take the high road to demonstrating idealized influence, which puts into practice the high moral standard of reconciliation emphasized in many of the world's religions. In a society that seems to value a mentality of vengeance ("an eye for an eye, a tooth for a tooth"), demonstrating forgiveness and mercy reflects idealized influence because it shows that the leader possesses keen moral awareness and selflessness.

When it comes to forgiveness, leaders need to use common sense in determining how many chances a follower gets before it is time to give up and move on. It may be difficult to forgive followers "seven times 70 times," as Jesus told Peter (Matthew 18:21–22). A series of small transgressions may balloon into habitual practices. Some significant errors can turn out to be career-ending events. However, less significant errors that are not repeated should be corrected and considered as learning experiences.

To summarize, the transformational leader demonstrates idealized influence when she helps the errant follower to learn from the experience, works to restore the relationship, and removes any residuals of negativity from her own psyche. This brings us to the 15th principle which describes the idealized leader's ability to forgive, but not necessarily forget, the transgressions of followers against her or the organization.

PRINCIPLE

15

Leaders and followers are fallible human beings, subject to folly, malice and error. Instead of carrying the burden of negativity stemming from grudges or vengeance, leaders need to show mercy and forgiveness towards followers who've let them down. When we forgive them, we restore the trust required to sustain successful leader-follower relationships and regain our sense of self-control in shaping the best we are capable of becoming.

Humility

One of the things that prevents people from forgiving others is their ego. People are often too proud to concede that they have been "done in" by others, let alone forgive them. Pride assumes that life is a competition: a zero-sum game where "if you win, then I lose," and vise versa. In our highly competitive Western culture, notions of pride are glorified as "noble" quests for establishing one's self-esteem and self-worth. You can see these values advocated in many popular self-help and career advancement books. You also see them in today's "reality" television shows, such as *Survivor* or *The Apprentice*, that promote a "survival of the fittest," or "kill or be killed" attitude. Or you can see them in organizations that still have not figured out ways to get people to work together collectively and reward them that way.

Nowhere is pride more poisonous than in leadership positions. We know that transformational leaders are very confident of their vision and their ability to lead. If they weren't, people wouldn't follow them during the difficult times that call for their leadership. But some of these leaders may suffer from what the Ancient Greeks called *hubris*. This form of exaggerated pride or excessive self-confidence was a common character flaw of many Greek and Roman heroes. For example, Odysseus, Jason, and Oedipus all possessed hubris and were punished by the gods for it. These icons of ancient literature possessed *narcissism*, the idea that one is better than others and deserves special attention and admiration from them. Narcissistic tendencies are reflected in many of the Ugly Eight vices discussed above and aspiring authentic transformational leaders need to be wary of them.

It is psychologically healthy for leaders to think good of themselves, to think that their work is important, and to see themselves as making a positive difference in the world. However, too much pride or narcissism can blindside leaders and put them on the track for career derailment. Consider the downfall of leaders at Enron and WorldCom, as well as the unfortunate case of "Chainsaw" Al Dunlap. Such leaders are not able to make accurate assessments of their personal and organizational accomplishments. They live in a world of distorted reality where they are not open to new ideas, contradictory information and good counsel from others. They are not able to accurately perceive how their leadership behaviors affect followers. They often over-estimate their ability to display the positive styles of leadership and under-estimate their use of more negative styles of leadership.

In contrast, leaders like Warren Buffet, who aspire to display authentic transformational leadership, tend to be more humble and modest than narcissistic. Research on humble/modest leaders who under-estimate their display of transformational leadership indicates that they are excellent mentors and highly trusted by followers.[12] Mentoring is an essential part of individually considerate behavior. Followers are willing to trust leaders who display idealized influence and achieve high levels of performance in their organizations. This leads us to the 16th principle regarding the necessity for leaders to be humble and let their achievements speak for them.

PRINCIPLE **16**   No follower or associate likes a pompous, self-promoting, or narcissistic leader. Instead, followers like to be around leaders who show humility because these leaders are seen as being more concerned for the development of followers and less concerned for their own agendas. Such perceptions by followers make it easy for leaders to show individually considerate behavior and be seen as idealized leaders who let their performance speak for them.

Prudence

While humility can keep a leader's ego in check, prudence can keep his immediate desires from potentially ruining his bright future. Aristotle included prudence as one of his cardinal virtues because of its guiding function. As Andy Grove's story illustrates, prudence can help an individual to assess and manage trade-offs in personal and organizational costs versus benefits that accrue over time. As the woman in Figure 8.3 realizes much too late, to be prudent is to consciously make wise decisions today that help to achieve the long-term goals of tomorrow.[13] As John Milton noted, "Prudence is the virtue by which we discern what is proper to do under various circumstances in time and place."

Consider the example of two newly hired managers straight out of college. For the first time, each manager has responsibility for and authority

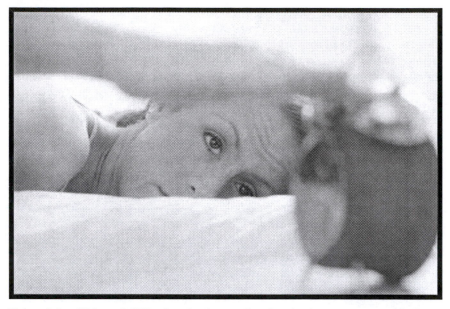

Figure 8.3.   *Wakeup Call.* Prudent leaders realize that the future comes much faster than we realize, so proper planning and care in making choices is always required.

over a budget. One invests in the future of the business while the other spends money on frivolous purchases. The prudent manager focuses on using the money to generate new clients and create a return on investment on her division's accumulated earnings. In contrast, the less careful manager spends a significant portion of the budget on setting up an opulent office space for herself. In her quest to create a professional impression, she overlooks her responsibilities to use her budget to build a client base that can generate new sources of revenue in the future. The former manager is prudent because she understands the time value of money and knows how to make it work for her division. The latter manager is focused on the present at the expense of her career and her division's future.

Leaders are responsible for helping to shape the future for their followers. They engage in strategic planning where they consider the trends in their industries and pose several questions to themselves. What challenges do these trends present for the organization? What opportunities do they present? What organizational strengths can we harness to take advantage of these trends? What organizational weaknesses do we need to address before we can leverage these trends? Based on these deliberations, leaders make projections of what the future will be like when they consciously ponder and then formulate their vision.

Prudence can be very helpful to transformational leaders when they display inspirational motivation. Prudence empowers leaders to take a foresighted stance about the future of the organization. Foresight is necessary for shaping an evocative vision. Thinking about long-term goals presented in the vision, linking the goals to important traditional values that excite followers, and aspiring to achieve these goals are all aspects of inspirational motivation. Prudence can also help leaders to integrate the multiple goals of followers, customers, stockholders and other organizational constituents and the interests into a coherent and inspiring vision.[14]

Prudence also benefits transformational leaders who wish to gain attributions of charisma from followers. Attributions of charisma involve followers believing their leaders to be trustworthy and capable of high performance now and in the future. Leaders who exhibit idealized influence demonstrate extraordinary capacities regarding their ethics and performance levels that set them up as role models for followers. When a leader is prudent, she is skilled at resisting self- or organizational-defeating impulses and persists at activities that may not be immediately appealing or beneficial, but may have large payoffs in the future. Such foresight or farsightedness is an important character strength that can benefit leaders and followers. It helps them to see the big picture of their conduct and to be pragmatic and disciplined in achieving long-term goals. Therefore, the 17th principle requires leaders to act prudently in their role as decision-makers so that the long-term successes associated with their farsightedness sets them up as inspiring role models for followers.

| PRINCIPLE 17 | Leaders who are prudent think and care about the future of their organization. By carefully and cautiously planning for their long-term goals in a deliberate and practical way, these leaders are able to achieve success. Their success stories, written through their hard work and personal sacrifices, serve to inspire and guide followers to higher levels of effort and performance. |

Self-Control

Self-control, which is integral to prudence, also plays an important role in the character strength of self-awareness. But self-control goes one step further than self-awareness. In most leadership situations, it's not enough to hold back on behaviors, but sometimes it is necessary to bring behaviors back in line by adjusting them. Look at Figure 8.4 and think of a time when you were irked by a comment that someone made while you were giving a public speech. "How dare that clown make such a stupid comment!" you

Figure 8.4.   *Making the Right Impression Helps Leaders to Influence Followers and Constituents.* Self-regulation and self-control are character strengths essential for displaying authentic transformational leadership, especially in a public forum.

thought to yourself privately. But publicly, you brushed it off unemotionally and moved on. Without knowing it, you were self-regulating your behavior.

To understand this concept, consider a household thermostat that is part of an air conditioning system. The thermostat regulates the temperature of the house by constantly comparing the actual temperature to a specified (standard or control) temperature. If the actual temperature hovers at or below the maximum requirement of the specified temperature, the system is considered to be in a steady-state and no action is required. However, if the actual temperature goes above the maximum requirement of the specified temperature, then the air conditioning system turns on and proceeds to cool down the house until it once again reaches the steady-state.

This process is similar to how individuals exert control over their own behaviors and how they respond so that they can live up to their own standards.[15] Applied to individuals, standards represent personal values, ideals, beliefs, or group, organizational or societal norms. All of these standards serve as guideposts for behavior. Control theory proposes that individuals compare their actual behaviors against their standards based on feedback from others.[16] This is how individuals are able to adjust their behavior and make the right impression so they can "fit in" with social groups within families, at work, or in the community.

Transformational leaders need to be aware of the impressions they make while communicating with their followers and others in order to sustain long-term organizational effectiveness. Indeed, Scott McNealy of Sun Microsystems, Steve Jobs of Apple Computer, and Carly Fiorina formerly of Hewlett Packard represent charismatic leaders who vary in terms of their awareness of the images they present to the public, yet these leaders have produced a range of organizational outcomes. According to self-awareness theory,[17] the self-ratings of behavior when compared to observers' ratings, are an indication of self-awareness and self-regulation. A self-aware leader would compare his/her behavior against a standard or new information such as others' evaluations of the self (e.g., 360 degree feedback), and incorporate those assessments into his/her self-evaluation. Incorporating these processes may help leaders to develop strategic self-presentation that is designed to package information about the self to get others to form the "right" impression.[18]

Much of the research that my colleagues and others have done on self-awareness of transformational leadership behavior points to several benefits of self-awareness and self-regulation for leaders. Self-aware/self-regulating leaders possess a strong pro-social purpose-in-life. This helps them to display idealized behavior, gain attributions of charisma from followers, and formulate compelling and inspiring organizational visions. They are very much like Nelson Mandela. Despite receiving "bum deals" in the past, they possess a very positive attitude which is helpful in formulating and articulating their vision to followers. They are committed to their organizations and are trusted by followers. As such, they are more trusting of their followers than leaders who under-estimate or over-estimate their transformational leadership behavior. Trust is essential to the leader-follower identification processes that emerge with idealized leaders.

Leaders who self-regulate their frequent display of transformational leadership do things that make them effective. They adapt their behavior based on feedback and therefore improve themselves and those around them. They are also good mentors. These behaviors can help them to display individualized consideration. They exude positive behaviors which helps them to serve as role models and reflect idealized influence. Their ability to be positive enables them to display inspirational motivation. They also are effective rational persuaders who make good decisions. This rational inclination helps them to use intellectual stimulation. As a result of such behaviors, these transformational leaders reap the benefits of very positive and innovative organizational performance outcomes.[19]

This brings us to the 18th principle, which involves pursuing long-term goals in a calm and collected manner, learning from the feedback we receive from others, and regulating our behavior to meet organizational, industry and societal expectations for excellence.

PRINCIPLE 18	Leaders who self-regulate their transformational leadership behavior pay attention to the feedback followers give through verbal and non-verbal expressions of approval or disapproval. These leaders adjust their behavior to meet or reshape norms or expectations of followers by controlling their impulses, feelings, thoughts and emotions. Their self-control allows them to serve as positive role models, to inspire and teach others how to behave in a moral fashion, and to use logic (intellectual stimulation) while pursuing long-term goals.

LIVING THE PRINCIPLES

The remainder of this chapter presents suggestions on how you can put these four principles into practice. By living these principles, you can build your leadership character through temperance.

Practicing Principle 15: Forgiveness

When leaders forgive followers for their mistakes or transgressions, they teach them how to separate the person from his behavior, to learn from their mistakes and to restore broken relationships. These are important lessons for building long-term relationships based on loyalty and trust, especially since employee turnover can be quite costly. Here are a few helpful hints relevant to the 15th principle:

- Separate the bad behavior from the person. Most people are not inherently evil. But when we feel victimized by someone who has hurt us, we often attribute very negative overall traits to our transgressor. Or we incorrectly attribute their behavior to internal factors under their control rather than to external factors that are out of their control. Instead, try to put the offense into perspective by hating the offensive behavior and not the offender. This tactic is one way you can demonstrate idealized influence.

- Don't obsess or ruminate over the offensive behavior or mistake. The more you think about the offense, the less likely you are to forgive the offender. Instead, seek an apology from the offender, discuss how to better handle the problematic situation in the future, and move on. Idealized leaders who forgive take the high road and their burden becomes light.
- Recall times when you made mistakes and were grateful for receiving forgiveness from others. By putting yourself in the offender's shoes, you begin to empathize with your offender. Empathy is the first step towards forgiveness. We can all learn from each other's mistakes.

Practicing Principle 16: Humility

When Hank Paulson, the highly authentic CEO of Goldman Sachs, teaches his people about accountability and leadership, he starts by talking about some of his own mistakes and how he constantly learns from them.[20] By demonstrating such humility, Paulson is able to show his people that he is human rather than infallible, approachable rather than aloof, and flexible rather than rigid. These perceptions make it easy for leaders to be individually considerate role models for their followers. Here are a few helpful hints relevant to the 16th principle:

- Think about your results from the Ugly Eight Vices checklist shown in Table 8.1. If your results indicated that Hubris and Excess Love of Praise were problem areas, then you need to make some changes in your life. First, discount comments made by others who say that you are superior to others. These manipulative remarks serve to over-inflate your ego. Second, try not to always compare yourself with others. Frequent comparisons with others make you hyper-competitive and perpetuate your hubris. And don't be a slave to popularity, appearance or perfectionism. These illusory goals only serve to exacerbate your self-focus.[21] By making these changes, you can help to temper your ego and present your "new and true" self—a self that is more approachable to your followers. Remember that being approachable is the first step in becoming an idealized leader.
- Take a 360-degree feedback review (and repeat when necessary). Such assessments of your leadership can provide humbling feedback. Hearing both positive *and* negative things about your leadership can

be an eye-opening reality check useful in developing transformational leadership over time.

- Perform menial chores inside or outside of the organization from
time to time. By performing tasks that most would consider to be
beneath a person of your status, you role model the need for all followers to value humility and self-sacrifice. You also show them that
people should not be defined by their positions, but rather by their
behavior and willingness to serve others.

- Attend religious services or programs on character development and
philosophy. These learning experiences foster changes in perspectives that can shift distorted attitudes of self-importance and power to
outlooks of modesty and submission. Such tempered attitudes go a
long way in shaping the character of an idealized leader.

Practicing Principle 17: Prudence

A prudent leader is able to delay gratification of immediate rewards in
favor of more substantial rewards to be attained in the future. She is also
able to envision, plan and work for future possibilities. Here are a few suggestions pertaining to the 17th principle:

- Exercise caution before proceeding on business initiatives or decisions. Always try to base your decisions on data (not just emotions or
opinions). Yes, transformational leaders are known for their "bold
moves," but they are also known for their valuing of intellect and
logic when they use intellectual stimulation with followers.

- Think about not only the immediate payoffs of decisions, but also
the long-term effects of your actions or decisions. Such future-oriented thinking can help to envision possibilities that can inspire,
energize and bond your associates to your long-term goals.

- Work towards being more conscientious on the job. Paying attention
to detail and focusing on what is truly important helps you to think
things through more thoroughly and execute tasks more effectively.
By doing this over time, you can build a reputation as an idealized
leader who truly cares about your work and organization.

Practicing Principle 18: Self-Control

This principle deals with adapting to the work environment by presenting yourself in an appropriate manner to project images of authentic transformational leadership. By being aware of the cues from the environment,

such as comments or non-verbal signals from others, self-regulated leaders are able to use this feedback in ways that are productive and motivational, rather than counter-productive or demoralizing. Here are some ways you can put this principle into practice:

- Keep a journal of critical leadership events from your day. Briefly describe both the positive and negative events and how you reacted to them. What did you do right? Where are areas for improvement? Reflect upon these events and make a conscious effort to improve your behavior in the future.
- Work on your public self-awareness. Start by making a conscious effort to pay attention to maintaining good posture as you walk, stand, and sit. More importantly, always be careful regarding what you say and how you say it. Carefully listen to what others are saying in your conversations. Notice the reactions people give you. Pay attention to your emotions, such as happiness, sadness, anger, or fear, while interacting with others. Don't let the negative emotions get the best of you. Corporate training or university courses on emotional intelligence are great ways to learn these skills. Over time, you will learn what is and is not appropriate in a variety of situations. Also, learn by observing and modeling other successful authentic transformational leaders.
- Learn to sense and control your impulses. It helps to know what your vices are, so that you can work to temper them before they harm the way you interact with your followers or associates. One means to this end is to review your results of the Ugly Eight Vices checklist shown in Table 8.1. Pay particular attention to issues concerning Anger/Impatience, Self-Will, and Jealousy because they can cause you to lash out and do or say things that you might regret. Control your anger and impatience through counseling or executive coaching. Temper your jealousy by appreciating all that you have. And tame your self-will through character development and religious or spiritual studies, which are fundamental to the virtue of transcendence discussed in the next chapter.

NOTES

1. http://news-service.stanford.edu/news/2005/june15/jobs-061505.html (Accessed January 4, 2006).
2. Collins, J. (2001). *Good to great: Why some companies make the leap and others don't*. New York: HarperCollins.
3. Steele, J. (1999). *Warren Buffet: Master of the market*. New York: Harper.

4.　Avolio, B.J. (2005, April). Personal communication; Buffett, W. (1998). *Thoughts of Warren Buffett: Thirty years of unconventional wisdom from the sage of Omaha* (compiled by S. Reynolds). New York: Harper Business; and O'Laughlin, J. (2003). *The real Warren Buffett: Managing capital, leading people.* Yarmouth, ME: Nicholas Brealey.

5.　Grove, A.S. (1996). *Only the paranoid survive.* New York: Doubleday; Grove, A.S. (2002). *Swimming across: A memoir.* New York: Warner Books; Tedlow, R.S. (2006). *The American: The life and times of Andy Grove.* Boston: Harvard Business School Press; and http://www.intel.com/pressroom/kits/bios/grove/bio2.htm (Accessed January 5, 2006).

6.　Mandela, N. (1995). *Long walk to freedom.* New York: Little Brown & Co.; McDonough, Y.Z. (2002). *Peaceful protest: The life of Nelson Mandela.* New York : Walker & Company.;and Mungazi, D.A. (2005). *We shall not fail: Values in the national leadership of Seretse Khama, Nelson Mandela, and Julius Nyerere.* Trenton, NJ: Africa World Press.

7.　Cook, B.W. (1992). *Eleanor Roosevelt, Volume 1: 1884–1933.* New York: Viking; and Goodwin, D.K. (1994). *No ordinary time: Franklin and Eleanor Roosevelt and the home front in World War II.* New York: Simon & Schuster.

8.　Neal, S. (2002). *Eleanor and Harry: The correspondence of Eleanor Roosevelt and Harry S. Truman.* New York: Scribner; and Youngs, J.W.T., & Handlin O. (1999). *Eleanor Roosevelt: A personal and public life.* New York: Longman.

9.　Kets de Vries, M.F.R. (1994). The leadership mystique. *Academy of Management Executive, 8* (3), 73–93.

10.　Graen, G.B., & Uhl-Bien, M. (1995). Relationship-based approach to leadership: Development of leader-member exchange (LMX) theory of leadership over 25 years: Applying a multi-level multi-domain perspective. *The Leadership Quarterly, 6* (2), 219–247.

11.　Peterson, C., & Seligman, M.E.P. (2004). *Character strengths and virtues: A handbook and classification.* New York: Oxford/American Psychological Association.

12.　Godshalk, V.M., & Sosik, J.J. (2000). Does mentor-protégé agreement on mentor leadership behavior influence the quality of mentoring relationships? *Group & Organization Management, 25*(3), 291–317; Sosik, J.J. (2001). Self-other agreement on charismatic leadership: Relationships with work attitudes and managerial performance. *Group & Organization Management, 26* (4), 484–511; and Yammarino, F. J., & Atwater, L. E. (1997). Do managers see themselves as others see them? Implications of self-other rating agreement for human resources management. *Organizational Dynamics, 25,* 35–44.

13.　Peterson & Seligman (2004) as cited in Note 11.

14.　Peterson & Seligman (2004) as cited in Note 11.

15.　Peterson & Seligman (2004) as cited in Note 11.

16.　Carver, C.S., & Scheier, M.F. (1998). *On the self-regulation of behavior.* Cambridge, UK: Cambridge University Press.

17.　Wicklund, R. A. (1979). The influence of self-awareness on human behavior. *American Scientist, 67,* 187–193.

18.　Sosik, J.J., & Jung, D.I. (2003). Impression management strategies and performance in information technology consulting: The role of self-other rating agreement on charismatic leadership. *Management Communication Quarterly, 17*(2), 233–268.

19.   For a concise review of the research on self-other rating agreement on transformational leadership see Sosik, J.J., Jung, D.I., Berson, Y., Dionne, S.D., & Jaussi, K.S. (2004). *The dream weavers: Strategy-focused leadership in technology-driven organizations.* Greenwich, CT: Information Age.

20.   Tkaczyk, C. (2005, December). Follow these leaders. *Fortune, 152* (12), I9–I10.

21.   Peterson & Seligman (2004) as cited in Note 11.

CHAPTER 9

TRANSCENDENCE

Strengths for Inspiring Greatness

The most beautiful thing we can experience is the mysterious. It is the source of all true art and all science. He to whom this emotion is a stranger, who can no longer pause to wonder and stand rapt in awe, is as good as dead: his eyes are closed.

—Albert Einstein

In November 2005, I ran a leadership forum on global citizenship and transformational leadership to promote Penn State Great Valley's graduate business degree programs. Panelists included the daughter of a former slain president of Liberia, a sociology professor specializing in African culture, a former executive from the WorldVision organization, and a Penn State graduate student who traveled to Liberia on a social entrepreneurship mission. The community responded well to our event and we drew a large and diverse audience. But one individual who was not able to attend was especially impressed by the event.

Shortly after the event, I received a business envelop postmarked with "INMATE MAIL PA-DEPARTMENT OF CORRECTIONS." It contained a letter from a 48 year-old African-American male inmate from Graterford Prison. Evidently, he heard about our event from an article in a regional newspaper that compelled him to write a letter of thanks. The letter

Leading with Character, pages 169–197
Copyright © 2006 by Information Age Publishing
All rights of reproduction in any form reserved.

described his turbulent life journey toward "the cognitive awareness that as human beings, we must all learn to live peacefully on Mother Earth." He wanted to make his presence known through the letter because, in his words, "regrettably my journey of self-actualization included a stop in the penal system of the State of Pennsylvania." He went on to say that he was very grateful that our campus was sponsoring such an event and hoped that in some way he could learn more about the topic. He wrote, "But as [a] seeker of the Source of our people's former greatness, I would truly be honored, if forethought was taken into consideration that there are probably [other] prisoners who would love becoming affiliated with the teaching of this philosophy."

I showed the letter to a few of my colleagues, who after first drolly dubbing me "Johnny Cash-Sosik," thought it was "a very unusual source of recognition." However, one colleague remarked that she was touched by the impact we were having on people regardless of their place in society. Her remark got me thinking about what transcendence really means. Here we were holding an event whose impact was able to transcend not only racial barriers, but also physical and spiritual barriers that we never intended to cross. For the prisoner, the event provided a sense of hope and a confirmation that we are all connected in some way. For me, the prisoner's reaction to the event taught me what transcendence is all about.

Transcendence is a form of reaching out spiritually and psychologically in ways that rise above barriers or limitations that are placed on us by others, or that we have placed upon ourselves. Transcendence helps us to connect with others and with God. It makes us both more human and more divine. How? In the prisoner's case, he was able to transcend his circumstances by being grateful for the presentation of a topic that he could identify with. He did not let his incarceration hold him back from connecting with the forum through his letter. He also transcended by appreciating the ideals of excellence and messages of self-actualization that were presented in the forum. This gave him hope that what he believed in was being encouraged in the outside world for the benefit of others.

All of us face barriers, limitations, setbacks and challenges in our business and personal lives. What are the walls that imprison you by holding you back from healthy relationships with your followers? Have your professional and/or personal circumstances condemned you to a life that ignores appreciating the beauty and excellence reflected in colleagues? Has your own self-centeredness made you so cold that you rarely show gratitude to those who have helped you become who you are today? How can you use humor and spirituality to break out of your bondage of the vices of self-excess described in Chapter 8? Read on and reflect upon what you might discover on the way to finding answers.

LEADERS OF TRANSCENDENCE

To overcome the trials and tribulations of life, we need to find "the Source" (as the prisoner wrote in his letter) of power and knowledge that gives our lives meaning and motivates us to develop others. Mastering the virtue of transcendence through its associated character strengths can guide leaders to the Source. This can help transformational leaders to better appreciate their followers through gratitude. It can help them to live in a state of awe at the variety of beauty and excellence that the world and its people have to offer. This is raw material for a leader's vision! It can provide leaders with reasons for hope, which also fans the flames of an inspiring vision. It also helps them to make better connections with their followers and the Source through spirituality and humor. For these reasons, transcendence is the most important virtue from which many other virtues and character strengths tap their energy. Let us now learn from four leaders of transcendence who have tapped the Source until their cups were overflowing with success (see Figure 9.1).

The Nutty CEO

Herb Kelleher, Chairman and former CEO of Southwest Airlines, is famous for finding something to laugh or joke about even in difficult times. Kelleher is not just a comedic businessman; he is a trained attorney, workaholic and brilliant corporate strategist. Indeed, there is a method to his "madness." Kelleher is well-known for his zany antics such as dressing like Elvis, or rapping with employees at company events. He's also famous for telling his employees to find humor in tense situations.

One very interesting situation occurred after a period of prolonged legal disputes with Stevens Aviation over the use the phrase "Plane Smart" in both Southwest and their adversary's advertising. In 1992, Kelleher suggested that he and Stevens Aviation's CEO settle the dispute with a televised arm-wrestling match with the winner keeping the rights to the slogan. Kelleher lost the match, but won the war. After the loss, as he was being carried off the stage in a stretcher, a reporter said to him, "I bet that this event is bringing you and your company a lot of publicity." In reply, Kelleher quipped, "Noooo, you really think so?" In fact, the event generated so much good will and exposure for Southwest that Stevens let them keep the catchphrase.[1]

Kelleher's offbeat personality and work ethic are the product of his upbringing. Kelleher's family was devastated by World War II. During that period, his father died and his older brother and sister left home. Another brother was killed in the war. His sense of loss was partially allayed by the

Figure 9.1.   *Leaders of Transcendence.* Herb Kelleher, Anita Roddick, Johnny Cash, and Fred Rogers.

close and nurturing relationship he had with his mother. She taught him about being idealistic and egalitarian, and valuing the dignity of all people. They would stay up late into the night philosophizing about politics, social responsibility and morality. As a young boy, Kelleher would do yard work for neighbors with a dutiful yet fun-loving demeanor. Kelleher used the lessons he learned from his mother and his early days growing up in Haddon Heights, New Jersey to shape the positive, fun-loving and family-like culture at Southwest.[2] Often we try to make up for, in later life, what we lack in our early years.

After earning a bachelor's degree from Wesleyan University and a law degree from New York University, Kelleher met his wife Joan and moved to

Texas intending to start a law firm or business. In the mid-1960s, he met Texas businessman Rollin King, who came up with the idea of creating a low-fare no-frills airline that would fly within the state of Texas and escape financially-burdensome federal regulations. In 1971, King partnered with Kelleher, who served as his attorney, to launch Southwest Airlines, and as they say, the rest is history. Southwest has grown to become the fourth largest U.S. airline. Southwest's organizational strategy and culture are topics of discussion in many top business schools. Its practices of selecting and hiring people who are a good fit for the culture, treating them with respect, and empowering them to make good decisions and have fun on the job are emulated by competitors as well as companies in a host of other industries. However, while many other U.S. airlines are on the brink of bankruptcy at the time of this writing, Southwest continues to be profitable. Even during the period immediately following the events of 9/11, Southwest was able to stay out of the red.

The phenomenal *sustained* success of Southwest stems from its bold strategic moves and idealistic organizational culture, both products of Herb Kelleher's persona. In particular, Kelleher's fun-loving disposition exemplifies the character strength of humor. When he uses humor, Southwest's employees have the opportunity to stand back and reevaluate their routine work approaches for continuous process improvement, and translate their ideas into company goals. His humor breaks monotonous tasks and creates an atmosphere that, together with his earnestness and devotion, draws Southwest employees together into a tightly-knit group—just like a family. Kelleher's humor also decreases the perceived social distance between him and his followers, thereby allowing them not only to learn on the job, but also to translate their intuitive learning to collective insights and institutional knowledge. In essence, this is how he helps his followers to learn about and strengthen Southwest's culture. Kelleher's example teaches us that it is indeed possible for funny things to happen on the way to the bottom line.

The Global/Social Entrepreneur

How many of today's CEOs can you think of who actually focus their business and service activities on an appreciation of beauty and excellence? And do all of this profitably over time? And then go on to promise to give away an accumulated fortune of $104 million dollars? These questions really narrow the field down to a sample of one—the one and only Anita Roddick. As founder and CEO of The Body Shop, Roddick's 30-year old global company has approximately 6,000 employees in 1,980 stores that serve over 77 million customers in 41 countries.

Most people are familiar with The Body Shop, an international cosmetics company that uses its products and stores to help promote human rights and environmental issues. It is a company with a conscience that manages to sustain growth while also making positive contributions to society. The mission of The Body Shop embodies the essence of the character strength of appreciation of beauty and excellence. The Body Shop's products celebrate and enhance the natural beauty of a woman's appearance. But the mythical image of Barbie and her 38-18-34 dimensions that most advertisers seem to glorify is not what Roddick has in mind. In 1997, Roddick and The Body Shop championed the Self-Esteem Campaign to expose the myth of the perfect female body, thereby showing appreciation for the beauty of physical diversity among women.

The Body Shop has also promoted its corporate values of social responsibility, respect for human and animal rights, the environment, and Community Trade. By appreciating excellence in organizational values, The Body Shop has served as a role model for all organizations. In fact, Roddick's activism has produced influential results in her crusades against giant oil multinationals such as Shell and Exxon-Mobil and their abuse of the Nigerian people and land and their contributions to global warming. In this way, Roddick is fighting to show an appreciation for the beauty of the natural environment and spirituality's emphasis on humanity's connection to it (see Figure 9.2).

Roddick has always been a fighter. A self-proclaimed rebel *with* a cause (her childhood hero was James Dean), Roddick always felt like an outsider because she was born into an Italian immigrant family living in Littlehampton, England. Her mother's frugality during World War II gave her the idea to use refillable containers later on at The Body Shop. She was trained as a teacher, but soon found herself inspired by participating in social causes. Her lifelong interest in spirituality propelled her into action based on her moral outrage against issues ranging from the Holocaust to the raping of the environment by greedy oil companies.

Roddick spent much of her early adulthood traveling the world, where she learned about important social issues and was exposed to the body rituals of women all over the world. After opening a restaurant and hotel in Littlehampton with her husband, she began to question her motives about being in business. She decided that if she was to pursue a career as an entrepreneur, she would use her business not only to make money, but also to strive to advance human rights, the environment and creative dissent.[3]

Anita Roddick's work toward attaining these goals has made her successful and led to her being knighted by Queen Elizabeth in 2003. In a world where waste is the norm, Roddick's advocacy of recycling and refilling containers has encouraged others to protect the global environment. In a society that venerates unrealistic expectations and images of perfection, Roddick's emphasis on appreciating women as they are, leveraging diver-

Figure 9.2.   *Appreciating the Beauty of the Environment Helps Leaders Refresh the Mind and Spirit.* When was the last time you spent quality time with Mother Nature?

sity, and valuing human rights rather than simply maximizing corporate profits is quite refreshing. As a patron of the Association for Creation Spirituality and global activist, Roddick has demonstrated the spiritual interdependencies among cultures, nations, corporations, and the environment.

Take one look at the impressive list of causes that Roddick has participated in and lists on her resume (visit www.AnitaRoddick.com for details) and you will agree that she has found a way to bring values into an industry that is not value-laden. Building upon her many successes, she has now started her own communications and publishing company to share her values with people around the world through "weapons of mass instruction." Indeed, Anita Roddick has transcended the norm by showing us how to better appreciate humanity and spirituality.

The Man in Black

Few others are idealized more by our society than the sinner who has been redeemed, or the underdog who has transcended difficult life circumstances to achieve greatness. Johnny Cash certainly fits both of these descriptions. To many people, Cash represents what country music is all about, with its attention to basic aspects of life such as love, faith, failure, death and redemption. Prior to his death in 2003, he was considered to be a living legend and a rebel leader whose work expanded the boundaries of country music. With his dark suits and introspective demeanor, Cash was able to produce a body of work that transcended musical genres and generations, and inspired many of his listeners to transcend the difficulties and limitations within which life circumstances had placed them. As Bob Dylan once said, "…Johnny was and is the North Star; you could guide your ship by him—the greatest of the greats then and now."

Cash was a man whose character was shaped by several trigger events that propel leaders into reflective introspection and positive changes in life. In 1932 he was born into a dirt-poor family in Arkansas. He was part Cherokee and later on would feel great compassion for the American Indian and other disadvantaged groups. *Walk the Line* (2005), the Golden Globe and Academy Award-winning film about Cash's life, portrays Cash as a boy working in the cotton fields and saw mills with his beloved brother Jack.

One such trigger event for Cash occurred when Jack was killed in a horrible table saw accident at the mill. Cash suffered deeply from the loss of his brother, especially because he was not with Jack at the time of the accident. Cash chose to go fishing instead of working at the mill that fateful day. His decision and the guilt he felt as a result of not being there with his brother haunted him for the rest of his life. It also planted the seeds of his strong religious faith based on Jack's deathbed comments regarding seeing and hearing angels.

A second trigger event occurred for Cash after he had achieved considerable success in country music by the mid-1960s. Because of the relentless touring and recording schedule he kept, Cash became severely addicted to amphetamines and barbiturates. His drug abuse and subsequent alcoholism impaired his performances and landed him in jail several times for misdemeanors. One night, much to the bewilderment of the audience, the stoned Cash kicked out the footlights of the stage at the Grand Old Opry. On another occasion, he was arrested for drug possession in El Paso, Texas. Cash never served a prison sentence, but his brushes with the law and his brief experiences with jails caused him to connect with the plight of the prisoner. He was famous for his performances at prisons such as San Quentin and Folsom.

Perhaps the most significant trigger event for Cash occurred when, in the late 1960s, he realized all the hardship that his drug and alcohol addiction had caused for his family and himself. He literally hit rock bottom when he crawled into a cave in Chattanooga, Tennessee because of his guilt and depression stemming from his addictions and perceived self-centeredness.

He intended to die there. But instead of succumbing to the forces of darkness, Cash said that he felt the warming presence of God that gave him a new purpose in life. He was charged by the Lord to serve as a role model of transcendence—a person who had overcome his demons in order to show others how to improve their character and rise above their circumstances.

Inspired by this new sense of purpose, Cash became known as "The Man in Black," often donning dark suits and projecting a virile, yet somber and wise, persona. Bono, the lead singer of the rock group U2 and social activist, once quipped that "Every man knows he is a sissy compared to Johnny Cash." But Cash used his "tough man" image to help many down-and-out and under-privileged groups, such as the Pima Indians, abused prisoners, as well as many social and political causes.[4]

Over the years, Cash dressed in black to point out the plight of the poor, the down-trodden, the hopeless, the forgotten prisoner, the uneducated and illiterate, the old and lonely, the drug addicts, and the martyred. If you listen carefully to the lyrics of Cash's song entitled *Man in Black*, you can understand why he chose this persona. He pointed these issues out in order to question the status quo and initiate positive change, promising that when these issues were addressed we'd see him dressed in white. In his last video for the single *Hurt* made right before he died, we see Cash still dressed in black. Perhaps in death he is now adorned among those in white.

Reflecting upon the legacy of Johnny Cash, it is easy to simply portray him as an iconic pop star and influential leader in country music. After all, he recorded about 150 albums, earned 11 Country Music Awards, 14 Grammy Awards, and one MTV Video Music Award. But Cash represented much more than that. In many ways, Cash defined the essence of transcendence. He was a deeply spiritual man, who like St. Peter, had fallen from grace but later achieved redemption through self-reflection and good works. He expressed his spirituality in many of his songs, his writings on the Apostle Paul, and his call to serve as a common man in a small Christian church near Nashville. His songs gave great hope to many people, those imprisoned by steel and stone walls, and those held captive by their personal vices and sense of hopelessness. Despite his somewhat somber and dark persona, he had a good sense of humor that he showed off in his songs such as "A Boy Named Sue," "One Piece at a Time," and "Sam Hall." Indeed, Johnny Cash's life teaches us that to demonstrate the character strengths of spirituality, hope, and humor, it doesn't necessarily take innate abilities. It just takes time for the man to come around.

Mr. Rogers

Each of us was once a child. In some ways, many of us still are. Think back to when you were a child. Every afternoon a man filled with grace would invite us all into his neighborhood and home. He would always follow the same routine of slipping out of his sport coat into a sweater, and changing from shoes to slippers. Then in his warm and comforting voice, he'd begin to talk to us about things that seemed to matter most—our sense of self, our relationships with others, and our worries about life's challenges. Could it be that Mr. Rogers actually taught leadership principles of the Saint to children for over four decades?

Fred McFeely Rogers was born in 1928 into a wealthy family from Latrobe, Pennsylvania. Rogers was the son of overly protective parents who instilled in him a deep faith and a love for music. His childhood was lonely; he would construct puppets to serve as his imaginary friends. College life offered him an expanded source of social opportunities and he graduated from Rollins College with a bachelor's of arts degree in music composition. He intended to enter the seminary after graduation, but got sidetracked into television when he landed a job as a puppeteer at WQED in Pittsburgh. Ironically, he disliked the low quality of shows that were on television in its early days and considered much of its content to be a waste of time. But then he thought "Wouldn't it be nice to be able to use the power of television's reach to spread grace (instead of waste) across the country?" He had found his purpose in life in Pittsburgh. There he also found the love of his life, Joanne Byrd; they married in 1952 and had two sons.

After a successful start in television at WQED and the Canadian Broadcasting Corporation, Rogers began developing concepts for a show that eventually became PBS' long-running series *Mister Roger's Neighborhood.* During the early 1960s, he was ordained a Presbyterian minister and attended the Graduate School of Child Development at the University of Pittsburgh. Building upon his education, he got his big break in 1968 when his show aired across the U.S. on National Educational Television (NET) which later became PBS. The show was an immediate hit. With its focus on the healthy emotional growth of children and their families, PBS produced his show from 1968 to 2001. It won four Emmy awards. In 1971, Rogers formed Family Communications Inc. as a medium for producing his show and other educational materials that reflected the development of character strengths in children and their families. Throughout his life, Rogers spread the philosophy of positive psychology in the over 900 episodes of his show, his numerous children's books, and many books he wrote for adults. He died of stomach cancer in 2003 leaving a rich legacy of leadership lessons for us all.

Who was this man that many affectionately called Mr. Rogers? Some of his detractors fault Fred Rogers for his "wimpy" behavior and calm demeanor that may not be appropriate as a role model for young boys hoping to develop into strong men. While Rogers may have been gentle on the outside, he was actually very tough on the inside. His power came from his strong value system, crystal-clear purpose-in-life, and deep faith in God.

Throughout his life, Rogers showed his inner strength by reaching out and connecting with forgotten or troubled children. One example involves a boy born with cerebral palsy who was abused by his hospital caretakers. Besides experiencing the physical handicaps of the disease, the boy suffered psychologically due to mistreatment. As a result of these cruel events, he would hate and hit himself. He didn't like who he was—both on the inside and outside.

But the boy always loved watching Mr. Rogers on TV. After hearing about the boy's condition, Rogers visited the boy and the two chatted for some time. Rogers left after requesting that the boy pray for him. This request had a significant effect on the boy. He realized that he was being asked to do an important thing for a person who was close to God. If Mr. Rogers was close to God and Mr. Rogers liked him, then God must like him too. Therefore, the boy reasoned, he should stop hating himself and start liking who he was and who he could be. In this case, Fred Rogers' inner strength transcended physical and psychological boundaries to build the self-esteem of a poor child who had become crippled inside. How many of us are strong enough to reach out to our followers who also are crippled on the inside?

Then there was the time Rogers met a belligerent little boy in New York's Penn Station who carried a big plastic sword—a Star Wars death ray toy. At first the boy looked at Rogers with a hostile glance of contempt when he approached him at the train station. The boy didn't know who Mr. Rogers was. But Fred Rogers knew why he carried the toy sword and he wanted to help shape a more positive self-concept and future for him. Rogers asked the boy if he knew that whenever a little boy carries a sword like that he wants other people to know that he is strong on the outside. The boy shook his head "yes" and finally looked at Rogers with the eyes of a child. The boy needed to realize that he was also strong on the inside.[5] Telling people that they too are strong on the inside has been Rogers' mantra for many years.

Inner strength is sustained through strong conviction and authentic behavior. Two different episodes in Rogers' life demonstrate his dedication to his personal values and willingness to take a stand on important issues. The first involved his logical and eloquent testimony in 1969 before the U.S. Senate Subcommittee on Communications. He was able to persuade John O. Pastore, the famously crotchety and edgy curmudgeon of a committee chairperson, to increase PBS' funding to $22 million. The second involved his vital testimony in the famous VCR trial, the 1979 case known as *Sony Corp. of America v. Universal City Studios, Inc.* Here he served as one of the most prominent and effective witnesses arguing that he had no problem with the home video recording of television shows.[6] These events illustrate two of the ways Rogers sustained his inner strength.

Fred Rogers personified the character strengths of spirituality and gratitude. Perhaps his most important personal value was striving to live in a state of grace. As a spiritual perfectionist, Rogers paid attention to the little things in life that made children feel good about themselves. This put them at peace. He always seemed to be very much at peace with himself. Finding peace within himself and sharing it with his viewers was how Rogers was able to bring spirituality into their homes through television. When he was onstage accepting Emmy's Lifetime Achievement Award, Rogers made a request of his audience: "All of us have special ones who have loved us into being. Would you just take, along with me, ten seconds to think of the people who have helped you become who you are…Ten seconds of silence…May God be with you."[7] By demonstrating gratitude, Rogers was able to teach an audience of self-interested celebrities the lesson he had taught children over the years: be grateful for what you have, who you are, and where you came from. You are the sum total of connections with people you have made in the course of your life.

HOW TRANSCENDENCE BENEFITS TRANSFORMATIONAL LEADERS

Character strengths that reflect transcendence enable leaders to display several aspects of transformational leadership. Perhaps the most important role that a transformational leader takes on is inspiring followers to work together toward a vision.

Vision: Appreciating Beauty and Excellence

The vision must be compelling, evocative, and perhaps even *beautiful* in the mind's eye of followers. Vision usually represents a utopian condition that is a vast improvement over the status quo. Describing visionary conditions involves setting high expectations for performance by defining what constitutes excellence. Transformational leaders, through their understanding of the people, things and events around them, construct and deliver compelling statements that inspire followers to accept their vision of the future and behave in ways that promote excellence.

To construct the vision so that followers find it appealing, leaders need to have a clear understanding of what constitutes beauty and excellence. Research on the content of visions produced by transformational leaders identifies *image-* and *emotion-*based words as being very effective. These words evoke positive feelings, pictures, sounds, smells and other sensations that arouse the motives of followers and get them excited about the work that needs to be done.[8] Adding excitement and meaning to work by "painting" an appealing verbal picture is what inspirational motivation is all about.

Leaders like Anita Roddick and Fred Rogers who appreciate beauty and excellence are able to recognize the best in people, processes and things. Recognizing the wonderful things in life provides standards of performance, suitable for setting lofty goals for followers. Idealized leaders value and promote aspects of beauty and excellence in themselves and others. They serve as role models who pay attention to only the best that the world has to offer. These leaders also take pleasure in recognizing people who have unique knowledge, skills and abilities and appreciate the individual differences associated with them. An appreciation of beauty and excellence certainly seems to make displaying individually considerate behavior more authentic and natural.

Appreciation of excellence and beauty is similar to the Big Five Personality trait of *openness to experience*.[9] This concept refers to an individual's interest in ideas, fantasy, and aesthetics, and having unconventional values. These interests and values are likely to be associated with leaders who display intellectual stimulation. Intellectually stimulating leaders encourage imagination, re-examine assumptions underlying problems, and encourage a broad range of interests. For example, a journey into *Mr. Rogers' Neighborhood* is full of examples of awe and imagery. Likewise, a conversation with Anita Roddick opens up a host of possibilities for improving the world's social and ecological conditions. This brings us to the 19th principle which describes the idealized leader's ability to take pleasure in the wonderful things in life, whether they are people or things, and to strive to achieve the highest levels of performance in their organizations.

PRINCIPLE 19

Leaders who appreciate beauty and excellence collect the raw material for setting standards of high performance for themselves, their followers and organizations. When we appreciate the best in people and things, we clarify what is valued by the organization and what is required for sustaining performance excellence. By communicating this understanding to followers, we can inspire, role model, teach and challenge them to strive for these ideals.

Gratitude

Transformational leaders not only appreciate the crème de la crème of their workforce, they are also grateful for followers who work hard, each and every day, but are not necessarily the stars of the organizations. These individuals get much of an organization's work done, and as a result, they make life easier for the leader. These people also deserve recognition. According to research conducted by the Gallup Organization, recognizing people for who they are, and celebrating their talents and strengths in the way that *they* value, helps to build a positive organizational culture.[10] The most gracious of leaders are quick to recognize and celebrate the achievements of these followers, and therefore demonstrate idealized influence.

Besides being thankful for these followers, gracious leaders, such as Fred Rogers, do not take things for granted. They appreciate the opportunities they are given to lead their organizations. They take note of the little things in life that can make them happy and share them with other people in their organization. They try to maintain a sense of goodwill with people, preserve a positive attitude, and show a warm sense of appreciation for their people.[11] A transformational leader can show gratitude when she displays individualized consideration by encouraging a two-way exchange of views and personalizing interactions with followers. A personalized conversation with a follower shows that the leader values the follower as a partner and a human being. When a follower feels valued, she is likely to become more motivated, satisfied and engaged in her work. Therefore, Principle 20 involves showing gratitude to followers as a way to point out role models within the organization and promote their continuous self-development.

PRINCIPLE **20**   Leaders who behave gratefully towards their deserving followers and associates recognize their achievements. When we recognize people for their excellence, we send the message that the ideals of authentic transformational leadership can indeed be achieved. When we appreciate the people and events that contribute to our success, we role model dedication to our organization and valuing its members.

Hope

The Chinese have often looked to the future with an appreciation for their rich past. One ancient Chinese proverb reads: "Hope is what you find in the woods when there was nothing before. But as the people began walking in the same place, there appeared the path." Today's transformational leaders are the ones who, through their vision, are able to find hope for clearing a path even in the darkest of hours. When Chrysler faced the real possibility of bankruptcy in the late 1970s, Lee Iacocca initiated several re-

structuring initiatives, encouraged innovative design projects, such as the
K-car or Minivan, and acquired an unprecedented loan guarantee from
the U.S. Congress. These actions provided hope to the employees of the
failing company that eventually spurred the economic recovery of
Chrysler.[12] In 2005, Iacocca was keeping hope alive by serving as Chrysler's
ad man in several television commercials advertising the company's
Employee Pricing Plus program.

Hope involves faith that allows leaders to set higher goals and work dili-
gently to achieve them. Hope, and its related concepts of optimism, future-
mindedness and future-orientation, is an important element of Positive
Psychological Capital discussed in Chapter 3. Remember, Positive Psychological Capital allows individuals to think about the future, hold positive
expectations, and feel confident that the expectations will be achieved in
the future.[13] Hope is more than just "pipe dreams." It allows a person to
focus on and work toward attaining goals. Hope is also an intrinsically satisfying condition for humans. It is a top-ranked character strength when it
comes to providing life satisfaction.[14]

Hope is also a powerful motivational mechanism and a positive attitude
that can be learned. The degree to which you can learn to be hopeful
depends on how confident or *self-efficacious* you are regarding whether or
not you have what it takes to successfully perform a task.[15] A self-efficacious
individual is more apt to greet and meet challenges as they arise. Taking on
such challenges with a strong will establishes a high degree of self-confidence. This allows for an increased willingness to take on greater and more
frequent challenges. Research suggests that transformational leaders display high levels of hope for a better future when they share their visions
with their followers and connect with them on an emotional basis.[16]

Followers are attracted to leaders who offer a vision of hope and a sense
of optimism. Who wants to follow a pessimistic leader? Hopeful leaders
look on the bright side of things and exude positive emotions. When they
enter into a competition, they expect to win, and if they don't win, they
view their loss as a learning experience. They find a silver lining in every
cloud. They expect the best and have a clear picture of what they want to
happen in the future. Jesse Jackson's classic "Keep Hope Alive" speech
given at the Democratic National Convention in 1988 is a great example of
the power of hope and its contagious emotional effects on followers. In this
speech, Jackson used inspiring language to paint a picture of an American
society capable of overcoming its many challenges such as disaffected
youth, poverty, inequality among races and genders, and disease.[17]

Hopeful leaders, such as Johnny Cash, provide the optimism and future-
orientation needed to display inspirational motivation. To genuinely inspire
followers, leaders need to be able to think ahead to take advantage of
unforeseen opportunities. The foresight often associated with hope can pro-

vide leaders with this capability. To inspire followers, leaders also need to be able to present an optimistic and attainable view of the future. The optimism often linked to hope can provide leaders with this capability. To inspire followers, leaders also need to create self-fulfilling prophecies of success. Hope can move leaders to look to the future, expect the best, and influence followers to share these positive expectations. Therefore, the 21st principle requires leaders to keep a sense of optimism for a better future, even despite difficult challenges and crises, in order to inspire followers to carry on.

PRINCIPLE **21**	No follower or associate will believe in a pessimistic or self-doubting leader. Instead, followers like to be around leaders who are optimistic because hope can be a very satisfying and motivating force. Such effects on followers make it easy for leaders to use inspirational motivation to mold expectations and create self-fulfilling prophecies of success.

Humor

Realistically, things do not always turn out as we hoped they would. Disappointments and set-backs are part of life. These letdowns can have devastating and de-motivating effects on followers. To help allay these negative effects, transformational leaders sometimes use benevolent and appropriate forms of humor (not inappropriate racial or sexual humor) to take the edge off of frustrating events. They use humor to get their followers out of a gloomy mood and to brighten their day. They like to have fun and to be around followers who also are jovial. Organizations such as Ben and Jerry's Ice Cream, The Geek Squad, Sun Microsystems, and Southwest Airlines credit their success, in part, to cultures that value humor. And those kinds of organizational cultures are shaped by what happens in top levels of management as we saw with Herb Kelleher.

Besides working for top executives, humor apparently serves as a "social lubricant" that makes interactions easier in meetings—even in the federal government. Ronald Reagan used self-deprecating humor to teach his cabinet members not to take themselves so seriously. When Secretary of State George Schultz and Secretary of Agriculture John Block became frenzied in a debate over seemingly unimportant details, Reagan reached into a bowl of jelly-beans, started picking out his favorite colors, winked, and quipped "I always had a hard time deciding between these." It's that same devil-may-care attitude that helped Reagan to react with humor to being shot and to verbal attacks by his political adversaries.[18]

Reagan's genius was his ability to use intellectual stimulation to generate simple solutions to complex problems and communicate them in a clear message that followers could understand. This was the case when he spoke at the Brandenburg Gate of the Berlin Wall in 1987. His speech's powerful and intellectually stimulating words helped to promote the fall of communism. The following excerpt illustrates the essence of intellectual stimulation to create a readiness for changes in thinking.

> General Secretary Gorbachev, if you seek peace, if you seek prosperity for the Soviet Union and Eastern Europe, if you seek liberalization: Come here to this gate! Mr. Gorbachev, open this gate! Mr. Gorbachev, tear down this wall!"[19]

Besides having positive effects on thinking, humor can also have positive effects on a person's health according to some physicians. Stories abound about Norman Cousins, who is said to have laughed his way back to health. Cousins was diagnosed as having ankylosing spondylitis. This disease causes the breakdown of collagen, the tissue that holds together the body's cells. Almost completely paralyzed and given only a few months to live, Cousins checked himself *out* of the hospital and into a hotel room. There he gave himself high doses of vitamin C and humor. Cousins claims to have cured himself by watching funny movies and television shows to produce belly laughs that promote the release of *endorphins* from the brain. These chemical healing agents can enhance the immune system, relieve pain, reduce stress, and postpone the aging process.[20] That good belly laugh triggers the release of endorphins which speed up the healing process by helping us develop greater optimism and joy—reflections of the character strengths of hope.[21] Two character strengths for the price of one! Imagine that.

Then there is the case of Hunter "Patch" Adams—pioneer clinician, physician and subject of the film *Patch Adams* starring Robin Williams. Adams talked about his values of humor, creativity and love that supported his mission to create a holistic organization for medical care-giving. Adams founded the *Gesundheit! Institute* in 1972 and began working to establish the world's first hospital based on sustaining joyful service to its patients. Adams infused fun and foolishness into the normally somber hospital environment so that it seemed more like an amusement park.[22] Adam's use of humor illustrates how truly intellectually stimulating a leader can be when he forces others to reconsider how healthcare provision can be funded, and how patients can be treated compassionately as real people.

Humor is also effective in helping managers with their performance and getting followers to accomplish organizational goals. In a study of 115 managers and their 322 subordinates at a large Canadian financial institution, my colleagues and I discovered support for the practical value of humor in the workplace. We found that managers who displayed transformational

Figure 9.3.　*Funny Business.* Appropriate humor has many beneficial effects for leaders and followers and also can lead to increased innovation and managerial and business unit performance.

leadership used more humor in interactions with their followers than managers who used transactional (exchange-based) or laissez faire (avoidant) leadership styles. More importantly, we found that the use of humor had a direct positive effect on managers' performance evaluations and the bottom line performance of their business unit. In other words, the more humorous the manager, the higher his performance review and more financially successful his business unit (see Figure 9.3). Therefore, not only are transformational leaders more fun to work for, they are more effective than leaders who rely on other styles of leadership.[23]

What is it about transformational leadership that makes it work so well with humor? To answer this question, we need to carefully examine the concept of humor by considering what makes something funny. Have you seen the episode of the television show *Seinfeld* where Cosmo Kramer uses the drawers of a very large antique dresser as sleeping compartments for his four "vertically-challenged" (read very short) Asian friends who can't find lodging? What makes *that* funny? That's funny because we normally don't use dresser drawers as beds. It's also funny because it demonstrates a playful and novel use for the dresser—it's something that actually could be done, but something we probably wouldn't do.

This *Seinfeld* moment shows us that humor involves the playful recognition, enjoyment and creation of incongruity. In other words, humor allows us to take two seemingly different ideas and juxtapose them in a novel way that presents a solution to a problem. In the *Seinfeld* episode, the dresser and very short people are put together in a way that solves a lodging problem. The witty idea generation and juxtaposition of concepts accomplished through humor are similar to several of the intellectually stimulating behaviors that transformational leaders display. These leaders exhibit intellectual stimulation when they are willing to put forth or entertain seemingly foolish ideas, such as Herb Kelleher's armwrestling match. They exhibit intellectual stimulation when they use appropriate forms of humor to address personal and task-related problems that plague followers. They also demonstrate humor when they use their imagination to think of alternate states of being. These seemingly ridiculous or impossible conditions may not reflect what is presently acceptable, but what, with a little work, can be an appropriate and practical solution to a problem.

Good humor comes across as being funny because much of it is based on manipulation of ideas, changes in scale, and absurdity. Consider the ironic manipulation of ideas in these words printed on a sign posted on a convent in Pennsylvania: *"Trespassers will be prosecuted to the full extent of the law.—Sisters of Mercy."* Manipulation of ideas is intellectually stimulating because it gets people to re-think their basic assumptions about the ideas. Note the change in scale in the following amusing sign found in a clothing store: "*Wonderful bargains for men with 16 and 17 necks.*" Here the omission of the word "inches" is intellectually stimulating because it changes the focus from the number of inches to the number of men. Or think about the absurdity in this excerpt from a church bulletin: "*A bean supper will be held on Saturday evening in the church basement. Music will follow.*"[24] The low-brow absurdity of this last example may be intellectually stimulating, but definitely not pleasantly stimulating to the olfactory senses. These examples should get you thinking about how humor can intellectually stimulate your own followers.

This brings us to the 22nd principle that recognizes the use of humor as a valuable way for leaders and their followers to deal with stress, promote good health, support innovation and creativity, and help ease interpersonal interactions. Intellectual stimulation provides several behaviors that leaders can use to show their humorous side and transcend the idiosyncrasies of being human.

PRINCIPLE 22

Learn to take humor more seriously. When leaders use appropriate forms of humor, they not only enhance morale at work and produce positive physiological effects on themselves and their followers, but also create interest and present work to employees as intellectually stimulating. All of these positive effects can pay off in enhanced organizational learning and effectiveness.

Spirituality

Another transcendent approach to leadership involves spirituality. In recent years, a growing number of organizations have recognized the positive effects of spirituality in the workplace. For example, Aetna International's Chairman, Michael A. Stephen, advises employees to meditate and use spirituality to advance their careers. Hewlett Packard's senior management advocates development of the self and others. IBM's management studied the Chinese spiritual philosophy of *I Ching* to help deal with the stresses of corporate life.[25] Websites, such as www.spiritatwork.org and www.spiritualityatwork.com/ also highlight the good that can come from integrating spirituality into work.

These organizations and websites recognize that people have an inner life that nourishes and is nourished by meaningful work that occurs in the workplace and community. A leader's spirituality is important because it shapes her ethics, beliefs, values and behaviors. This set of personal characteristics helps to shape the ethical climate of the organization. As seen at Enron, WorldCom and other organizations, the corporate misconduct of CEOs and their top management can cascade down the chain of command. This can potentially spread a dark spirit of secrecy, self-aggrandizement, obfuscation, and deception into the rank and file. Such dysfunctions can bring down entire organizations.

The idea of spirituality is closely related to the inspiring behaviors of transformational leaders. To inspire means to "breathe into," to inject with spirit, to energize, or to fill with passion for the cause. In their training of cadets, the United States Military Academy at West Point highlights the importance of inspiration. West Point teaches its cadets that inspiring others by what one says and does gets them fully committed to the values of Duty, Honor and Country.[26] Inspirational motivation reflects spirituality since it arouses in followers an emotional acceptance of challenges. It also gets followers to believe that they can perform at higher levels than they ever thought they could. As a result, followers are energized to become totally involved in working toward achieving the organization's cause, because they now possess the esprit de corps.

Spirituality is not the same as religion. Religion represents the feelings, acts and experiences of individuals as they consider the divine within the framework of an institution and its practices, such as church attendance, worship services, or any set of rituals related to a particular faith group. Spirituality concerns an individual's considerations of connections between human and metaphysical systems to provide faith explanations of past and present experiences and, for some, to predict future experiences. Religion and spirituality may endow leaders' lives with meaning and purpose and give them hope in a better future.[27]

Religion and spirituality provide meaning for transformational leaders, particularly those who face hardships and suffering while leading missions of change. Without meaning and purpose, there would be no reason for transformational leaders to endure their struggles. In addition, transformational leaders generate faith by connecting behaviors and goals to a "dream" or utopian vision of a better future. Followers are often motivated by such faith because it is intrinsically satisfying. Anita Roddick, Johnny Cash and Fred Rogers represent transformational leaders whose purpose was influenced by their spirituality.

There are several noteworthy characteristics of spiritual leaders. First, they have a strong sense of purpose, much like some transformational leaders who display inspirational motivation. Their belief in God or some sort of Spiritual Source helps them to understand their purpose in life. Both Lou Gerstner, the corporate CEO/turnaround guru of American Express, RJR Nabisco, and IBM fame; and Vince Lombardi, former head coach of the Green Bay Packers, frequently looked to God for purpose, support and guidance. Each prayed and attended Mass on a daily basis during their leadership tenures. This helped them to understand the meaning of the events they experienced and the power to overcome adversity.[28] But they still were hard-hitting results-oriented task-masters who focused on winning. This goes to show that transformational leadership is not "feel-good" leadership—it can be a tough developmental experience much like what one would experience in basic training in the military. Perhaps it is the challenge that inspires leaders and their followers to work toward accomplishing great things.

Second, spiritual leaders focus on the development of self and others, much like transformational leaders who display individualized consideration. Spiritual leaders believe that God, or some Spiritual Source, is in all living things and that this spirit connects us to each other. As a result, they feel compelled to build up people in their organizations. For example, Joel Osteen, pastor of the Lakewood Church based in Houston, Texas, is a very dynamic and encouraging transformational leader. He teaches his followers about bringing out the best in people. Osteen's father founded the Lakewood Church in 1959. Today this church is one of the nation's fastest growing Christian congregations. Osteen presides over its weekly services that are televised on a variety of networks such as the Trinity Broadcasting Network. He also conducts numerous services and workshops across the U.S. One of Osteen's and his followers' key beliefs is that people possess the power to survive difficulties, learn from them, and then thrive by living an abundant life that has been promised to them by God.[29]

Third, spiritual leaders promote trust and openness, much like some transformational leaders who display idealized influence. Trust involves putting yourself in a vulnerable position by relying on another person to act in your best interest. Trust enables leaders to form healthy relationships that value open and honest communication with their followers. Openness is what some scholars refer to as *relational transparency*, which they define as "presenting one's genuine, as opposed to a "fake," self through selective self-disclosure to create bonds of intimacy and trust with close others, and encouraging them to do the same."[30] This aspect of spirituality is seen in the example of Warren Buffett in Chapter 8.

Fourth, spiritual leaders seek to empower their followers and associates, much like some transformational leaders who display individualized consideration. Spiritual leaders also tolerate follower expression of their diversity. Transformational leaders not only *tolerate* diversity, they appreciate and try to leverage its power to promote innovation. Former New York City Mayor Rudolph Giuliani gained wide acclaim for his effective leadership during and after the 9/11 terrorist attacks on the World Trade Center. Giuliani relied on his faith and belief that as a leader, he can't do it all by himself. Leaders need to rely on great teams to help them accomplish their tasks. According to Giuliani, great teams have diverse members who bring unique knowledge, skills and abilities (that the leader doesn't have) to the table. Great teams are empowered by the leader with the physical and psychological resources they need to get the job done. Giuliani is very proud of the empowered, diverse teams that he has assembled over the years.[31]

This brings us to the 23rd and final principle, the belief that a sense of faith or purpose is an important Spiritual Source that gives meaning and vitality to leaders as they encounter all kinds of resistance, strife and crisis in their professional and personal lives.

PRINCIPLE **23** Spirituality is an important source of meaning, refreshment and energy for leaders. Spirituality helps leaders to understand their purpose in life and why their work is important. It provides them with a moral code that guides their behavior as a role model. It also focuses their attention to development of their followers and associates, and away from selfish interests.

LIVING THE PRINCIPLES

In the rest of this chapter, several guidelines are offered that can help you to put these five principles into practice. By living these principles, you can build your leadership character through transcendence.

Practicing Principle 19: Vision

When leaders live with a sense of awe, wonder and amazement, they gain an appreciation for what defines excellence. By setting standards or goals defined by excellence, they inspire followers to achieve the highest levels of performance, while striving for continuous personal and organizational improvement required to sustain such performance. Here are a few helpful hints relevant to the 19th principle:

- Be more open to new experiences. Travel abroad when possible and pay attention to your surroundings. Carefully study the people and their customs, the natural environment, and how your "world" differs from theirs. Also try working on new projects that stretch your abilities and introduce you to people with different view points and skill sets. Pay attention to what they are good at and learn from them. These tactics provide you with material to intellectually stimulate and inspire your followers.

- Create a culture in your organization that actively searches for benchmarks of excellence. Then recognize them through quarterly reward ceremonies and performance evaluation systems. What gets rewarded gets repeated. That's how transformational cultures are built. At the same time, discourage attitudes that equate admiration with naïveté, and intelligence with cynicism. These unhealthy mindsets eat away at positive cultures.

- Take up a hobby that encourages the appreciation of beauty and excellence. Photography, for example, is a great pastime that naturally focuses the mind's eye on what is beautiful, outstanding or unique. Your photographs serve as vivid reminders of the people, places and times that have shaped who you are. They also serve as images you can use to inspire and challenge your followers. As they say, "a picture is worth a thousand words."

Practicing Principle 20: Gratitude

Principles 19 and 20 go hand-in-hand. We need to first appreciate standards of excellence in order to recognize and reward our followers for them. Since leadership effectiveness is built on a foundation of completed transactions, it is essential for leaders to show gratitude to followers in return for their work. Here are a few ways to put Principle 20 into action:

- Work to eliminate the enemies of gratitude: hubris, self-will and jealousy. Start by reviewing your results of the checklist shown in Table 8.1. Hubris makes us expect things from others based on narcissism and false entitlement. Self-will makes us ignore the interdependent and transactional aspects of leadership. Jealousy makes us unwilling to show gratitude to others since we feel that they are unworthy of their accomplishments. By tempering these vices, we can become more aware that our success as leaders, to a large part, depends on the efforts of others. To sustain these efforts often requires displaying little acts of kindness (individually considerate behaviors).

- Keep a "gratitude journal." Writing your thoughts down on a weekly or monthly basis forces you to reflect upon what you are thankful for, and how you can express your gratitude. This can keep you from forgetting the things that your followers do that often go unnoticed, but need to be recognized through individually considerate coaching and mentoring sessions.
- Build gratitude modules into leadership and organizational training programs at work. Books such as Tom Rath and Don Clifton's *How Full is Your Bucket* (2004, Gallup Press) suggest several ways to get your associates to be more grateful. These tactics are a nice complement to transformational leadership's emphasis on appreciating the unique talents and strengths of followers and rewarding their continuous personal improvement.

Practicing Principle 21: Hope

Remember what Napoleon once said: "Leaders are dealers in hope." A hopeful leader inspires followers to strive to achieve an evocative and appealing vision. The feeling that followers get from working with a sense of optimism and hope is intrinsically satisfying. To put Principle 21 to work, consider the following tactics:

- Reframe experiences of failure and trauma into learning experiences. Nothing kills hope faster than repeated disappointments. Try to understand and learn from the failures in order to correct the mistakes or eliminate deficiencies in skills that may have contributed to the failures. Just as people can learn to be helpless, they can learn to be optimistic.[32] University or training courses on building Positive Psychological Capital can be helpful to sustain your efforts to be an inspiring role model for your followers.
- Learn from the role models described in this book and those in your organization. Consider the life experiences of your parents, family members, teachers, coaches, or clergy whose optimistic outlook on life has helped them to overcome difficulties. Their stories can be quite inspiring and helpful.

- Attack your unbelief. Do this by reviewing results of the checklist shown in Table 8.1 regarding the vice of Unbelief. Attend faith community services or support groups and adhere to their teachings. Hope is an integral part of spirituality. And use the tactics described below to improve your spirituality through inspirational motivation of the self.

Practicing Principle 22: Humor

A humorous leader is able to intellectually stimulate and inspire followers to achieve higher levels of organizational learning and effectiveness. Here are a few suggestions for practicing the 22nd principle:

- Don't take yourself too seriously. Learn to laugh at yourself and the imperfections you share with humanity. When you put things into perspective, you begin to appreciate humor.
- Start a collection of jokes and funny anecdotes. These ditties are useful for starting speeches, for calming people down in tense meetings, or for helping people to find humor in stress. Remember that humor can be a much appreciated social lubricant.
- Make a conscious effort to be funny. "But I'm not a born-comedian like Jerry Seinfeld!" you might object. Realize that humor is a behavior and behaviors can be learned. You can learn by relaxing with funny TV shows or movies, or reading witty or satirical books. Pay attention to the funny things that happen to you and your associates at work. Talk about them in order to lighten things up as needed.

Practicing Principle 23: Spirituality

While much of your spirituality depends on your personality and upbringing, it can also be cultivated through important life events that trigger a need to become spiritual, develop faith, and find purpose. Faith and personal meaning are important motivational forces in most people. Spiritual leaders use these forces to rally others to achieve their mission. Some pathways for developing spiritual forms of leadership include:

- Pray. By having a meaningful conversation with God, you can tap into the Spiritual Source of all four transformational leadership behaviors and get physiological and psychological benefits (see Figure 9.4).
- Study the major world religions—especially their similarities and differences—and write brief summaries of their belief systems. Then use your summaries to consider reasons for major issues such as cre-

Figure 9.4.   *The Power of Prayer.* Leaders who pray can reap several benefits including decreased stress, anxiety, and lower blood pressure as well as greater perspective in coping with crises and other challenging situations.

ation, life, death, war, disease, good and evil, and character flaws and strengths. Such intellectually stimulating exercises broaden your knowledge base and provide meaning for what role you and your organization serve in the world.
- Start a monthly discussion group on issues of spirituality in the workplace. The discourse within these groups can be quite an inspiring source of "fuel" for those who get bogged down in the trivialities and seemingly meaningless tasks that we sometimes perform. Better yet, partner with faith community groups to provide much needed outreach to disadvantaged members of society. Such opportunities for service allow you to see that you are a small, but important, part of humanity.

- Write a personal leadership mission statement. Start by reflecting upon all the people in your life who have (as Fred Rogers once said) "loved you into being." How much of who you are today do you owe to them? Then ask yourself, who are you without your job and your money? What gives you the greatest joy and energy in your life, and how can you share it with others? If you were on your deathbed and you wanted to tell your children (or young people close to you) the two most important things that you've learned in your life, what would they be? How you answer these questions will determine what you value in life, and what your overarching purpose in life is. Remember that your purpose in life is supported by your most cherished values. People can't see your values, but people can guess what they are since your behavior reflects your values. Complete this exercise by writing a three paragraph mission statement. The first paragraph succinctly describes your purpose in life. The second describes your values, how you define them, and how they support your purpose. The third paragraph describes how your transformational leadership behaviors reflect your values. Revisit your mission statement from time to time and revise it as necessary.

Remember that *"When what you say is what you do, and you are true to yourself, then you are an authentic leader."* Only then will you be leading with character.

NOTES

1. Freiberg, K., & Freiberg, J. (1998). *Nuts!: Southwest Airlines' crazy recipe for business and personal success.* New York: Broadway Books.
2. Beldon, T. (2003, May 1). Southwest Airlines was really born in S. Jersey. *Philadelphia Inquirer,* C1, C4.
3. Roddick, A. (2005). *Business as unusual: My entrepreneurial journey.* West Sussex, England: Anita Roddick Books; Wheeler, D. (1997). *The stakeholder corporation: The Body Shop blueprint for maximizing stakeholder value.* New York: Pitman; and www.bbc.co.uk/london/communicate/anita_roddick.shtml (Accessed January 16, 2006).
4. Cash, J.R., & Carr, P. (1997). *Cash: The autobiography.* New York: Harper Collins; Miller, S. (2003). *Johnny Cash: The life of an American icon.* London: Omnibus Press; and Urbanski, D. (2003). *The man comes around: The spiritual journey of Johnny Cash.* New York: Relevant Books.
5. http://www.esquire.com/features/articles/2003/030227_mfe_rogershero _1.html (Accessed January 19, 2006).
6. Collins, M. (1996). *Mister Rogers' neighborhood: Children, television, and Fred Rogers.* Pittsburg, PA: University of Pittsburgh Press; Hollingsworth, A. (2005). *The simple faith of Mr. Rogers: Spiritual insights from the world's most beloved neighbor.* Franklin, TN: Integrity Publishers; and Rogers, F.M. (2003).

The world according to Mister Rogers: Important things to remember. New York: Hyperion.

7. Esquire.com web link as cited in Note 5.

8. Emrich, C.G., Brower, H.H., Feldman, J.M., & Garland, H. (2001). Images in words: Presidential rhetoric, charisma, and greatness. *Administrative Science Quarterly, 46,* 527–557.

9. Peterson, C., & Seligman, M.E.P. (2004). *Character strengths and virtues: A handbook and classification.* New York: Oxford/American Psychological Association.

10. Rath, T., & Clifton, D.O. (2004). *How full is your bucket?: Positive strategies for work and life.* Omaha, NE: Gallup Press.

11. Peterson & Seligman (2004) as cited in Note 9.

12. Iacocca, L.A. (1984). *Iacocca: An autobiography.* New York: Bantam Books.

13. Luthans, F. (2002). The need for and meaning of positive organizational behavior. *Journal of Organizational Behavior, 23,* 695–706.

14. Park, N., Peterson, C., & Seligman, M.E. (2004). Strengths of character and well-being. *Journal of Social and Clinical Psychology, 23 (5), 603–619.*

15. Bandura, A. (1986). *Social foundations of thought and action: A social cognitive theory.* Englewood Cliffs, NJ: Prentice-Hall.

16. Megerian, L.E., & Sosik, J.J. (1996). An affair of the heart: Emotional intelligence and transformational leadership. *Journal of Leadership Studies, 3* (3), 31–48.

17. Shamir, B., Arthur, M.B., & House, R.J. (1994). The rhetoric of charismatic leadership: A theoretical extension, a case study, and implications for research, *The Leadership Quarterly, 5,* 25–42.

18. Brookhiser, R. (2004). Reagan: His place in history. *American Heritage, 55* (4), 34–39.

19. http://www.reaganfoundation.org/reagan/speeches/wall.asp (Accessed August 4, 2005).

20. Cousins, N. (1979). *Anatomy of an illness as perceived by the patient: Reflections on healing and regeneration.* New York: Norton.

21. Fries, D.S. (2002). Opioid analgesics. In Williams DA, Lemke TL. *Foye's Principles of Medicinal Chemistry* (5th ed.). Philadelphia: Lippincott Williams & Wilkins.

22. Adams, P., & Mylander, M. (1998). *Gesundheit!: Bringing good health to you, the medical system, and society through physician service, complementary therapies, humor, and joy.* Rochester, VT: Healing Arts Press.

23. Avolio, B.J., Howell, J.M., & Sosik, J.J. (1999). A funny thing happened on the way to the bottom line: Humor as a moderator of leadership style effects. *Academy of Management Journal, 42,* 219–227. Additional evidence of the link between transformational leadership and humor can be found in Berson, Y., & Sosik, J.J. (2006, August). *Humor, leadership, and organizational learning: A multiple source examination.* Presented as part of a symposium on Leadership and Organizational Learning (D. Waldman, Chair) at the national meetings of the *Academy of Management,* Atlanta, GA.

24. Visit www.danielsen.com/jokes.shtml for more examples of such humorous anecdotes.

25. Tatar, R.R. (2000). Spirituality in corporations. *Literature: Essays by the creator.* Available at http://www.reemcreations.com/literature/corporations.html (Accessed August 4, 2005).

26. Lennox, W.J. (2002). *Cadet leader development system.* USMA Circular 1-101. West Point, NY: United States Military Academy.

27. Conger, J.A. (1994). *Spirit at work.* San Francisco: Jossey-Bass; and Sosik, J.J. (2000). The role of personal meaning in charismatic leadership. *Journal of Leadership Studies, 7*(2), 60–74.

28. Gerstner, L.V. (2002). *Who say's elephants can't dance?: Inside IBM's historic turnaround.* New York: HarperBusiness; and O'Brien, M. (1989). *Vince: A personal biography of Vince Lombardi.* New York: Quill.

29. Osteen, J. (2004). *Your best life now: 7 steps to living at your full potential.* New York: Warner Books.

30. Gardner, W.L., Avolio, B.J., Luthans, F., May, D.R., & Walumbwa, F. (2005, p. 357). "Can you see the real me?" A self-based model of authentic leader and follower development. *The Leadership Quarterly, 16,* 343–372.

31. Giuliani, R.W. (2002). *Leadership.* New York: Hyperion.

32. Peterson & Seligman (2004) as cited in Note 9.

CHAPTER 10

REACHING A HIGHER LEVEL OF LEADERSHIP AND PROSPERITY

Looking through the backyard of my life; Time to sweep the fallen leaves away...

—Sir Paul McCartney, "Promise to You Girl,"
from the album *Chaos and Creation in the Backyard* (2005)

Benjamin Franklin was among the most important of the Founding Fathers and early political figures of the United States. As a true "Renaissance Man" and epitome of pragmatic leadership, Franklin was not only a leading statesman, author, printer and inventor; he was a witty and wise philosopher as well. To this day, many people appreciate his words of wisdom found in *Poor Richard's Almanac,* and those reprinted in the issues of *The Saturday Evening Post,* the folksy magazine he conceived shortly before his death.

When Franklin was in his late twenties, he gave considerable thought to the function of virtues as guideposts for behavior and pathways to prosperity. He identified 13 virtues that he attempted to use in leading his life: temperance, silence, order, resolution, frugality, industry, sincerity, justice, moderation, cleanliness, tranquility, chastity and humility. (Any of these sound familiar?) Throughout his life, Franklin kept a ledger to account for how well his behavior reflected these virtues. Some weeks he faired well,

Leading with Character, pages 199–211
Copyright © 2006 by Information Age Publishing
All rights of reproduction in any form reserved.

others he went astray. He eventually gave up on the idea. He realized that even if he achieved success with the first 12 virtues, he would lack humility since he would therefore be superior to others![1]

It seems that Benjamin Franklin lacked the character to, in his words, "resolve to perform what you ought and perform without fail what you resolve." But he was wrong to have given up. As the examples in this book show, many authentic transformational leaders, such as Mother Teresa, Fred Rogers, and Pope John Paul II, were able to persist in their efforts to use virtue and character to exert great positive influence over others. While no one is perfect, it *is* indeed possible to follow virtue by practicing the principles described in this book. How? Study the principles reviewed in Table 10.1. Think deeply about how and when you can apply them in your leadership role and situation. Take time at the end of each week to evaluate your performance by comparing how you actually behaved versus how you intended to behave according to the principles. Then adjust your behavior in future interactions with your followers and associates. All it takes is thoughtfulness and hard work. As Franklin once wrote, "Diligence is the mother of good luck."[2]

Now is the time for you to "clean up" your leadership past and replace it with leadership based on the principles set forth in this book. Like the thoughtful man described in Paul McCartney's lyric whose identity is shaped by both his past and future, look to your past and rid yourself of any vices that are making you lose touch with your real self. Visualize the type of self you hope to become in the future. Realize your vision of prosperity by behaving in ways that reflect your ideals. Recall that *"When what you say is what you do, and you are true to yourself, then you are an authentic leader."*

Possessing the ideals, virtues and character strengths described in this book is a necessary, but not sufficient, condition for being an authentic transformational leader. To complete this noble personal goal requires you to *act* like an authentic transformational leader by practicing the principles in this book. Turn your attention from the self-development of your character to the development of character in others. This "other-orientation" is what political scientist, James MacGregor Burns, described when he challenged all of us to apply the concept of transformational leadership to solve the world's global poverty problem. He writes "While leadership is necessary at every stage, beginning with the first spark that awakens people's hopes, its vital role is to create and expand the opportunities that empower people to pursue happiness for themselves."[3] Recall that research from the field of positive psychology has demonstrated many social, spiritual, mental and emotional benefits associated with the character strengths described in this book. By helping others to develop character, we, as authentic transformational leaders, can help them to live long and prosper.

Table 10.1.   Summary of Leadership Principles and When to Use Them

Leadership Principle	Reflects the virtue of...	And Should be Used When Your Objective is...
1 *Creativity* allows you and your organization to challenge the status quo and identify opportunities. Your creativity fuels the inspirational motivation and intellectual stimulation of your followers.	Wisdom and Knowledge	Championing change and innovation
2 *Curiosity* makes you a more adaptive leader and your company a more learning-oriented organization. Curiosity is a powerful source of inspirational motivation and intellectual stimulation that can energize your associates to be more innovative.	Wisdom and Knowledge	Obtaining new information and ideas
3 A leaders' *open-mindedness* is the key for followers to participate and develop a sense of ownership. Participation and ownership in organizational initiatives are built by displaying inspirational motivation, intellectual stimulation and individualized consideration.	Wisdom and Knowledge	Fostering collaboration
4 *Love of learning* is an important foundation for leaders to identify new trends in the business environment and develop effective strategies for a new set of challenges. Through a love of learning, a leader can demonstrate inspirational motivation, intellectual stimulation and individually considerate behavior, so that followers can face the future more confidently and successfully.	Wisdom and Knowledge	Promoting continuous improvement of people, processes and products
5 *Perspective-taking* allows leaders to consider both sides of many paradoxes they have to face in today's business environment. The ability to understand these paradoxes through a broader perspective also allows you to show inspirational motivation, intellectual stimulation and individualized consideration to your followers. These transformational behaviors energize your followers to perform beyond expectations.	Wisdom and Knowledge	Thinking strategically and/or solving problems effectively
6 *Bravery* will demonstrate your willingness to act consistently with your values and beliefs. You can inspire the people in your organization by bravely acting on your most passionate beliefs. In essence, your bravery fuels your ability to inspirationally motivate and intellectually stimulate your followers.	Courage	Standing up for your values and beliefs and/or taking on risks
7 *Persistence* will allow you to win trust and loyalty from your followers. Persistent behaviors demonstrate your determination to practice your values and beliefs. Doing so allows you to display idealized influence and inspirational motivation to your followers.	Courage	Achieving long-term success

Table 10.1.   Summary of Leadership Principles and When to Use Them

	Leadership Principle	*Reflects the virtue of…*	*And Should be Used When Your Objective is…*
8	*Integrity* will make you a more confident leader because you know you are doing the right thing. Being true to yourself is the essential aspect of an authentic leader and integrity is the foundation of such leadership. To be an authentic idealized leader in the eyes of your followers is to possess integrity.	Courage	Being authentic and gaining respect
9	*Vitality* will make you a more dynamic leader with followers who feed from your contagious energy to produce extraordinary results. Vitality is the source of fuel for displaying idealized influence and inspirational motivation to your followers.	Courage	Leading in crises and sparking action
10	When you *love* your followers, you show real compassion for them as human beings. Showing compassion proves that you care for them as persons and not as things to be used to achieve some purpose. Love is the foundation for close relationships in which leaders and followers show trust, loyalty and commitment to each other, and followers go the extra mile for the leader.	Humanity	Building and sustaining healthy relationships
11	By showing *kindness* to your followers, you make a very important statement to them: They are more important than the tasks that you require of them. The tasks will always be there, but your people may not. The genuine kindness that you show to your followers sets a very positive example for them to follow (idealized influence), and shows that you recognize and appreciate their unique talents and skills (individualized consideration).	Humanity	Building and sustaining healthy relationships
12	Leadership is a *social influence* process. To effectively influence followers, leaders must be keenly "tuned in" to their own emotions, motives, actions, and concerns, and those of their followers. In addition, understanding the dynamics of organizational social systems helps leaders to act as an appropriate role model for followers (idealized influence), inspire followers to work harder (inspirational motivation), and identify and develop followers' talents (individualized consideration).	Humanity	Effectively communicating and understanding yourself and others
13	Leaders are good citizens of their organization and community. As good citizens, they are granted the right to work toward prosperity, as well as the responsibility to help others, show loyalty to their people, and be a good team player. Valuing *citizenship* shows your commitment to the common good that builds	Justice	Being a team player and fostering collaboration

Table 10.1.   Summary of Leadership Principles and When to Use Them

	Leadership Principle	Reflects the virtue of...	And Should be Used When Your Objective is...
	followers' trust, emotional attachment and dedication to you, and increases the amount of idealized influence your followers attribute to you.		
14	Leaders who value *fairness*, justice, and principled moral reasoning in their interactions with others become idealized by their followers. Leaders who value an ethics of care for the needs, interests and well-being of others display individualized consideration. Both behaviors build a sense of "oneness" in the organization, where people believe "if the organization succeeds, then I succeed."	Justice	Being a team player and fostering collaboration
15	Leaders and followers are fallible human beings, subject to folly, malice and error. Instead of carrying the burden of negativity stemming from grudges or vengeance, leaders need to show *mercy and forgiveness* towards followers who've let them down. When we forgive them, we restore the trust required to sustain successful leader-follower relationships and regain our sense of self-control in shaping the best we are capable of becoming.	Temperance	Fixing broken relationships
16	No follower or associate likes a pompous, self-promoting, or narcissistic leader. Instead, followers like to be around leaders who show *humility* because these leaders are seen as being more concerned for the development of followers and less concerned for their own agendas. Such perceptions by followers make it easy for leaders to show individually considerate behavior and be seen as idealized leaders who let their performance speak for them.	Temperance	Focusing on your organization's mission
17	Leaders who are *prudent* think and care about the future of their organization. By carefully and cautiously planning for their long-term goals in a deliberate and practical way, these leaders are able to achieve success. Their success stories, written through their hard work and personal sacrifices, serve to inspire and guide followers to higher levels of effort and performance.	Temperance	Thinking strategically about the future
18	Leaders who *self-regulate* their transformational leadership behavior pay attention to the feedback followers give through verbal and non-verbal expressions of approval or disapproval. These leaders adjust their behavior to meet or reshape norms or expectations of followers by controlling their impulses, feelings, thoughts and emotions. Their self-control allows	Temperance	Effectively communicating and understanding yourself and others

Table 10.1. Summary of Leadership Principles and When to Use Them

Leadership Principle	*Reflects the virtue of...*	*And Should be Used When Your Objective is...*
them to serve as positive role models, to inspire and teach others how to behave in a moral fashion, and to use logic (intellectual stimulation) while pursuing long-term goals.		
19 Leaders who *appreciate beauty and excellence* collect the raw material for setting standards of high performance for themselves, their followers and organizations. When we appreciate the best in people and things, we clarify what is valued by the organization and what is required for sustaining performance excellence. By communicating this understanding to followers, we can inspire, role model, teach and challenge them to strive for these ideals.	Transcendence	Communicating expectations of high performance and superior standards
20 Leaders who behave *gratefully* towards their deserving followers and associates recognize their achievements. When we recognize people for their excellence, we send the message that the ideals of authentic transformational leadership can indeed be achieved. When we appreciate the people and events that contribute to our success, we role model dedication to our organization and valuing its members.	Transcendence	Showing appreciation for your associates' efforts and results
21 No follower or associate will believe in a pessimistic or self-doubting leader. Instead, followers like to be around leaders who are *optimistic* because hope can be a very satisfying and motivating force. Such effects on followers make it easy for leaders to use inspirational motivation to mold expectations and create self-fulfilling prophecies of success.	Transcendence	Leading people into the future as a witness to hope
22 Learn to take *humor* more seriously. When leaders use appropriate forms of humor, they not only enhance morale at work and produce positive physiological effects on themselves and their followers, but also create interest and present work to employees as intellectually stimulating. All of these positive effects can pay off in enhanced organizational learning and effectiveness.	Transcendence	Boosting morale and group cohesiveness
23 *Spirituality* is an important source of meaning, refreshment and energy for leaders. Spirituality helps leaders to understand their purpose in life and why their work is important. It provides them with a moral code that guides their behavior as a role model. It also focuses their attention to development of their followers and associates, and away from selfish interests.	Transcendence	Providing purpose and meaning to life and work

DEVELOPING CHARACTER IN OUR CHILDREN

A good starting point in our quest to develop the character of others is our children; they represent the very best of what our future holds or the very worst of what we are capable of doing to ourselves and each other. In essence, our future depends on the character and moral fiber of our children. Why is it that today we see incidents like the Columbine shootings, teen pregnancy and suicides, and all-time low levels of self-esteem in young girls and boys? It is indeed difficult to find a complete answer to this question, for it seems that our children are enjoying much higher standards of living and opportunities than ever before. But perhaps on a large scale, they are lacking the one thing that children of the past abundantly enjoyed—face time with their parents, teaching them about virtue and character. Our hectic lives seem to preclude the traditional family dinner where parents and children can sit down and reflect upon the day in ways that teach children how to cope with the challenges in life by following the path of virtue.

Not long ago in my graduate class on leadership and lifespan issues, I could not help admiring a student who shared a very personal experience with us. His father had just passed away and he emotionally described how his father had shaped his love of leadership. His father owned a grocery store where he began working at the age of eight. Even at that early age, he got a first hand glimpse of what leadership was all about. He recalled hearing his father say "if you treat your people well, they will be good to you." He also remembered the impact this had on the store's employees. His coworkers would tell him "Your Dad is a good person." Later in life, the student became a successful manager in a large engineering firm. What a profound effect a positive role model can have on a youngster!

This does not mean that all children blessed with good mothers and fathers will turn out to be fine upstanding pillars of society or transformational leaders. Perhaps that would not be fair to those raised by only one parent, or those orphaned and dependent upon government or religious-based institutions to shape their character. Regardless of how and by whom a child is raised, the family unit, in any of its various forms, remains the first and foremost foundry that forges character as shown in Figure 10.1. During early childhood, we depend upon and look up to our parents and guardians; throughout our lives we learn from them through social learning processes that involve role modeling. And we grow in our character development when they actively engage us in discussions about the value of character and virtue, as in the case of Herb Kelleher. Children appreciate the time and effort parents spend teaching them life lessons; such time is fleeting, but precious. We must use it wisely to forge the character of our future leaders.

Figure 10.1.   *It All Starts in the Family.* Perhaps one of the noblest forms of leadership and character development is the parenting of children, where important values can be instilled and moral fiber shaped.

Beyond the family are our schools, civic organizations and faith communities. These institutions can provide an additional layer of character development. Both public and private schools can help in this regard (see Figure 10.2). Consider the variety of effects that good teachers can have upon our children's character development. They give children hope of a brighter future by pointing out which paths are worthwhile to pursue. They help children identify their innate talents and show them what professions will allow them to match their skills to a satisfying career. They help students to become more disciplined and focused. They build children's confidence level and self-esteem by showing them their value to their peers and to society. Through sporting or academic competitions, they teach students the value of teamwork, loyalty and organizational citizenship. Therefore, involvement in your child's PTA at school is an important way to be a part of this aspect of their lives and insure that character development programs exist and are being effectively implemented like the types championed by James Hunt in North Carolina.

Local civic organizations are another source of character development of our youth. Whether it's the Boy Scouts, Girl Scouts, YMCA, YWCA, Little League, Big Brothers/Big Sisters, the local Chamber of Commerce or the like, these organizations provide many opportunities for you to volunteer.

Figure 10.2. *Learning to Lead.* Schools provide social environments that can mold children's character by offering a variety of academic, sporting and service-learning activities that teach the virtues described in this book.

By getting involved, you can help to shape the content of the youth programs offered and practice the principles described in this book by mentoring a child. When you share your life experiences and values with a child, you can pass on your legacy of positive change to future generations. What a joy it is to see youngsters carry on the ideals that you stand for! Working with these children and other community-minded leaders is a truly rewarding way to put your positive values into action.

We must not forget about the important role that faith communities play in shaping and reinforcing character development of our youth. Through both formal and informal services, our places of worship teach religious beliefs that guide our children's behavior. Biblical passages and parables teach lessons about virtue and character strengths, as we saw in the example of Andy Griffith. Clergy and other faith community leaders are called upon to role model important values and to be authentic leaders in their own right. For people of all faiths, character development is a lifelong journey that is often sustained through increased faith, spirituality and service to others. Let us build upon our Spiritual Source and practice authentic transformational leadership. As the words of James 2:14 teach us, "What good is it ... if a man claims to have faith but has no deeds?"

DEVELOPING CHARACTER IN OUR COMMUNITIES

Crime, violence, pollution, traffic congestion, urban sprawl, drug addiction, the homeless, poverty, prostitution, child molestation, illiteracy, unemployment. Do any or all of these problems exist in your community? Yes? What are your community and local government officials doing about it? Not enough? Then, if you are truly an authentic transformational leader, what can you do about it?

To the authentic transformational leader, a problem or a crisis presents itself as an opportunity for character development. Remember how Anita Roddick responded when Shell and Exxon-Mobil were laying waste to the Nigerian countryside. Or recall how Dr. Martin Luther King Jr. reacted to the Montgomery Bus Boycott. Both of these leaders saw beyond injustice and seized the opportunity to demonstrate their leadership through character. You're probably thinking "Yes, but these are world-class leaders of big business and history. What can I do?" A lot.

At Penn State, we offer an award-winning course called Social Entrepreneurship and Community Leadership as the capstone experience in our Master of Leadership Development program. The message of the course is that business should be about more than just profits; it should be about providing a service or producing a product that introduces positive change into the community as well. During the course, students serve as mentors to small teams of high school honors students who work on a project aimed at solving a community project. Teams partner with local social services and non-profit organizations to provide help with strategic business planning and financial resource funding. The results have been phenomenal. Projects have included the GAD Beacon program which linked resources of rural and urban schools to provide strategic planning and operations. Other community organizations that have benefited from the course include a school for the autistic and emotionally disturbed, a civic organization raising money for a local town's 250th birthday celebration, and an organization devoted to providing literacy and social services to the Hispanic community, among many other noble community service projects.[4]

The success of this course shows that leaders of character step up and tackle such problems. They act as change agents in their communities. Through their hard work, they demonstrate for others the character strengths of citizenship and vitality. Over time, their collective action can build a culture of virtue and character.

If our students can do it, so can you. The trick is to find a social problem or cause that really gets you excited. What injustice or irksome problem really gets under your skin? What are you passionate about changing in your community? In what way would you like to add value to society? When you find answers to such questions, you have found your community call-

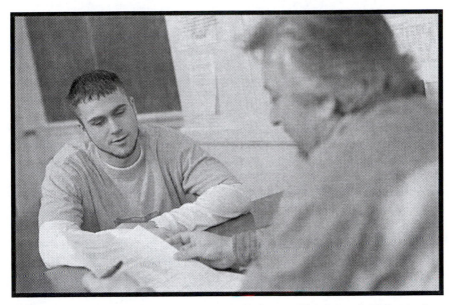

Figure 10.3.   *Character Development Crossing Generations.* This executive is mentoring a talented high school student on the fine points of leadership as they collaborate on a community service project.

ing. Follow this calling by becoming involved in a civic, school, governmental, or faith community initiative aimed at solving the social problem that you find insufferable. By partnering with others, you can provide maximum benefits to the community you serve and create cultures of character and virtue along the way, just like the executive shown in Figure 10.3.

DEVELOPING CHARACTER IN OUR ORGANIZATIONS

Developing character strengths and virtues in organizations pays off. In a recent study of 18 large corporations representing 16 different industries, researchers from the University of Michigan found that those companies whose workers reported demonstrating more of the character strengths and virtues described in this book were associated with higher levels of perceived and objective measures of organizational performance.[5] As the field of positive organizational scholarship matures, much more evidence that character in organizations pays off is likely to accumulate. How can you develop character in your organization?

Developing character in organizations goes hand-in-hand with developing strong organizational cultures. First, the organization's founders or top executive team must embrace, role model, and champion the cause of authentic transformational leadership. They must communicate stories of associates who have demonstrated character strengths over the course of the history of the organization. They must be committed to selecting and rewarding associates based on aspects of character. Herb Kelleher's participation in employee recognition events at Southwest Airlines illustrates this first step.

Second, a philosophy of character and virtue espoused by the top leaders needs to influence the criteria used for hiring. For example, MBNA's corporate values are printed on its employment applications and used in the selection process. By extension, leaders can use validated measures of corporate values and character strengths to screen job candidates. This helps to bring the future leaders of character into the organization because they are likely to share the values of the organization.

Third, it is essential that top executives role model the character strengths espoused by the organization. Their behavior sets the climate for what is and what is not acceptable behavior for associates at lower organizational levels. The example of Joe Namath's intolerance for racial bigotry and discrimination within the New York Jets organization in the late 1960s and early 1970s illustrates this step.

Fourth, socialization programs, such as orientation, leadership and team training, and quality conferences, can provide "booster shots" of character and virtue so that associates continue to talk about and display the behavior of authentic transformational leaders. Over time, associates become assimilated into the organization's culture of character if their personal values match those of the organization in the selection process and if the socialization methods that are preferred by top management are actually seen as valuable by new associates. The example of Bill Gates and the strong culture at Microsoft illustrates this step.

The U.S. Army has been extremely effective in using these steps to forge character in new recruits and sustain a culture of character over the years. Recruits learn about character through formal and informal education and training. This involves teaching Army values and demonstrating attributes of leadership through case studies, experiential exercises, and reflection and group discussions. Next, recruits comply with the principles taught in the first step. This involves reinforcing Army values and leadership attributes through feedback, socialization processes, and developmental exercises. Over time, recruits come to firmly believe in what they have been taught. They internalize Army values and character strengths associated with leadership. These attributes become part of who they are. This is how recruits grow into authentic leaders. As more and more recruits internalize these attributes, the Army's ethical climate and culture of character is shaped and perpetuated.

In all organizations, this process of character development can create a shared understanding of how we behave, what we value, and what we expect of our associates. By following this process, we can help organizational members realize that leading through character helps us to reach a higher level of performance, prosperity and peace of mind.

As this chapter ends, another begins. But this new chapter is not in the book you are now reading; it is in *your life*. And the next chapter in your life as a leader is yours to write. Will your chapter portray you as living to reap the social, psychological, spiritual, mental and physical benefits associated with character strengths and virtues? Will it depict you as leading by being true to yourself and devoted to the development of others? Will it show you leading by the principles in this book? What will be the real substance of your leadership? Will your followers appreciate the essence of your character?

As you turn the rest of the pages of this book, you will find words of recognition written by individuals like you who have witnessed leaders of character living among us. Their collective message is that the authentic transformational leaders described in this book are really not that unique. Most are *not* famous. Their achievements go unrecognized for years or even lifetimes. Until now. It is time for us to pay tribute to these unsung heroes. Their stories give us hope that we too can use our character strengths to promote prosperity and expand opportunities for happiness.

NOTES

1. Franklin, B. (2005). *The autobiography of Benjamin Franklin*. Philadelphia, PA: University of Pennsylvania Press.
2. Both quotes culled from Franklin, B. (n.d.). *Poor Richard's almanack*. Mount Vernon, NY: Peter Pauper Press.
3. Burns, J.M. (2003, p. 240). *Transforming leadership: A new pursuit of happiness*. New York: Atlantic Monthly Press.
4. http://www.imakenews.com/innovationphiladelphia/e_article000336037.cfm (Accessed January 24, 2006).
5. Cameron, K.S., Bright, D., & Caza, A. (2004). Exploring the relationships between organizational virtuousness and performance. *The American Behavioral Scientist, 47* (6), 766–790.

CHAPTER 11

LEADERS OF CHARACTER
AMONG US

You cannot dream yourself into a character; you must hammer and forge yourself one.

—James A. Froude

Adult working professionals, both men and women, from many different ethnic groups, organizational levels and industries contributed to this
final chapter. These aspiring leaders were asked to talk about their "ideal
leader." They each described a person who has had a significant influence
on their personal and professional development. As part of a contest, I
invited over 100 individuals, average age of 41, to send me an e-mail formally recognizing their "ideal leader" for his or her personification of the
virtues and character strengths described in this book. I would like to
thank those who participated in the contest. I reviewed their submissions
with two colleagues and we selected the ten best.

The e-mails of the contest winners appear below. I wanted the winning
e-mails to add clarity and extend the examples provided in the book to all
walks of everyday life. Their poignant words of recognition paint vivid and
descriptive portraits of the leaders of character among us, and the best that
humanity has to offer.

Leading with Character, pages 213–224
Copyright © 2006 by Information Age Publishing
All rights of reproduction in any form reserved.

LEADERSHIP AND LEARNING GO HAND-IN-HAND

I am proud to recognize my colleague, James R. Jones, for his exceptional leadership and his passion for learning. James R. Jones, MBA, CPCU, ARM, AIC and AIS, is the director of the Katie School of Insurance at Illinois State University. As director, James is responsible for ensuring that the Katie School offers the best possible curriculum for tomorrow's industry leaders. What makes James an inspirational leader is his passionate pursuit of wisdom and knowledge and his commitment to share it, his insatiable curiosity, and his dedication to the variety of people he serves.

The value James places on learning and the voracity with which he pursues education are reflected in his many academic achievements. However, his learning extends far beyond the classroom; he regularly participates in or conducts industry research, he teaches, he serves on the Board of the Insurance Education Institute, and he contributes his knowledge as a subject matter expert to a variety of committees. But he is not content to rest on his acquired knowledge. As long as there is more to learn about insurance and education, James seeks to learn it.

This abiding curiosity also feeds James' success as a leader. His interests encompass people, theories, ideas, processes, quality, and implementation. He embraces innovation as a means to achieve a better product or service. His creative ideas have initiated or contributed to many innovative programs and research that benefit the insurance industry, such as the work he conducted at the Center for Performance Improvement and Innovation, which he founded. James also created the Katie School Leadership Certificate Program, which recognizes and develops high potential students into leaders.

James considers every person he encounters as a learning opportunity to be embraced with humility and kindness. In getting to know James, I was not surprised to learn that he had served in the Peace Corps in Gabon, Africa. He unconsciously practices what is known as servant leadership: putting the needs of others ahead of his own. By creating opportunities to interact with his students, faculty, clients, and industry contacts, James learns what is important to each of them and finds ways to meet those needs. He always solicits people's ideas, opinions, and expertise, appreciating the variety of perspectives that leads to a better outcome and valuing the resulting richness in human relationships.

While the nightly news focuses on leadership in the highest levels of corporate America, the real newsmakers are the "everyday" leaders like James Jones who make it a practice to learn as much as they can, share the wisdom they acquire, and inspire others to follow their example. In my opinion, this is the core of authentic transformational leadership.

—Patricia Enright, President
ROI Performance Solutions
Glenside, PA

MEMORIES OF A SOLDIER

During a war that divided this nation in the 1960s, Ronald Watson was an inspiration to others and led his subordinates with bravery, vitality, and a keen sense of spirituality. This man's leadership style embodied many of the virtues and character strengths described in this book.

Born and raised in Texas, Ron was a talented and highly motivated young man who achieved significant accomplishments by his 24th birthday. Among them, he had been awarded his Doctorate of Philosophy in history from the University of California, Berkley, and had recently won the "Mr. Texas" Body-building Tournament. Believing in a strong mind and body, the focus of his endeavors soon turned to serving his country in its time of war.

I first met Ron in late 1968, while we were undergoing advanced counter-espionage training at a military intelligence facility in Maryland. Initially I knew little about him, however, during the course of this training our mutual respect and friendship developed. Ron's natural ability to understand and take command of various complex situations brought him the trust and admiration of those around him. At the same time, he continually encouraged me to complete my education, which at the time consisted of an associate degree. Ron's *love of learning* was an integral and important part of his makeup; he was passionate about the benefits of higher education and promoted its virtues with religious fervor. His dedication and commitment to the value of education was inspirational and motivational.

Upon completion of our training, we were both assigned back to the war in Vietnam. Six months elapsed and even though our assignments were classified and geographically apart, we were able to frequently communicate with each other. Even in the worst battlefield situations, he continued his unrelenting "educational barrage," focusing on the importance of completing my undergraduate degree. While serving our country with distinction and valor, Ron never allowed me to waiver on my commitment to him to finish my degree.

Ron died in 1970 during a classified mission in Laos. Although his body was never recovered, his name is inscribed on the Vietnam War Memorial in Washington, D.C. His leadership, friendship, warmth, and desire to see those around him succeed, lived on long after he lost his life. Shortly after his death, I returned to the University of Maryland to finish my undergraduate degree. Ron will always be with me in spirit, and I honor his memory by proudly completing my master's degree.

—Reuben M. Rosenthal
Gladwyne, PA

SUFFERING BREEDS CHARACTER,
CHARACTER BREEDS FAITH

Thanks for giving me the incentive to write this short essay. We don't always get the chance to let important influencers know how they affect our lives.

"My boss is a real character!" How often have you heard a friend or fellow employee describe their boss in those terms? If you have, the connotations of that statement are usually negative. I, too, however, have made that statement, but with *positive* implications attached. Webster defines character as "one of the attributes or features that make up and distinguish the individual: the complex of mental and ethical traits marking a person...."

I thought long and hard about the person who has most influenced my professional development exemplified by a virtue or character strength described in this book. The person that immediately came to my mind had not only one of those character strengths, but a combination of them all! The kudos go to my boss, mentor and friend, Lee Wagner.

My boss lies in a hospital bed connected to tubes and monitors. Outwardly, he is the skeleton of the man he once was, but inwardly he continues to exhibit the strength that has touched the lives of so many. His courage during these difficult years has been exemplary as he continues to forge onward with the persistence and the bravery of a hero. Withstanding chemotherapy, two bone-marrow transplants, transfusions and radiation, Lee continued to add value to the organization through phone conferences, e-mails, and, whenever possible, personal meetings. Working with Lee for ten years, I've had the joy of being on the receiving end of the wisdom he accumulated after years of successful consulting in the field of Organization Development (OD). Lee enjoyed nothing more than helping people and teams improve. Sharing his expertise and knowledge, Lee loved to elaborate on any aspect of employee and team development. A friend and colleague to those in the executive level, Lee's kindness and concern also reached down to the production workers and janitors as well.

Working with Lee on special projects proved to be fun and exciting. Always one for having a good time, we spent many hours joking as we creatively joined forces to write articles and proposals. Not only did Lee give me opportunities to develop as a trainer, editor and OD consultant, he gently guided me to a position of leadership where I could emulate those characteristics I saw in him. Thank you, Lee, for being my best boss!

—Jeanette Landgreen
Manager, Learning & Development
TEVA Pharmaceuticals USA
Quakertown, PA

SOWING THE SEEDS OF HOPE

As I waited in line at the American Embassy in Monrovia, Liberia, Africa, I met Patty Anglin. We chatted and it became clear that Patty was an unusual person and a very strong leader. Raised the daughter of medical missionaries in the Congo, Africa, she is the mother of 16 children (9 adopted). She is an outspoken advocate on adoption and founder and Executive Director of Acres of Hope, a U.S. national charitable organization. We became friends and I visited her orphanage later in the week.

Four years ago, Patty witnessed firsthand the devastation of Liberia after their 14-year civil war. Patty and her husband, Harold, adopted a son, Tucker, and saw many children impacted by the civil war which left them orphans and medically fragile. After their home in Wisconsin burned down, Patty used the insurance proceeds to establish Acres of Hope. Loving families in the U.S. and Canada have adopted approximately 300 Liberian children; 8,000 children eat daily; and 4,000 children now attend schools, which were previously non-existent in the bush country of Liberia.

A true transformational leader, Patty demonstrates all of the *Four I's*. She exhibits Idealized Influence through her behavior and attitude and serves as an example to all that know her; she walks the talk. Openly sharing her vision for Acres of Hope, she inspires and motivates those that work with her and others that donate to her worthy cause. She challenges each of us to make a difference in the world and proves that it can be done by doing it. I found her mission intellectually stimulating and agreed to help her; it felt like something I should do. Observing Patty working with her team, I saw that individual consideration is a major aspect of her style.

Patty displays several of the character strengths and virtues described in this book. As the founder and Executive Director of Acres of Hope in a war torn country, we witness great courage and humanity, and the virtues of bravery, persistence, integrity, vitality, kindness, love and social intelligence. We see creativity, open mindedness and perspective in her work and dedication to her cause, which are virtues associated with wisdom and knowledge. Establishing schools in the bush country demonstrates her leadership and teaching, and a sense of fairness comes through as she tries to balance the scales in such a difficult environment. These virtues of justice are combined with temperance: such a mission requires self-regulation and control, and, despite her success, she demonstrates humility. Patty is guided by her strong spirituality, showing gratitude and she is always hopeful for a better future— acres of it. Transcendence plays a big role in her life.

Patty's accomplishments go beyond Liberia. In the U.S., she has testified before Congressional hearings on adoption issues and has served on local, state and national boards whose missions include health care, advocacy, and adoption for children. As a public speaker, Patty has won numerous awards for her efforts in humanitarian work world-wide. Her advocacy efforts for women and children have earned her distinguished awards of excellence. She earned the Silver Medallion Award for her book entitled, *Acres of Hope....*

Recently, Patty and I met and discussed plans to help Acres of Hope in its efforts to establish economically self-sustaining villages in the bush of Liberia. Our plans include more schools, clinics and village co-operative farms. It is with great honor that I recognize Patty Anglin as my idealized leader.

—John Juzbasich, Partner
Merit Systems LLC
Wayne, PA

WILL YOU FORGIVE ME?

My father, Chacko Punnoose, has been an inspirational figure in my life since the very early stages of my childhood. He has played a significant role in molding who I am today through his ability to lead by example. As I consider the virtues and character strengths described in this book, I notice that my father's most prominent characteristics fall within the following virtues: Wisdom & Knowledge, Courage, Temperance, and Transcendence. To best depict the essence of my father, below is a salient memory from my childhood.

Another Saturday morning arrives and (as usual) my sister and I cannot agree on what to watch on TV. Being the older sibling, she decided to ignore my wishes and opted to watch the program she liked. Seeing this unfairness, I took it upon myself to decide that neither of us would watch TV that morning. I began talking very loud as I stood in the way of the television screen, at which point my dad entered the chaotic scene. My dad managed to calm us down and then advised that we each apologize to one another, starting with admitting our wrongdoing. Even though I didn't really want to, I muttered the words "I'm sorry."

That's not where this story ends... After what I thought was my apology, my father suggested that my apology was incomplete. "Why?" I asked. He replied "Saying 'I'm sorry' is meaningless unless you follow it immediately with another statement: Will you forgive me?" Saying "I'm sorry" suddenly became a much easier feat to accomplish, but the words "will you forgive me" took more out of me than I ever expected. It was through this critical life event that I had learned the meaning of humility and integrity. These two strengths are the most important qualities my father hoped to instill in his children.

Fr. Chacko Punnoose is a rare commodity amongst [Knanaya Syrian Orthodox] priests in my faith community today. His enthusiasm of learning, open-mindedness to change for the better, and sense of humor contribute to his distinct personality. These qualities are highly transparent and consistent in his daily communication, which makes him an authentic leader in my eyes.

—Sandy Chacko
Aetna
Philadelphia, PA

APPRECIATING BEAUTY AND EXCELLENCE

"Find the Good and Praise it." I often heard this quote from my aunt and those close to her, because her positivism transcended others. Although my aunt was a cultural and historical icon, to me and other family members, her humbleness just made her who she was—simply Aunt Betty. More specifically, I am talking about Betty Shabazz, the widow of one of the most charismatic leaders of the Civil Rights movement of the 1960s, Malcolm X. Although she was taken from us about nine years ago, my memory of her and the values she possessed will be with me forever.

One of the most important things that she valued was education or "Wisdom & Knowledge." She proved that education was important in her life, by earning her PhD and becoming a professor after her husband's death. She also instilled a foundation of education in me, by giving out college savings bonds, which could not be cashed until I entered college. She believed that education was the great equalizer because the more you learn, the more your capital is increased, both in knowledge and finances. Aunt Betty also believed that knowledge is power, and without it you will not improve your situation in life.

She was not only an advocate for her family, but also for her students as a professor at Meager Evers College in New York. She routinely mentored the students who were having problems with course work and those who were having issues in the family. Through her leadership many of her students went on to graduate and do great things in their lives and careers.

She was a woman of high integrity and courage, because she took the hand that God dealt her and played it. Although she witnessed the brutal murder of her husband, she never allowed that to define her. She was a person of high ideals and morals which she instilled into all her family. I choose Aunt Betty as my ideal leader because she is someone who was truly ideal in her leadership. I hope that the morals and ethics that I gained from her can be shared with other generations, especially "to find the good and praise it."

—Parris O. Sandlin
Philadelphia, PA

HE MADE THE WORLD A BETTER PLACE

To those of us who loved him, Reverend John L. Taylor, or JT as we called him, was truly an authentic transformational leader. You may not think this surprising as he was a leader of the Marshallton United Methodist Church in Marshallton, Pennsylvania. He changed the lives of many individuals, including mine, and he left a lasting legacy in this community.

Beyond his amazing and personal influence in the lives of many individuals, he led this church to undertake and successfully complete a significant, multi-phase building expansion that had been attempted unsuccessfully several times in the previous three decades. The community realized that in order to grow, more physical space was needed, particularly an "education wing." The existing facility was located in a small, densely built village setting. There were several very ambitious hurdles that had to be overcome in order to achieve this goal. A neighboring property had to be purchased. Hundreds of thousands of dollars needed to be raised. Our poor congregation had to take on significant debt to finance the project. And people in the congregation needed to form and work in committees to advance the project.

All of this was possible because JT was a teacher. In fact, his first career had been as a school teacher, before he responded to being called to be a spiritual leader. He preached great weekly messages. He encouraged others to speak openly about their faith, life challenges and joys. He modeled this behavior. While leading this congregation to undertake and achieve the major physical expansion, he actively grew new leaders in the group. He left the congregation stronger and more capable than he found it. This was a critical factor in his church's ability to withstand turmoil that occurred under its next leader.

As the new education wing reached its completion, JT moved on to lead another faith community. Very sadly, not too long after that he was diagnosed with pancreatic cancer and only lived a few more months. He continued to teach faith and life lessons even as his days in this life waned.

JT's strongest virtues and character strengths were Transcendence and Spirituality, Humanity and Love, Temperance, Forgiveness & Mercy, Justice, and Citizenship. He demonstrated other key character strengths and attributes, too. JT demonstrated Courage as he approached his death.

My relationship with JT occurred before my formal study of leadership theory and development. But, from our first meeting, I was always aware of JT's impact on my life and faith. I am so blessed to have had JT on my life's faith journey. And I am pleased and proud to be able to share his story of transformational and servant leadership. He left me and many others better people. Part of his legacy is the expanded church that is now able to support a larger congregation and more community programs. The world is definitely a better place because JT was here.

—Janet Hutchison
Downingtown, PA

CHARACTER TEMPERED BY LIFE

Col. Joseph Patterson Davisson has been a mentor and role model for me for years. Col. Davisson is one of seven children. He grew up in Philadelphia and served in the Army for 25 plus years. He showed great courage by leading his troops in multiple battles during the war. He also showed great persistence in continuing the fight, even after finding out his brother died while they were both in the Battle of the Bulge.

Fast forward a few years. Pat, as he was called, moved into business, first in banking as a Vice President and then later in sales for the former Beeline Fashion Company. In this latter position, he worked with his wife to become the highest selling team in the company. One of the perks to this was a "gold" Cadillac (much like Mary Kay's pink one). Pat succeeded in business much like he did in the Army. Pat and his wife were both placed in the Beeline "Hall of Fame" as a result of their team's ability to succeed. Great teams need to have great leaders to show them the way. Pat and his wife were those leaders.

Pat used many of the skills he learned in the Army and in business to make up his "Portfolio." He had four children of his own that were moved around when he was stationed at different places around the country. He was always fair. You may not like what he had to say, but he treated everyone fairly. Pat always loved being around family and friends. He loved to "teach" others, often times you did not realize what he taught you until later, sometimes years. He was a religious man, devoting many hours to the Catholic Church, and various charities. He was always willing to give back to the community that supported him for many years...

Why do I discuss Col. Joseph Patterson Davisson? Because he taught me what it takes to be a true leader. He has shown me that even in the worst possible scenario, such as war, you can rise above your circumstances and be strong. He has shown me to love my family, my wife, and to keep everything else in perspective, because nothing is more important than family and friends. He has shared with me his wisdom, he has shown me what it takes to be a leader and that you always are learning, and that it doesn't stop when you finish school. He taught that you need to feel connected to the community, because they will support you when you need it, even if you never do. He showed me to enjoy life for what it is...and make it a better place.

Many of these characteristics sound like something you would want from a father or grandfather, but I would argue that they are some of the same traits you would want from a leader. Ronald Reagan was often seen as someone you would want as a grandfather...and he made the world a safer place. Leaders need to have some of the same characteristics in order to lead their companies, divisions, departments, and teams to be better. And why does Col. JP Davisson sound like a grandfather? Because he was mine.

—Scott Carpenter
The Vanguard Group, Malvern, PA

NO GREATER LOVE OR LEADERSHIP

My mother Emma H. Berardi is the person that I would like to recognize as the person who most influenced my life. This year she will be 83 years old. She now is in great pain from osteoporosis and a very brittle spine. Mom lives in a skilled nursing unit of a retirement home about 20 miles north of Malvern, Pennsylvania.

She was born in 1923… Her father was an Italian immigrant and worked as a carpenter building many houses in Philadelphia, PA… My mother at a very young age had to cook meals, shop for food, clean the house and take care of her younger brother. She was one of a family of nine. While my grandparents worked, she had to take care of the household and still managed to go to school and get straight A's. She began to work right after high school in an office as a secretary. She saved and went to night school at Moore College to study art and fashion design, which she loved. She married my father…when he returned from the Army after World War II…

My mother possesses so many of the virtues and character strengths described in this book. She raised us with them…It is hard to describe this completely, but here goes…

Wisdom—She encouraged my creativity, which led me to be a chef. She enjoyed and passed on the love of learning; all of my siblings graduated from college. We were the first generation in our family to do so. She always encouraged education since she really did not have the chance to complete her education. She claims this is her most rewarding achievement—that we all have at least a Bachelor's degree.

Courage—Sincerity, you will never find a person more sincere, with absolutely no pretenses. Truth was demanded; telling a fib was like a life threatening event, which was only used under the most extreme circumstances. If she had to tell a fib, I'm sure she would say a few extra Rosaries that evening. She said the Rosary daily, without fail for as long as I remember.

Humanity—She was the most nurturing and caring person. She did not work outside the home, so she was always there for us. She loved us more than anything, and encouraged us to be kind to any and all. My siblings were always there for each other and treated each other with love and respect.

Temperance—Mom would forgive and forget. We always had a second chance and were never criticized. Instead we were redirected in a manner to learn from our mistakes and to try to avoid falling into the same behaviors…She is very humble. A few years back, a painting that she did was featured as a Best of Show in Chester County Magazine. She really did not want any credit. The painting is a beautiful scene of a barn on a farm. She is not one to brag or expect anything.

Transcendence—Mom taught us to appreciate nature, flowers, gardening, art, and being aware of our surroundings. She encouraged us to thank anyone that gave us gifts or helped in anyway. Mom would always help anyone that was in need and encouraged us to do the same. As a devout Roman Catholic, my mom taught us to attend Mass every week…I remember praying with the family at home as a child. We were taught that we were very fortunate, and to be thankful for everything that we had because there were so many who had nothing or were less fortunate.

From her very humble beginnings as a child of immigrants, my Mom influenced my life more so than anyone else. I'm very thankful that I've had many opportunities, and look forward to doing anything I can to continue in the manner of such a beautiful person. I love her very much for always being there for me and giving me such a great path to follow.

—Chuck Berardi
Regional Executive Chef
Wegmans Food Markets
Downingtown, PA

UNCOMMON VIRTUE

After a long and storied career, it is very hard to pick one person. If I had to pick one, it would be LTC (then CPT) E. John Deedrick, Jr. He was my last Team Leader on ODA-156 and my Company Commander when I was a First Sergeant. I personally believe John reflects most of the virtues and character strengths described in this book.

The strength he most demonstrated would have to be courage. At 6'4" 240 lbs, he is not really built for Special Forces. We were in Bangladesh, jumping Chinese parachutes; John had to put the chute on his back and then lay down on his back with his legs in the air in order to connect the leg straps. The team would have understood if he said he wasn't going to jump. But John is a leader who never asked of his men anything he wouldn't do himself.

When John requested to take command of my company, he was warned that he could be putting his career in jeopardy. He had already had a "branch qualifying" job and it would be "risky" to take on a command he did not need for promotion. John told them he was an Officer in the United States Army and his responsibility and duty was that of commanding soldiers in the field. He stated "if I fail it would not be for a lack of trying." Upon completion of his command he was promoted to Major in what is referred to in the Army as "below the zone" or ahead of his peers. Of the approximately 600 Captains in Special Forces, only seven are promoted annually to Major "below the zone." Not bad for someone who was advised to not take the command.

When John was the Assistant Battalion Operations Officer, he was the unfortunate victim of Army politics. The Group Commander did not like the Operations Officer and felt that John's loyalty and hard work was a sign of some sort of misguided allegiance to the Operations Officer. The Group Commander gave John a performance rating that basically ended his future opportunities to command troops. John was very disappointed and hurt. He felt he did the right thing by giving 100% everyday, no matter what his feelings were for his boss. The irony of the situation is that he did not agree with all of the decisions the Operations Officer made either. However, his values of loyalty and integrity would not let him give anything less than 100%.

A couple of years later John was assigned to work for the same Commander that had given him the adverse rating. Having personally seen John's performance and witnessed his character, he realized his previous rating had been a mistake and he worked hard to make it right. Last year John was selected for Battalion Command after having been passed over once. This was a history making event. No officer in the history of Special Forces had ever made the Battalion Command list after such an adverse rating.

In my 25 years of service in the Army, John Deedrick is the only officer I ever served with who did what was right for his soldiers *everyday.* He lived the Army values daily and they were the foundation of the decisions he made and how he lead his soldiers as an authentic transformational leader.

—Darrell Davis

First Sergeant, United States Army Special Forces (Retired)

Wilmington, DE

ABOUT THE AUTHOR

Dr. John J. Sosik is Professor of Management and Organization and Professor-in-Charge of the Master of Leadership Development program at The Pennsylvania State University, Great Valley School of Graduate Professional Studies. He earned his Ph.D. in management specializing in organizational behavior and human resource management from the State University of New York at Binghamton. He teaches behavioral science in business, leadership, strategic high-tech leadership, and managerial and financial accounting courses. He received the 1999 Penn State Great Valley Award for Teaching Excellence, and the 1998 and 2006 Arthur L. Glenn Award for Faculty Innovation, and the 1997 and 2001 Penn State Great Valley Awards for Excellence in Research and Scholarship.

Dr. Sosik's research interest focuses on effects of transformational and charismatic leadership on individuals, groups, and organizations, 360-degree feedback, group/team dynamics, and mentoring. He is an expert on charismatic/transformational leadership, having published over 70 articles, proceedings and book chapters and presented about 50 papers at academic conferences since 1995, conducted training and organizational development programs, and serves on the editorial boards of *The Leadership Quarterly* and *Group & Organization Management*. His excellence in reviewing the scholarly work of colleagues in his field has been recognized by both the *Academy of Management* and *Institute of Behavioral and Applied Management*. He is the lead author of *The Dream Weavers: Strategy-Focused Leadership in Technology-Driven Organizations* (2004, Information Age Publishing). He was awarded a grant from the National Science Foundation to study e-leadership of virtual teams at Unisys Corporation. Dr. Sosik also is a certified public accountant and certified management accountant, having worked in corporate industry prior to entering academia.

INDEX

Printed in the United States
136430LV00001B/8/A

9 781593 115418